4XR: Developing Excellence in Reading

Nikki Gamble

4XR: Developing Excellence in reading
Copyright © 2016 Nikki Gamble. All rights reserved.
First paperback edition printed 2016 in the United Kingdom

A catalogue record for this book is available from the British Library. ISBN 978-0-9935624-0-2

Published by Just Imagine Story Centre Ltd

For more copies of this book, please email: info@justimaginestorycentre.co.uk

Tel: 01245 267748

Designed and set by Steven Woods

Printed in Great Britain by C3 Imaging print and graphics

Acknowledgement: This book is based on work undertaken in nine schools in the London Borough of Richmond. It would not have been possible without the hard work and dedication of the lead teachers who trialled and developed teaching approaches in their classrooms, and the participation and thoughtful feedback from their students. Thanks are due to the head teachers, staff and students at Barnes Primary School, East Sheen Primary School, Kew Riverside Primary School, Lowther Primary School, Richmond Park Academy, Sheen Mount Primary School, St Mary Magdelen's Catholic Primary School, St Osmund's Catholic Primary School, The Queen's School. We learnt so much from all of them. In particular, the following teachers have contributed case study material, exemplification of teaching and reflections on professional development and the process of change:

Mary Jane Blease
Debbie Canner
Judy Corry
Clare Durling
Camilla Garofalo
Scott Griffin
Theresa Guarino
Leanne Lisney
Suzanne Maille

Laura Martin
Rachel Marshall
Deborah O'Gorman
Marguerite Rodrigo
Carla Ruocco
Judy Shaw
Emily Treble
Kayleigh Squires
Rachel Wilson

Special thanks to consultant Ginny Germaney who efficiently maintained our records and data, coached the teacher researchers in schools and contributed to the film section to this guide.

Contents

CONTENT

Project Overview

4XR Developing Excellence in Reading project was set up to investigate the needs of high attaining students in years 6 – 8, to identify the most effective pedagogies to move learning on, and to increase attainment in reading. Within this frame of reference, the project sought to:

• cultivate teacher excellence and subject knowledge

• enable cross-school learning and a shared understanding of outstanding practice

• create new teaching resources to support ongoing professional learning

• further develop existing activities already tested and positively evaluated.

Project schools

The project was conducted in nine schools (eight primaries and one secondary) in the London Borough of Richmond from April 2014 – September 2015.

• Richmond Park Academy

• Barnes Primary School

• East Sheen Primary School

• Kew Riverside Primary School

• Lowther Primary School

• Mary Magdalene Primary School

• Saint Osmund's Primary School

• Sheen Mount Primary School

• The Queen's School

Expert teachers from each school were appointed as teacher researchers to work alongside consultants in order to develop and test ideas and strategies.

Project design

The project was conducted in eight phases:

• literature review

• baseline data collection

• gap analysis

• framework design

• training and development

• post-delivery data collection and analysis

• evaluation

• production of handbook and website.

LONGMAN STUDY GUIDES

GCSE

Music

Richard Lambert

LONGMAN

LONGMAN STUDY GUIDES

SERIES EDITORS: **Geoff Black and Stuart Wall**

Titles available

Biology	Mathematics
Business Studies	Mathematics: Higher Level
Chemistry	Music
Design and Technology	Physics
Economics	Psychology
English	Religious Studies
English Literature	Science
French	Sociology
Geography	Spanish
German	World History
Information Technology	

Addison Wesley Longman Limited
Edinburgh Gate, Burnt Mill, Harlow,
Essex CM20 2JE, UK
and Associated Companies throughout the World.

First published 1990
Third edition 1997

British Library Cataloguing-in-Publication Data
A Catalogue record for this book is available from the British Library.

ISBN 0582-30497-0

Set by 30 in 9.75/12pt Sabon
Produced by Longman Singapore Publishers Pte
Printed in Singapore

CONTENTS

> ## AUTHOR'S NOTE

You will have purchased this Study Guide because you enjoy music and wish to do well in the GCSE examination. No matter which syllabus you are following, the book provides useful information to maximise your success in all aspects of Listening and Appraising, Performing and Composing. Although it contains many hints and ideas on final revision before you sit a written paper or submit your coursework compositions, it also contains many helpful suggestions for your various practical examinations.

The various syllabuses are clearly outlined, with their requirements explained in detail. Specimen and actual past questions from the different Exam Groups are reproduced, enabling you to familiarise yourself with different styles of question. Some have typical student answers with suggestions for improvement; others provide you with a tutor's model solution. Much emphasis is placed in this book on musical analysis – primarily to help you with the various types of questions on your set works, but also to illustrate the essential construction of many pieces, in a wide range of styles. This will also help you with your composition coursework.

Several glossaries are included at the end of the book for you to look up any information you may require on composers, instruments, people in music and theoretical terms.

I hope that this book will help you to achieve your best in the examination, and further stimulate your musical appetite.

Richard Lambert
October 1996

This book has been written as a course companion for use throughout your GCSE course in Music. The first chapter focuses on examination requirements, including information about the aims of a GCSE in Music, assessment, skills required, advice about techniques that can be applied when preparing coursework or sitting examinations, and details of the grading schemes. The second chapter gives details about the topic areas common to all music syllabuses. For further details on your syllabus requirements you should obtain a copy of the syllabus set by your Exam Group. The addresses for the Exam Groups are found in Chapter 1. Please read these first two chapters carefully as they give invaluable advice which will be useful throughout your Music course.

Each of the remaining chapters, 3 to 14, deals with an important aspect of music. Each chapter starts with a **Getting started** section which is an introduction to the chapter. This includes a **Topic chart**, a table which, at a glance, shows which parts of the chapter are relevant to a particular Exam Group's requirements. You should use this to identify whether topics in a specific chapter are covered by your examining board. The chart can also be used to check your study and revision progress over the two years. A Topic Chart looks like this:

IGCSE	LONDON	MEG	NEAB	NICCEA	SEG	WJEC	TOPIC	STUDY	REVISION 1	REVISION 2
✓	✓	✓	✓	✓	✓	✓	General aims			
✓	✓	✓	✓	✓	✓	✓	Assessment objectives			

Key to the initials

IGCSE	The International General Certificate of Secondary Education
London	EDEXCEL Foundation (formerly ULEAC)
MEG	Midland Examination Group
NEAB	Northern Examinations and Assessment Board
NICCEA	Northern Ireland Council for the Curriculum, Examinations and Assessment
SEG	Southern Examining Group
WJEC	Welsh Joint Education Committee

Each topic listed is then explained in the **What you need to know** section – the core of the chapter. This section seeks to explain the topic area in detail, giving examples where appropriate, and questions and answers to test your understanding. There are also examples of student answers in some chapters which will help you to see what problems are identified by examiners and how you could improve your own approach.

At the end of each chapter there is a **summary box** which briefly identifies the key points about topics covered in the chapter. You should check that you know, and understand more fully, each of the key points listed.

At the end of the book there are four glossaries for you to use as reference, these include:

1. Composers mentioned in this book.
2. Musical words.
3. Musical instruments.
4. Well-known performers, past and present.

ACKNOWLEDGEMENTS

I am grateful to the following Examining Boards for permission to quote from their syllabuses and to reproduce questions which have appeared in past examination papers. Whilst the Boards have granted permission to reproduce the questions, I accept full responsibility for any solutions provided.

EDEXCEL Foundation
International General Certificate of Secondary Education
Midlands Examining Group
Northern Examinations and Assessment Board
Northern Ireland Council for the Curriculum, Examinations and Assessment
Southern Examining Group
Welsh Joint Education Committee

I am grateful to the following schools for permission to include students' work:

St Christopher School, Letchworth, Hertfordshire
Coopers School, Chislehurst, Kent
Meridian School, Royston, Hertfordshire
Chislehurst and Sidcup Grammar School, Kent

Thanks to Adrian Pitts, Noel Morgan and Christopher Weaver for help with students' compositions; to Stuart Wall and Geoff Black for their encouragement; and to my son Tristan for his thorough scrutiny of my text and invaluable wordprocessing skills!

GCSE Music

▷ **GETTING STARTED**

Music in secondary schools is now thought of as a practical subject. Over the last ten or twenty years the class music lesson has changed its emphasis from factual knowledge ('knowing that...') to a direct practical experience of music-making ('knowing how'). Gone are the lessons with dictated notes on composers' lives, gone is the old-fashioned harmony lesson where all examination students applied countless rules which produced similar stereotyped exercises.

It is now accepted that the music teacher is no longer the single source of musical experience for pupils. With music on record, tape, television and radio so fully available to everyone, music teachers rely on this valuable resource and can expect differing interests and achievements from their pupils.

It was realised that the previous music examination at 16+ (Ordinary level) was catering for a small minority of pupils – an elite who were well experienced on an instrument or two before they even started the exam course. The exam groups could exempt candidates from one paper (usually the harmony paper) if they produced evidence of a Grade 5 pass or above on an instrument. This was a very stimulating course for pupils who loved their exclusive diet of classical music and were considering an Advanced level music course, and perhaps a music degree to follow. However, it excluded large numbers of pupils who enjoyed different styles of music, perhaps because they were less fortunate in their previous experience of listening or playing.

IGCSE	LONDON	MEG	NEAB	NICCEA	SEG	WJEC	TOPIC	STUDY	REVISION 1	REVISION 2
✓	✓	✓	✓	✓	✓	✓	General aims			
✓	✓	✓	✓	✓	✓	✓	Assessment objectives			
✓	✓	✓	✓	✓	✓	✓	Coursework			
✓	✓	✓	✓	✓	✓	✓	Written examinations			
✓	✓	✓	✓	✓	✓	✓	Differentiation			
✓	✓	✓	✓	✓	✓	✓	Addresses of the Examining Groups			
✓	✓	✓	✓	✓	✓	✓	Grade descriptions			
✓	✓	✓	✓	✓	✓	✓	Glossary of terms used			
✓	✓	✓	✓	✓	✓	✓	Coursework and examination techniques			
✓	✓	✓	✓	✓	✓	✓	Good listening			
✓	✓	✓	✓	✓	✓	✓	Personal response			
✓	✓	✓	✓	✓	✓	✓	Note taking			
✓	✓	✓	✓	✓	✓	✓	Practice habits			
✓	✓	✓	✓	✓	✓	✓	Coursework: composing			
✓	✓	✓	✓	✓	✓	✓	Revision			
✓	✓	✓	✓	✓	✓	✓	Types of question			
✓	✓	✓	✓	✓	✓	✓	In the exam			

▷ **WHAT YOU NEED TO KNOW**

The General Certificate of Secondary Education (GCSE) was first debated in1984 and courses began in 1986. The first candidates sat their GCSE examination in l988. Although the GCSE initially caused some controversy and worry amongst teachers, courses are now well established, and it is fully accepted that the exam allows pupils of all abilities the opportunity to show what they understand, know and can do. Also, the added bene-fit of assessed coursework removes some of the pressure of having an examination on a particular day.

The GCSE sets out to reward an absolute level of achievement, without any comparison between candidates. Since it is designed for **all** pupils of 16+, it will range widely from a basic level of competence to an extremely high level of achievement in each subject. GCSE tests memory and factual knowledge as before, but with much more emphasis on under-standing, practical skills and the ability to apply your knowledge. The National Criteria (standards that courses and assessment must meet) contain *grade descriptions* which clearly inform you what you need to know, understand and be able to do in order to achieve a particular grade for any subject. You will read about these grade descriptions later in this chapter.

Following the Dearing review of the National Curriculum new national criteria were introduced. This meant that there would be important changes to all GCSE music syl-labuses for 1998. It has been nationally agreed that GCSE students in music should experience three essential activities: **Listening and appraising, performing and composing.** Although we shall consider these separately for the sake of clarity, it must be emphasised immediately that a good musical education will successfully combine these three activities. Indeed, you will soon see how important this combination really is: most of the elements in GCSE music are an obvious synthesis of the three. For example, an *improvisation* is a form of instant *composition*, and a composition on paper only comes to life when it is successfully *performed* before an audience. It was necessary to separate the activities for ease of assessment.

▷ **General aims**

The National Criteria for Music (published by SCAA) set out the educational purposes of following a GCSE music examination as follows:

(a)   To develop sensitivity towards music through personal experience by the exercise of imagination and the acquisition of skills and knowledge.

(b)   To continue and develop musical activities previously undertaken in the classroom.

(c)   To stimulate and develop an appreciation and enjoyment of music through an active involvement in the three musical activities: listening and appraising, performing and composing.

(d)   To develop performing skills to enable candidates to participate in the wide range of musical activities which can be found at present in the school and in the community.

(e)   To provide intellectual and aesthetic stimulation.

(f)   To develop a perceptive, sensitive and critical response to music of different styles in a cultural and historical context.

(g)   To encourage the understanding and expression of thoughts and feelings which may be more readily accessible through music than through other forms of communication.

(h)   To encourage the development of memory and the acquisition of skills of a more gen-eral nature such as analysis, inventiveness and co-ordination.

(i)   To provide an appropriate body of knowledge, promote understanding and develop skills as a basis for further study or leisure or both.

Whichever syllabus your school has chosen for you to follow, it has been designed to build on all the knowledge, skills and understanding that you have gained up to the end of Keystage 3 of the National Curriculum. The syllabus will also provide a good foundation for further study, including A-level.

▷ **Assessment objectives**

Aims are an important part of a syllabus, but not everything that we feel or think about music can be readily assessed. This is why the music exams of the past sometimes tested a candidate's *knowledge* of composers' lives, for example – facts which were either right or wrong, and so were easy to mark. This sort of testing has little to do with musicianship. After all, an intelligent but totally unmusical person can learn historical and factual information. The GCSE Exam Groups set out to encourage more satisfactory ways of providing musical experiences which pupils would find enjoyable and challenging; it therefore encompasses many more styles of music than was previously the case.

An *assessment objective* describes an ability or achievement which can be readily measured. For examination purposes everything that you write or perform has to meet these agreed objectives. Your teachers will prepare coursework tasks that will test them; the question papers will be set with the objectives in mind; and you will have to demonstrate that you can meet them! We can consider these objectives within our three essential activities and the examination will assess your ability to demonstrate:

1. **With listening and appraising:**
   (a) the ability to identify and compare distinctive musical characteristics from a wide variety of styles and traditions;
   (b) the ability to express views by critical judgements about music and using a musical vocabulary.
2. **With performing:**
   (a) technical control, appropriate interpretation and expression by performing a solo part or piece (a solo is defined as playing a significant part);
   (b) technical control and a sense of ensemble, by performing an individual part with others or rehearsing and directing a group.
3. **With composing:**
   (a) the ability to create and develop musical ideas by composing music.

External candidates

Everything that is explained in this book applies to candidates in full-time education, where a two-year course is the normal time span for GCSE. External candidates may enter, but should write to their nearest regional exam group for further details. Addresses are given later in this chapter.

▷ **Coursework**   The National Criteria for Music specifies that a certain percentage of the marks have to be allocated for *coursework* (Composing).

In some subjects, the coursework has to be done by specified times during the course. With music – although you should be composing all the time – the final selection does not have to be made until shortly before the exam (probably the end of the Spring term in the examination year). Your teacher will have all these details, but do fully understand your commitment:

▶ Make sure that you know the number of pieces and the minimum duration required for submission.
▶ Make sure that you compose to the best of your ability, with all written work neatly done.
▶ Check up on the format for presentation. Do I need to make a tape? Do I need to write a commentary?
▶ Make sure that your coursework is not lost. Most teachers keep pupil compositions at school. If your work is not with your teacher, do make certain that it is kept in a safe place. You are permitted to make photocopies of your *own* compositions!

Presentation

Presentation of your coursework must follow the guidelines set down in your syllabus. Speaking generally, the exam groups give great flexibility; written scores are encouraged, but a detailed commentary and/or annotated tape is sometimes satisfactory. Check your own syllabus (and Chapter 2) for precise details.

Sometimes it is hard to know **how much help** you are allowed with coursework. You will probably have to sign a form declaring authenticity – that is, that the coursework is your own work. Do remember, though, that it is acceptable for your teacher to give you initial ideas, and to discuss with you any problems arising with the writing of a piece. However, records of assistance must be kept and acknowledged when your work is submitted for assessment.

Organisation

What is the best way to **organise** coursework? Some people make a diary of deadlines for the completion of each piece; your teacher will probably have done this anyway. It is certainly best to complete your folder or folio of compositions in good time before you start your proper revision period.

There is a generous proportion of the full exam which is allotted to *Composing* coursework; but in many ways the *Performance* section can also be regarded as coursework. Although your performing has to be tested on a certain day, you will need to plan the programme and polish your performance in your own time, well in advance of the actual day. You will benefit from a conscientious attitude throughout the course; it is impossible to master these skills in last minute frantic practice.

With careful **planning** you should be in a confident position when the examination time arrives. Your composition folio should be finalised and out of the way. Your performance section (much of it chosen by you) should be well prepared, leaving time for you to concentrate on your revision.

▷ **Written examinations**

The *written paper* for *Listening and Appraising* will test your knowledge, understanding and response to a wide range of music. Make sure that you fully understand how many marks are available for each section of the paper. A question worth only one mark, for example, is best answered with a word or brief phrase. As with every GCSE subject the aim of assessment is that you are given marks for what you can do, rather than losing marks for what you cannot do. This is why some questions are differentiated – to allow all candidates to show what they have learned. There should be no real surprises in your written paper, because everything has been spelt out so clearly in the syllabus. If you work hard in class, taking careful note of all requirements for coursework and prepared tests, and revise properly towards the end, you will emerge with a good GCSE grade.

▷ **Differentiation**

Setting an examination is an extremely difficult task because GCSE covers such a wide ability range. Some subjects have solved this problem by incorporating 'hurdles' – cut-off points where you can proceed no further if you do not reach a set standard. The music GCSE does not include hurdles. Instead it uses a method known as *Differentiation by Outcome*. This means that **all** candidates answer the same questions and are free to choose which ones they will answer, subject to certain requirements. This method enables all candidates to respond positively, showing what they know, understand, and can do.

Differentiation is provided automatically in the *Composing* and *Performing* sections, as candidates will compose and perform at their own ability levels. In the *Listening* section, differentiation is achieved by using *structured questions* which allow personal response at an individual level of experience and knowledge. In this way, a question may be answered 'correctly' by one candidate, while another may get more marks by offering more depth and perception in his or her answer.

▷ **Addresses of the examining groups**

There are six Examining Groups which cover the whole of England, Wales and Northern Ireland. The IGCSE (International) has been formulated for Overseas Candidates. These seven groups are constantly referred to in this book.

International General Certificate of Secondary Education (IGCSE)
IGCSE Office
University of Cambridge Local Examinations Syndicate
Syndicate Buildings
1 Hills Road Cambridge
CB1 2EU
Tel: (International) + 44 (1223)553311
Fax: (International) + 44 (1223) 460278

EDEXCEL Foundation (London)
Stewart House
32 Russell Square
London
WC1B 5DN
Tel: (0171) 331 4000
Fax: (0171) 331 4044
Advice line for subject information: (0171) 753 4586

Midland Examining Group (MEG)
Purbeck House
Purbeck Road
Cambridge
CB2 2PU
(01223) 411211

or Elsfield Way
Oxford
OX2 8EP
(01865) 54421

Northern Examinations and Assessment Board (NEAB)
Administering Office for the 1392 Syllabus
Devas Street
Manchester
M15 6EX
Tel: (0161) 953 1180
Fax: (0161) 273 7572

For general despatches and publications:
12 Harter Street
Manchester
M1 6HL
Tel: (0161) 953 1170
Fax: (0161) 953 1177

Northern Ireland Council for the Curriculum, Examinations and Assessment (NICCEA)
29 Clarendon Road
Belfast
BT1 3BG
Tel: (01232) 261200
Fax: (01232) 261234

Southern Examining Group (SEG)
Oxford School Examinations Board
The Associated Examining Board
Central Administration Office
Stag Hill House
Guildford
Surrey
GU2 5XJ
Tel: (01483) 506506
Fax: (01483) 300152

Welsh Joint Education Committee (WJEC)
245 Western Avenue
Cardiff
CF5 2YX
Tel: (01222) 265000
Fax: (01222) 575994

▷ **Grade descriptions** Your grade is determined by your overall performance in the examination and it might conceal a weakness in one area which is balanced by a stronger performance elsewhere. The following three grade descriptions are provided to show the standards of achievement likely to have been demonstrated by candidates awarded those particular grades. The grade descriptions are printed identically in all exam group syllabuses except the IGCSE, which are given on page 7.

Grade descriptions are provided to give a general indication of the standards of achievement likely to have been shown by candidates awarded particular grades. The descriptions must be interpreted in relation to the content specified by the syllabus; they are not designed to define that content. The grade awarded will depend in practice upon the extent to which the candidate has met the assessment objectives overall. Shortcomings in some aspects of the examination may be balanced by better performances in others.

Grade F

Candidates perform a simple piece at an appropriate speed with some fluency and control of the resources used. They maintain an individual part within an ensemble or direct a group, giving clear instructions when to start and finish and selecting an appropriate tempo. They compose music which shows some organisation of musical ideas and uses appropriate resources. They describe musical features using a simple musical vocabulary and show some justification of opinions expressed.

Grade C

Candidates perform music with control, making expressive use of phrase and dynamics appropriate to the style and intended mood of the music. When performing with others they fit their own part within the group performance knowing when to take the lead and when to support. When directing a group they bring several parts together and suggest improvements during rehearsal. They compose music which develops musical ideas, uses conventions including simple harmony and explores the potential of musical structures and resources. They compose music which fulfils a given or chosen brief. They assess music critically, identifying musical characteristics and change and continuity in musical styles and traditions. They justify opinions and preferences, using a musical vocabulary and showing knowledge of conventions used in different times and places.

Grade A

Candidates perform music with a sense of style and command of the resources used. When performing with others they demonstrate a sense of ensemble making appropriate gradations of speed and dynamics as a member of a group. When directing a group they coordinate several parts making use of balance and expression to interpret the mood and style of the music. They compose music which shows coherent and imaginative development of musical ideas and consistency of style. They exploit musical structures, resources and conventions and produce compositions which fulfil a given or chosen brief. They assess music critically and identify specific times and places through a knowledge of musical conventions. They show an understanding of how and why musical traditions change or stay the same across time and place, including the contribution of composers and performers. They articulate opinions and preferences, using an accurate and extensive musical vocabulary.

Grade A*

There is an A* (A star) grade which is awarded to outstanding candidates. It is higher than the ordinary A grade.

This is how IGCSE group presents its grade description

	Examples of Grade F attainment	Examples of Grade C attainment	Examples of Grade A attainment
Domain A: Listening			
The demonstration of:	*Candidates should be able to:*	*Candidates should be able to:*	*Candidates should be able to:*
musical language – staff notation and rudiments	– recognise longer/shorter higher/lower notes	– recognise time (meter) – transcribe an aural rhythm	– transcribe an aural melody
an elementary harmonic sense	– recognise chord change (aurally)	– identify chords I and V, – recognise major minor (aurally)	– identify chords I, IV, V, VI – identify cadences (aurally)
instrumental and vocal timbre and texture	– recognise solo/accompaniment, strings, woodwind, brass, keyboard	–identify the more common instruments, SATB	– identify instruments playing in bass, etc.
structural and expressive elements	– recognise changes of mood (e.g. sad, cheerful, etc.)	– recognise repetition, variation, binary/ternary	– recognise derivation, sequence, imitation, fugato
an awareness and recognition of past and present musical styles	– recognise a genre such as jazz	– identify music of different periods and cultures, and the more common forms within any genre, e.g. 'blues'	– identify as Baroque, Classical, Romantic
selected works, with some knowledge of their composers		– identify structural features in any given extract	– relate any given extract to the complete work
Domain B: Performing			
The demonstration of:	*Candidates should be able to perform:*	*Candidates should be able to perform:*	*Candidates should be able to perform:*
singing or playing individually	– a simple piece played/sung adequately	– a piece of moderate difficulty played/sung with reasonable fluency and accuracy, and with a degree of sensitivity	– a piece demanding a good technique played/sung with good accuracy, intonation and style
singing or playing individually as a second instrument	as for 'singing or playing individually', but allowing for a piece of a lower technical standard		
singing or playing in an ensemble	– an easy part in a simple ensemble (e.g. elementary recorder consort) played adequately	– a part in an ensemble of moderate difficulty played/sung with some accuracy and a sensitive awareness of the other parts (e.g. a brass ensemble of moderate difficulty)	– a part in an ensemble posing some difficulties in both the part and the ensemble, played with sensitivity and style
	Candidates should be able to make:	*Candidates should be able to make:*	*Candidates should be able to make:*
repetition of musical phrases given aurally	– a barely recognisable repetition of the rhythm/melody	– a reasonably accurate repetition of the rhythm/melody	– an accurate repetition of the rhythm/melody, with a good flow if played, and with good intonation if sung
performance of previously unseen music	a recognisable attempt to play/sing sight reading Test 1 (e.g. a violinist would be required to use basic fingering in first position)	– a reasonably accurate attempt to play/sing sight reading Test 2	– a near accurate performance of sight reading Test 2, at a good tempo and with some expression
instrumental or vocal improvisation	– a repetition of the given material with just a few alterations	– a moderate attempt at improvising on the given idea, showing some variation or extension	– a musical and finished improvisation on the given idea, showing some imagination and development
Domain C: Composing			
The demonstration of:	*Candidates should be able to compose:*	*Candidates should be able to compose:*	*Candidates should be able to compose:*
composing or arranging in a variety of genres or styles	– short pieces in a simple form (e.g. binary unaccompanied song) with simple rhythms, reasonably accurately presented	– rather longer pieces with a more imaginative use of ideas and resources (e.g. a short march for trumpet, synthesiser/piano and percussion with a contrasting middle section)	– 'free' compositions of imagination that will clearly work well, and at least one example showing some competence in the handling of traditional harmony or counterpoint

▷ **Glossary of terms used**

You will probably hear or read most of the following words at some stage in your course. They are not musical words as such (there is a separate glossary for those at the back of the book), but words used in an educational context.

Aesthetic A word which relates to the appreciation of beauty.

Assessment The marking of your work; it is assessed according to criteria (assessment criteria) which have been nationally agreed and accepted by all the Groups.

Attainment targets The knowledge, skills and understanding which pupils of different abilities and maturities are expected to have by the end of each National Curriculum key stage.

Coursework Work for assessment that is produced during your course and, therefore, without the pressure of exam conditions. Composition is your main coursework.

Differentiation by outcome All candidates are free to answer the same set of structured questions which are then assessed according to your ability, and without comparison between candidates.

Free response A type of question where you have the opportunity to show your knowledge through feeling and experience. The answer will not be right or wrong as such.

Grade descriptions An account of the skills considered appropriate for a particular level of achievement. Your syllabus will have three grade descriptions (for grade F, grade C and A). You then work out the other grades from these.

Moderation The examiner's adjustment (up or down) of the marks awarded by your teachers so that they conform to the agreed standards.

National criteria Nationally agreed standards which your course and its assessment must meet. There are general criteria as well as subject-specific criteria for each of the subjects.

National curriculum A document containing provisions relating to attainment targets and programmes of study. These statutory requirements were first introduced for Music in September 1992. Music is now a foundation subject in Key Stages 1–3. Continuation of the study of music at GCSE level is not compulsory and corresponds in other subjects to Key Stage 4. The attainment targets for Key Stages 1–3 are similar to those formulated for GCSE: AT1 – Performing and Composing: AT2 – Listening and Appraising.

Rubric Explanatory instructions in an examination paper.

SCAA The Schools Curriculum and Assessment Authority which is in control of all the GCSE examinations.

Weighting The proportion of the total marks available that is given to one part of the examination.

▷ **Coursework and examination techniques**

We hear music around us all the time – in the supermarket, the restaurant, while watching a film – and much of it is inevitably filtered out from our minds. Sometimes we only notice when it stops! In many ways there is too much muzak (as this perpetual background music is called); it makes concentrated listening to music of quality more difficult, as we become accustomed to being surrounded by this 'wallpaper music'.

There is a world of difference between listening with concentration to an expressive piece of music, and playing the Top Ten on your Walkman as background entertainment. Try to develop good *listening habits* from the very start of your GCSE course. Have a notebook and pen handy so that you can jot down any responses and thoughts as they occur at the time. These need not be lengthy, but making notes, which you can later refer to, is a good way of organising your thoughts. Keep a list of all the pieces that you listen to, with brief details of who played, sang, and conducted, and also your feelings about each piece.

If you listen to too much at first, you will probably 'switch off' your attention, and what you are hearing will revert to background music. Any music that you hear in your class lessons is likely to be in short, concentrated amounts as your teacher is experienced in these matters, and realises how much is appropriate. Out of class, therefore, plan your listening in similar concentrated bouts; then think about what you have heard. Did you enjoy it? Is it a style you would like to hear more of? If you have been studying the piece at school, discuss it with your teacher and friends in class.

▷ **Good listening**

Try to follow your teacher's suggestions as to the choice of listening. Ask to borrow the tapes he or she has used for lesson material, or join your local record library, and reinforce a class topic by further listenings in your own time. When you have listened to a piece on tape or record, listen to it again a few days later. Are your responses the same? No doubt you will notice more details about the piece during the second hearing; you will continue to perceive new things with each hearing, as you become more familiar with it. Do not expect to 'understand' it first time; you will have a response straight away, but good music is very concentrated, and full of complex emotion. 'Meaning' in music is a very difficult topic. For now, perhaps you should listen innocently, without trying to analyse the meaning of the music; one thing is certain – that you will discover new things each time you return to a work.

We mentioned earlier how muzak fills up our every silence. As an experiment, try listening to film music, or TV jingles, in a new way. Concentrate on how they enhance or detract from the action. Consider whether the style is suitable for the mood of the film at any moment. Is there too much music? Would silence be effective?

There is, of course, no substitute for live music. However good your hi-fi equipment, the reproduction and atmosphere can never replace the concert hall or stage auditorium. If you have the chance to attend music in theatres, a church or concert room, notice how the musicians have been placed. Why do you think they are sitting or standing in that particular position? Is the acoustic a resonant or a 'dead' one? Did you like the way the sound carried in that particular atmosphere?

Returning to recorded music, as that is how you are likely to hear most of your music, start to be more fussy over the quality that you accept. Are the controls on your hi-fi adjusted correctly? Should there be a little less treble, and more bass for a particular piece? Most hi-fi sets now have graphic equalisers (EQ) which allow you to adjust the low, middle and high frequencies to your preferred settings. Experiment with these, and aim to be more critical with your demands for recorded music. Don't accept second best if you can help it.

▷ **Personal response**

In addition to testing your factual knowledge about a piece of music, the examiners may also be interested in your *personal response* to it. Obviously, this must come from you alone – it cannot be taught; this is why you are recommended to listen so carefully and make notes as you go along. You can be taught the things to listen for, together with numerous technical terms and signs and general musical vocabulary, but in the end a response to a piece is very much an individual thing.

Do be careful to discipline your responses. You are not asked to use music as a trigger for nostalgic experiences ('This piece is great because it reminds me of the time I went scuba diving...'); try to base any feelings you are asked to describe on the piece alone.

▷ **Note taking**

In class do write down suggestions or factual statements made by your teacher. These notes will help you with any assignments that you are given throughout the course, and will be invaluable during your revision period.

The importance of recording your feelings when listening to music has already been stressed. You should develop the habit of writing down anything which could be useful at a later stage. When listening, also jot down brief details of instrumentation/voices, the words used (if applicable), the style or period, and any other relevant notes that could enhance your appreciation of it.

When working at your practical pieces, you may need to write down short notes during your lesson so that you will remember essential points for further practice later. If you have private lessons your instrumental teacher will be discussing speeds, dynamics, light and shade in expression, pauses, breathing/fingering/bowing and a wealth of other details. You may be asked to practise certain exercises, studies or scales to improve a particular technique. Write it all down!

When composing, you may need to make several sketches before you arrive at your final result. A 'theme' or idea may come to you at any time, so write it down immediately, before you forget it! Even a few squiggles on a scrap of paper will mean something later on, and can then be worked into something of musical value when you have time. You may like to keep a compositional sketch-book so that all your ideas are in one place.

▷ **Practice habits**

One of the new things about the GCSE music examination is that you are expected to perform on an instrument (or sing) – as a soloist and/or as a member of an ensemble. The examination is encouraging the making of music, as well as the responding to it with intelligent listening. You will need to plan out your time so that you are practising regularly and to the maximum possible effect. Your instrumental teacher will have recommended (many times, no doubt) how often you should practise, and for how long. This depends on your ability, and your particular instrument, of course, but make sure you organise your time well.

Ask yourself, am I practising correctly? Some people have the habit of playing the same thing over and over again without really trying to correct faults. Isolate a mistake, work out the best way to solve it, and when you are satisfied put it back into its context. You will 'kill' a piece if you play it too many times for the sake of it.

Do respect these recommendations. It may be that you are the sort of person who has no problems with organising time for practice; but many people 'forget' or are too 'busy' for several days at a time. As a serious music student (and it is assumed that you are, or you would not have purchased this book!) this is now an area that must not be neglected.

Depending on the options that you choose, remember that you will need to practise your solo pieces, ensemble pieces, (perhaps) improvisation, or rehearsing/directing an ensemble. You may even choose to use a second instrument, and it all requires regular work and self-discipline if you are to make real progress.

The 'doodle bug'

This is rather a silly title for a serious habit which you should start to acquire. 'Doodling', or experimenting on your instrument, is very beneficial as well as being great fun. It can lead to proficiency in improvisation, give you ideas for composition, improve your sense of pitch and, in the case of guitar or keyboard, your sense of harmony. Composition is a long process of selecting sounds, and by experimenting fully with textures, chords and melodies before you start to write you will gradually evolve a style that you find pleasing – a style of your own. Whenever you find yourself with a few spare moments, shut yourself away quietly and improvise something. It need not be in exam format, but a fun piece where you will start to discover sounds of your own.

Performing experience

If you are an advanced player, you will hold no fears for performing in front of your GCSE examiner. Most likely you will have played before an audience several times at school concerts or other events, and will be fairly confident that nerves will not spoil your performance.

Less experienced players should endeavour to gain some performing experience, however small. You should try, ideally, to perform often throughout the course, but if this is not possible, your chosen performance programme must be played in class or before your friends. They may be able to make constructive comments on musical details, posture, or your placing in the room, as well as inspire you with confidence!

▷ **Coursework: composing**

Since the start of your course, you will have been composing, but not all of your work will be assessed for the exam. The good thing about GCSE is that it is all about achieving – not failing. Some of your pieces will not be your best work. You may have been under the weather when a certain piece was done, or uninspired by a certain style in which you were asked to compose. You will probably think of your first attempts as insignificant, but by the end of the course you will almost certainly have some fine pieces of work from which you can select the appropriate number for assessment.

The various Groups have different requirements for submission of compositions, and you would be well advised to re-read the assessment objectives in your syllabus from time to time. Since your teacher will be assessing your work initially anyway, it will be a good idea to listen to your teacher's suggestions on what to include or discard. You may feel you could re-write an earlier piece rather better, if you have the time; but not if your teacher has already marked it as a final assessment – that is not allowed.

Have confidence in your composing. Each piece will probably be better than the last, so that nothing is ever wasted – it is all good experience. Don't make the mistake of writing only the number of pieces that are required for submission; write as many as you are able, and select from these. Plan out your time to allow yourself regular composing periods, and you will find this a satisfying and fulfilling activity.

▷ **Revision**

How can you best prepare for the exam? There is no one way to revise; everyone must work out a way that best suits them. The following suggestions may help you formulate your own revision plans, but do discuss this with your teacher – he or she knows your work better than anyone, and can advise how you could work to best advantage.

▸ Check all the requirements for the examination very carefully in your syllabus: re-read the assessment objectives – the questions will be formulated around these. Check any details that you are unsure of – the numbers of pieces, length of programme, composition requirements etc. (Details for obtaining a syllabus are given in the Summary of this chapter.)

▸ Be absolutely certain which options you have been entered for, and what each option aims to test.

▸ Find out the actual dates of your final music exams as soon as you can, then, using your classnotes, decide on your priorities for revision. You should base your weekly revision around your weakest area. Your teacher can best advise you on your strengths and weaknesses, and your mock exam will have probably shown these. Try to organise your classnotes into topics first of all, and then put these into sections. Subdividing your work in this way may help you focus your revision. Simply re-reading notes will not help very much at all; apply them to the musical topics so that they start to mean something.

▸ Look at as many past questions as you can. You should be able to purchase past papers quite easily. (Addresses for the various Boards are given on page 4–5.) Notice the rubric (instructions in the questions). What is each question really asking? Notice the number of marks that each question carries, for this tells you what the examiners regard as important – you can then give extra revision time to these topics and skills. It is easy to waste marks by spending too long on one question, or by not reading another carefully. Practise some of these questions against the clock so that you become used to the timing.

▸ If you have a computer, perhaps you can program it so that you can test yourself, on musical terms or theoretical knowledge. Spelling should not count against you if it is clear what you mean, but do try to be accurate; your computer may be able to help here.

▸ If your school allows you to borrow records or tapes, listen to extracts as if they were exam material – test yourself with imaginary questions on instrumentation/structure/style/period/personal response etc. You may be allowed to borrow some past examination tapes.

▸ Use your teacher if there are any elements of the syllabus that you are unsure about. Ask to go through a topic in class if you are unclear about it. Avoid going into an exam worried about something that you could have checked out beforehand.

▸ Revising with your friends and testing each other can be a useful way of revising, as long as you stick to work and don't waste time! Your family may be able to help too; you could play over your performance pieces to them, or ask them to test you on some questions.

▸ Most importantly – know when to **stop** your revision. If you have organised all your work, and kept to your revision timetable you will be able to enter the exam with confidence.

▷ **Types of question**

In the written (*Listening and Appraising*) paper you will come across different types of question. Examples of these are given in Chapter 3. These may include:

(a) multiple choice questions
(b) one-line answers
(c) paragraph answers
(d) longer answers
(e) adding detail to a score
(f) response to a score (graphic or staff notation)

You will have read about Differentiation by Outcome. Some of the questions in your written paper will be structured so that credit can be awarded for depth of perception and knowledge within the answer. Obviously the number of marks allowed for a question will indicate the amount of detail that is expected for full marks. It is important to notice these when you read the question.

▷ **In the exam**   This is common sense but worth stating. If you have worked until the small hours, or been up since first light, you will not be in peak condition for taking an examination. Try to be relaxed, and wear comfortable clothes if you are allowed to do so. Also make sure that you have all the necessary equipment for writing or playing.

Read the examination paper very carefully. The rubric in the questions is usually very well worded to avoid any confusion; make sure that you have clearly understood what is expected of you before you begin your answer. How many marks is each question worth? You will be well prepared by having worked through past papers, but don't spend too long on each question make sure that you have time to finish the paper. If you have studied hard, practised well and revised thoroughly you have nothing to worry about!

SUMMARY

▷   Get a copy of your syllabus for the year you take the exam by writing to the Publications Department of your Examining Group (the addresses are given on page 4–5 of this chapter), or ask your teacher how to go about it.

▷   Know exactly what is expected of you – how much coursework and when it must be completed; what to listen to; what to perform.

▷   Organise your time and stick to it.

▷   Keep taking notes.

▷   Keep up with your regular music practice!

Chapter

2

Topic areas for all music syllabuses

▷ **GETTING STARTED**

The National Criteria for Music have stressed the importance of *Listening and Appraising, Composing* and *Performing*, and emphasise the importance of combining these activities wherever possible. The GCSE examination has to consider them separately to facilitate accurate assessment, but your teacher has probably organised your lessons in such a way that you are regularly experiencing all three activities simultaneously.

Chapters 3–12 consider these GCSE elements separately with relevant details for all the examining groups. Although this can be a book to 'dip into', it is recommended that you work your way through the exercises and specimen questions **during the course**, as they are calculated to reinforce your musical understanding, even if a particular topic is not required by your syllabus.

This chapter will cover the elements in general, describing the requirements of the various examining groups, before getting on to more detailed information later in the book. It is recommended that you obtain your own copy of the syllabus that your teacher has chosen – not to check up on him or her, but to take it upon yourself to discover exactly what GCSE Music will require of you. You will then be in a better position to plan your method of **work, practice** and **revision** for the duration of the course. Your teacher will have worked out an appropriate music course for you to follow that covers all aspects of the chosen syllabus, but you may not be fully aware of the weighting marks for the various elements. You will find some of this detail in the chapters that follow, but there is no substitute for looking at the current syllabus itself. You will find addresses for the examining groups in Chapter 1.

For basic information about the various courses read the following paragraphs carefully, with reference to your particular syllabus. *Listening and Appraising* and *Composing* requirements are outlined fully here, but further details on *Performing* components will be found later on in the book, near the beginning of each relevant chapter.

IGCSE	LONDON	MEG	NEAB	NICCEA	SEG	WJEC	TOPIC	STUDY	REVISION 1	REVISION 2
✓	✓	✓	✓	✓	✓	✓	Listening			
✓	✓	✓	✓	✓	✓	✓	Composing			
✓	✓	✓	✓	✓	✓	✓	Performing			

▷ IGCSE

Table 2.1 IGCSE GCSE Music syllabus

Core Curriculum Grades available: C to G	Extended Curriculum Grades available: A to G
Paper I: Listening (1 hr max.) Sections A to C, 4-option multiple-choice, and short-answer questions	Paper 1: Listening (2 hrs) Sections A to E, 4-option multiple- choice, and answers requiring single sentences and longer paragraphs
80 marks	160 marks
Practical assessment	
Component 2: Performing	120 marks
Component 3: Composing	120 marks

For **Listening and Appraising**, there is a written paper based on a recording. The first part of the test, comprising sections A–C, is for all candidates. Sections D and E are targetted at candidates aiming for the higher grades.

Sections A–C (for both Core and Extended candidates) will be structured as follows:

Section A

Folk (or ethnic) music selected from European, Latin American, African, Indian and Far Eastern traditions. No detailed study need be made of the music or instruments of non-Western European cultures. It will always be possible to answer any question using the descriptive terms associated with Western music.

Section B

This will use extracts selected from the *Baroque*, *Classical* and *Romantic* periods, and may be instrumental and/or vocal. You will be asked questions relating to rudiments, instruments, structure, effects, style or mood. You may be required to identify the period and suggest a possible composer.

Section C

Based on four extracts associated with *sounds of the twentieth century*, selected from a variety of styles: classical, non-classical, European and non-European.

Section D (extended candidates only)

You may be required to identify chords I, IV, V and VI and cadences aurally, and to insert rhythm or melody in a skeleton score.

Section E (extended candidates only)

You must prepare any *two* of three set works. There will be compulsory questions on a taped excerpt from each work, and a choice of questions where you demonstrate a detailed knowledge of one of these works.

The **Performing** section will consist of both *prepared* and *unprepared* performing:

Prepared

Candidates must offer:

  (i) individual singing/playing (1 piece/movement)
       and *either*
 (ii) individual singing/playing as a second instrument (1 piece/movement), *or*
(iii) ensemble singing/playing using first or second instrument (1 piece/movement).

Unprepared

Candidates must offer:

(iv) musical phrase repetition as (a) a rhythm, (b) a melody
and *either*
(v) a performance of unseen music, *or*
(vi) improvisation (vocal or instrumental) on a chosen stimulus.

For further details and guidance, refer to Chapters 5, 6, 9, 8 and 10 respectively.

For **Composing** you should present *three* pieces of differing character (in a folder and/or on tape cassette), preferably representing more than one of the categories given below. These categories probably do not cover all the possibilities. They are mainly given to suggest ideas and to encourage variety.

Candidates aiming for grades A and B should include at least one piece qualifying, and marked, as Group B. The bracketed numbers are a guide to potential marks. For example, short genres, and those imposing a structure such as (iii) will not generally enable high marks to be given, say, for Form. However, it will be possible for really outstanding tariff (1) compositions to obtain the highest marks.

Group A

These may be in any style or idiom, using any traditional, electronic, experimental or local medium. Scores (which could be the result of computer technology) are desirable, but not essential. Non-traditional notation may be used *if appropriate*, and experimental genres must include an annotated tape.

(i) an unaccompanied melody or song	(1)
(ii) an unaccompanied song, setting the candidate's or other words. The accompaniment may be for any instrument (piano, electronic organ, guitar, percussion, local instruments, etc.)	(2)
(iii) the addition of a vocal or instrumental descant above and/or below a given song	(1)
(iv) an accompanied instrumental solo (including guitar solo)	(2)
(v) a keyboard solo	(2)
(vi) a piece for two or more voices, with or without any additional accompaniment	(2)
(vii) a piece for two or more melody instruments (any chamber ensemble, steel pans, etc.)	(2)
(viii) an arrangement or variation of an existing vocal or instrumental piece	(1,2)
(ix) a piece for unpitched percussion	(1)
(x) a piece for percussion, some of which must be melodic	(1,2)
(xi) any experimental genre requiring electronic media	(1,2)
(xii) a descriptive piece using any traditional or experimental media	(1,2)
(xiii) any non-electronic experimental/avant-garde genre	(1,2)
(xiv) any local genre, using local instruments if desired	(1,2)

Group B

These must be in a 'traditional' European harmonic or melodic style and a written score (not derived from computer technology) must be included (*nb* Group A genres if written within the constraints of Group B, may qualify as Group B. For this they need not obey all the formal academic rules but the score must exhibit explicit or implied traditional harmony):

[Formal Completion-type Composition]

(xv) the harmonisation in four parts (as for SATB) of a given short melody and/or bass	(1)
(xvi) the addition of an instrumental or vocal part to a given part, making interesting two-part counterpoint	(1)

[Free 'Pastiche' Composition]

(xvii) an original piece for SATB in homophonic style (e.g. a hymn)	(2)
(xviii) an original piece for two or more parts in some contrapuntal style	(2)

(xix) an original piece for one or more voices/instruments with additional
accompaniment   (2)

(xx) an original piece for one or more voices/instruments in any other traditional
European form   (2)

▷ **London**   With this group there are two courses: the Full Course (first examination 1998) and the
Short Course (first examination 1997).

London Full Course

Candidates take three compulsory papers and one option as in Table 2.2.

Table 2.2 London Full Courses

		Component	Weighting	Mode of assessment
C	Paper 1	Performing	30%	Internal (External if required)
O	Paper 2	Composing	30%	Internal then moderated
R	Paper 3	Listening and Appraising	30%	External
E				
O	Paper 4	A: Performing on a second instrument		
P		B: Improvisation		
T		C: Commissioned composition	10%	External
I		D: Set work		
O		E: Music technology		
N				
S				

Paper 1: Performing (30%)
For details see London, Chapters 5, 6.

Paper 2: Composing (30%)
For guidance refer to Chapters 11, 12.
   You must submit two compositions lasting at least three minutes altogether. They will be
marked by your teacher and sent for moderation. You should give information on the given or
chosen brief, a notated score or commentary, and a tape recording. Arrangements are acceptable instead of compositions but they must be a new version, not just a simple transcription.

Paper 3: Listening and Appraisal (30%)
For guidance refer to Chapters 3, 4, 13, 14.
   This will be a 90-minute written paper with questions based on recorded extracts. Part 1
will be General Listening, and Part 2 Further Listening and World Music. You will need to
show an awareness of (a) music from Western traditions, (b) music from popular culture
(pop, folk, jazz etc.) and (c) non-Western music (Indian, African, Gamelan, Latin-
American, Caribbean etc.). Questions will include multiple choice, grid completion and
free response style, as appropriate.

Paper 4: (10%)
You choose one option from the following:

Option A: Performing on a Second Instrument (10%)
For details see London, Chapter 5.

Option B: Improvisation (10%)
For details see London, Chapter 10.

Option C: Commissioned Composition (10%)
For guidance refer to Chapters 11, 12.

You are asked to submit a single piece, lasting 1–2 minutes, from a choice of three commissions: (a) a musical idea, (b) a genre piece (e.g. a wedding march), (c) a word setting. You must send in a recording with *either* (i) a score written by you, *or* (ii) a commentary where you outline the process of composition, *or* (iii) a computer score. You will be allowed four weeks to complete your composition, and it will be marked externally.

Option D: Set work study (10%)
For guidance refer to Chapters 4 and 14.

You will study one work from a choice of three, all of which are based on a written score. You will be allowed an unmarked score in the examination. The 30-minute paper will be taken, after a short break, following Paper 3. Some questions may be based on extracts from a recording. You will need to show an understanding of form, development of material, and musical detail (phrase structure, cadences etc.).

Option E: Music Technology (10%)
For guidance refer to Chapter 12.

You are required to produce a sequenced performance of one piece lasting between two and five minutes. It should include at least three different timbres used simultaneously throughout. It may be an existing piece or one of your own compositions (including work submitted for Paper 2). You will be marked on performance quality – not composition quality. You must provide a copy of your source material – a tape recording or a score, and a log detailing all equipment and processes used. You will be expected to show accuracy in notation and general musicality. It will be marked externally.

London Short Course

The name Short Course is misleading. It was introduced to give greater flexibility to teachers and students. The course can still be a normal two-year course but you might have a reduced teaching time. Alternatively, you could take the examination after a year. The main benefit of the Short Course is that with the opportunity to specialise in Composing or Performing, differing timetabling arrangements in schools or colleges can be accommodated. Effectively it amounts to half a GCSE as the range of skills to be developed and the amount of knowledge to be acquired is reduced.

There are two options available: Listening and Appraising with Performing and Creative Skills (Table 2.3), *or* Listening and Appraising with Composing and Realisation (Table 2.4).

Table 2.3 London Short Course – Option 1: Listening and Appraising with Performing and Creative Skills

Paper	Section	Description		Requirements
I	A (i)	Solo performing	30%	I piece
	A (ii)	Viva	10%	I–2-minute evaluation of performance
	B (i)	*Either* Improvisation	20%	I improvisation based on a range of stimuli
	B (ii)	*Or* Music technology	20%	I piece – own choice
3	Part I of Full Course Paper 3	Music from Western traditions, including popular culture	40%	I-hour written paper

Table 2.4 London Short Course: Listening and Appraising with Composing and Realisation

Paper	Section	Description		Requirements
2	A (i)	Composing	30%	I–2 pieces
	A (ii)	Viva	10%	I–2-minute discussion of realisation of pieces
	B (i)	*Either* Performing	20%	Performance of piece(s) composed
	B (ii)	*Or* Rehearsing and Directing	20%	Organisation and realisation of piece(s) composed
	B (iii)	*Or* Music technology	20%	Sequencing of piece(s) composed
3	Part I of Full Course Paper 3	Music from Western traditions including popular culture	40%	I-hour written paper

▷ MEG

Table 2.5 MEG (1678) GCSE Music syllabus

Component	Name	Duration	Weighting
1	Listening Question Paper	$1\frac{3}{4}$ –2hrs	30%
2	Further Listening Question Paper (Terminal Task)	30 mins	10%
3	Performing (Coursework)	–	30%
4	Unprepared Performing (Terminal Task)	–	10%
5	Composing (Coursework)	–	30%
6	Composing using a given stimulus (Terminal Task)	–	10%

All candidates take the Listening Question Paper (Component 1), *one* Terminal Task (Component 2, 4 or 6) and *two* Coursework components (Components 3 and 5).

For details of the Performing components, see Chapters 5, 6 and 7 as appropriate. See Chapter 8 for Component 4 – Sight Reading.

You are required to submit two pieces of music composed during the course. You may compose in a traditional or contemporary style, including free composition, pastiche and experimental work. It is expected that you will be given, in conjunction with your teacher, a starting point from which you will develop a more detailed brief setting out your intentions. Though not a pre-requisite of the examination, credit will be given where evidence of composing in different genres can be demonstrated. This will be done by offering a third piece of composing.

For the compulsory Listening Question Paper, you will be expected to answer questions on music in a variety of styles and ensembles from:

▷ the Western tradition, from Gregorian Chant to the present day;
▷ twentieth century popular music;
▷ cultures of the world – extracts of music will be taken from a repertoire influenced by the cultures of Europe, India, Africa, Latin America and the Caribbean.

The paper will consist of two sections, which will be given in two sessions with a break in between. There will be up to twelve questions, and you will be required to answer them all.

For Component 2 (Terminal Task) – Further Listening, there will be a thirty-minute examination on musical extracts, and you must answer all three questions.

▷ NEAB

Table 2.6 NEAB (1392) GCSE Music syllabus

Component	Weighting	Description	Assessment
Listening and Appraising	40%	A test of listening skills in two Parts using excerpts on a pre-recorded cassette	2-hour written examination
Composing	30%	A folio of compositions with a total duration of 5 minutes	Internal assessment and external NEAB moderation
Performing	30%	*Two of the following:* ▷ performing a solo part/piece ▷ performing an individual part within an ensemble ▷ rehearsing/directing an ensemble	Internal assessment and external NEAB moderation

The requirements and further details for the performing element will be found in Chapters 5, 6 and 7 respectively.

Composing, which may include arranging, must be submitted as *either* a score with a cassette recording wherever possible, *or* a cassette with a detailed annotation on the appropriate Report Form. You may offer *either* one substantial composition *or* a folio which shows some variety of musical styles. You must demonstrate the ability to compose in response to given or chosen briefs, and may work in any appropriate medium or style.

For Listening and Appraising, questions will be set on musical excerpts from a wide variety of styles and periods. Musical notation will be required in some of the questions, and you will be expected to use a suitable musical vocabulary in your answers. Questions will be set on Western art music from 1550 to the present day; well-known styles of pop, jazz and contemporary music; folk music of the British Isles; and the traditional music of North and West Africa, Central and South America, including the Caribbean, and the North Indian classical tradition.

▷ NICCEA

Table 2.7 NICCEA GCSE Music syllabus

Component	Weighting	Assessment
Composing (coursework)	30%	Teacher assessment with moderation by the Council
Performing: Individually *and* in an ensemble *or* rehearsing and directing an ensemble	30%	Terminal assessment conducted by the Council's visiting assessors
Listening and Appraising	40%	Terminal assessment by aural perception exam, externally marked

Requirements and further details for the Performing components can be found in Chapters 5, 6 and 7 respectively. For Composing, your folio should consist of notated scores and/or annotated tapes, with a performance time of four to six minutes. Annotation sheets, giving details of chosen or given stimuli and the process of development for submitted compositions, must be included within folios. Your folios will be assessed in relation to the following criteria and percentage weightings:

1. organisation and development of musical ideas   12%
2. sense of completeness   9%
3. use of timbre and texture   6%
4. variety within the folio *or* application of music technology   3%

Criteria 1–3 will be applied to individual pieces within the folio; criterion (4) will be applied to the folio as a whole.

For Listening and Appraising, you will need knowledge and understanding of musical styles, idioms and conventions from the Renaissance to the twentieth century (including 'art' music, folk music, blues, jazz, and rock/pop idioms). You will study a number of set works and/or extracts.

▷ SEG

Table 2.8 SEG (3360) GCSE Music syllabus

Coursework 60%			
Performing Paper 1	**30%**	**Composing Paper 2**	**30%**
Solo Performing	15%	Composing Coursework consisting of:	
Either Ensemble Performing	15%	*Either* 2–4 pieces of music	
Or Rehearsing and Directing an Ensemble	15%	*Or* 1 substantial composition (lasting 4–5 minutes in performance)	
		together with Candidate's Commentary on each piece	
All coursework will be teacher assessed and moderated by SEG			

+

Written examination Paper 3 40%
Based on recorded excerpts of music, played on tape. There will be up to 10 compulsory questions

Further details for the Performing requirements can be found in Chapters 5, 6 and 7 respectively. For Composing you are expected to include with your commentary a statement of intention and an analysis of the outcome. Your compositions should be recorded in the most suitable form using scores and/or audio tapes as appropriate. Graphic scores must be accompanied by a recording.

The written Listening and Appraising paper will last about 1½ hours and will require you to:

▶ identify and compare distinctive characteristics of music from a wide variety of styles (Western European 'classical' from Renaissance to the present day; folk, pop and music in African, Asian, South American and West Indian traditions);
▶ relate the music to its social, historical and cultural context;
▶ make critical judgements about music, expressing and justifying views using a musical vocabulary.

You will need to be familiar with different notations – staff, graphic and chord notation (the use of letter names to represent major/minor chords e.g. Dm7).

▷ WJEC

Assessment component	Component weighting		Assessment method
Performing:			
Solo Performance	15%	30%	Externally by WJEC visiting examiner
Ensemble or Directing	15%		
Composing:			
Creating and Developing	15%	30%	Internally by teacher/moderated by WJEC
Meeting chosen/given brief	15%		
Appraising:			
Listening Examination		40%	Externally by WJEC

For details of the Performing components, see Chapters 5, 6 and 7 as appropriate.

Your Composing folio will normally contain a selection of three or four pieces, with a total playing time of 2–4 minutes, but a single work consisting of one or more movements will also be acceptable. Composing includes free composition, arranging, and pastiche (imitation of other composers' styles), and you have free choice as to genre, medium or elements used. Your compositions may be submitted as notated music and/or recordings. If you are unable to supply a score, your recording must be accompanied by an explanatory commentary.

The Listening and Appraising paper is in two parts. In Part 1 you will be expected to answer questions on stylistic and compositional detail, and you will be expected to add detail to a skeleton outline of a musical extract. You may be required to:

▶ complete rhythm and/or pitch of part of an extract;
▶ identify and correct errors in rhythm and/or pitch;
▶ identify primary triads;
▶ name/identify cadences;
▶ add phrase marks;
▶ identify changes of key/mode;
▶ identify time signatures or changes of time;
▶ identify instruments;
▶ insert appropriate musical terms and signs;
▶ recognise simple forms;
▶ compare different presentions of the same/similar material;
▶ express and justify views using a musical vocabulary.

In Part 2 you will be expected to answer questions on the work set for Detailed Study, where you will be allowed to use an unmarked score. There will also be works set for general study, this time without the use of scores. Finally, you will be expected to answer questions on unprepared musical extracts. This may include the identification of stylistic periods, instrumental and vocal sounds, structure and texture.

▷ A FINAL STATEMENT

Having now studied your relevant syllabus thoroughly, you should have a clearer idea of what is expected of you in GCSE Music. The following Chapters will break down the three main components of Listening and Appraising, Performing and Composing, so that you can more easily meet the objectives for all elements of the examination. By all means 'dip' into this book for advice or suggestions, but do try to work at the questions and exercises that have been included. There are model questions and actual examination questions; pupil answers and compositions. There is plenty here for everyone.

Good luck!

SUMMARY

▷ Obtain your own copy of a syllabus (addresses are given in Chapter 1) and read it thoroughly.

▷ Make sure that you know exactly what is expected of you in all three areas – Listening and Appraising, Performing and Composing.

▷ Choose any options carefully so that you use your strengths to the full and so that you enjoy what you are preparing.

Listening and appraising

GETTING STARTED

You will have read in Chapter 2 of the different requirements specified by the exam groups for the Listening component. The old-style GCE and CSE (Certificate of Secondary Education) exams encouraged an interest in, and an awareness of, music of different periods, by giving set works and selecting a particular period of musical history to be studied. While this may have been successful with those students who enjoyed and appreciated the serious music of the Western European tradition, it excluded large numbers of pupils who showed a preference for pop, jazz, rock, or the wealth of other musical styles from around the world. These were not included in the syllabuses at that time.

GCSE makes up for this 'oversight' by encouraging 'a perceptive response to music, including the aural recognition and identification of musical features and the critical appraisal of the expressive and structural characteristics of music' (National Criteria 1.3.1). The exam groups continue to draw on the styles and trends from Western Europe, but now include Afro-American styles and other traditions, such as Chinese, Japanese, Indian, Balinese, and Latin American, as well as the aforementioned popular styles.

In Chapter 14 the first five sections cover the main developments in Western music, its styles and composers from 1550 to the present day. Read these carefully and follow the suggestions for listening and follow-up work. You can also read about jazz, its development and important musicians, folk and pop music from 1950 onwards in the later sections of Chapter 14.

IGCSE	LONDON	MEG	NEAB	NICCEA	SEG	WJEC	TOPIC	STUDY	REVISION I	REVISION 2
							Ethnic music: music from non-Western-European cultures			
✓	✓	✓	✓		✓	✓	Indian music			
✓			✓			✓	Chinese music			
✓			✓				Japanese music			
✓	✓	✓	✓		✓		African music			
✓	✓		✓		✓		Indonesian music			
✓	✓	✓	✓	✓	✓	✓	Afro-Caribbean music			
✓	✓	✓	✓	✓	✓	✓	Listening and appraising			
✓	✓	✓	✓	✓	✓	✓	Practice questions			
✓	✓	✓	✓	✓	✓	✓	Summary			

▷ **WHAT YOU NEED TO KNOW**

▷ **Ethnic music: music from non-Western-European cultures**

Part of this chapter aims to cover music from around the world. As you listen to some recordings of music from other traditions, try to consider the following points. What instruments are being used? Are they similar to instruments that you know? Are there whole families of these instruments, or are they played singly? How do you respond to the music? What sort of mood does it convey?

Although the list is by no means complete, you should be aware of the main characteristics and instruments used in the music from the following areas:

(a) India
(b) China
(c) Japan
(d) Africa
(e) Indonesia
(f) Afro-Caribbean

The following information about music from these parts of the world, although deliberately concise, is quite sufficient for the sort of questions that you are likely to encounter in GCSE. It is essential that you should hear some examples of music from these countries for words are never adequate for describing music. Try, too, to find some illustrations of the instruments mentioned in a good book on musical instruments; it will help you to see the similarities between instruments from different countries.

Indian music

You will possibly have heard the sitar and tabla in a rock recording at some time: The Beatles, Pink Floyd, The Rolling Stones and several other groups have used these Indian instruments, with their evocative timbres. For this study you should obviously become familiar with an authentic Indian raga.

Melody is the fundamental component in Indian music. Each raga portrays a different mood or emotion which is developed through the musical skills of a particular artist, and it has its own scale pattern which can be different in its ascending and descending forms. Ragas can be associated with a certain time of day, a colour or a season, and every performance (which is totally improvised after the chosen raga is played) will try to convey the feelings of that particular raga.

The most commonly used melodic instrument is the sitar with its seven melody strings and approximately twenty 'sympathetic' strings (so-called because they vibrate in sympathy when the main strings are plucked). The neck has adjustable frets which are moved to accommodate the chosen raga scale. You may also notice a perpetual drone when listening to Indian music. This will be played on the tamboura, which resembles the sitar but has only four strings. This somewhat hypnotic drone is provided by a continuous strumming of the strings. In the absence of a tamboura, the drone is provided by a harmonium.

The tabla is the most popular of all the many kinds of drum in Northern India. The full name is tabla-banya, the tabla being the right-hand drum and the banya the left. The tabla is usually tuned to the tonic, dominant or sub-dominant of the raga. Tuning is done by knocking blocks, held by braces on the side, into place. The rhythms produced on the tabla are very sophisticated.

In the raga the most important part is at the beginning (the alap), when the mood of the raga is set in a slow, rhythm-free exposition where each note is made fully important. In the jorh and jhala some rhythm is introduced but still without percussion. Now the raga is developed in complex variations and the tabla will join the main instrument for the final section. Here rhythm is very important and both soloist and percussionist improvise a complex dialogue with each other. The Indian musician does not consciously use harmony, but will embellish notes with a slide. Their virtuosity is shown to the full here, and the increasing speed and complexity of the variations generate great excitement.

Fig. 3.1 shows some examples of well-known ragas. These notations provide only the rising and falling note patterns with the Western middle C representing the Indian SA or tonic.

Bhairav:

Darbari:

Todi:

Fig. 3.1

Having listened to some Indian music, what will you remember most about it? Did you enjoy it? Write down your thoughts and feelings on listening to it, and it will help you with further recognition.

Here are some specimen questions on extracts of Indian music.

Specimen questions

Question 1

This 'extract' will be played TWICE with a silence of half a minute between each playing. After the second playing you will have ONE minute to complete your answers.

(a)   Name the percussion instrument heard in this extract.

   Instrument _____   *(1)*

(b)   (i)   From which part of the world does the music come? Choose your answer from the following list and underline the correct area.   *(1)*

   Bali (Southeast Asia)   America   Caribbean
   Russia   Japan   India

   (ii)   What do you hear that suggests your answer?

   Reason _____   *(1)*

Note: make sure that your answers are pertinent to the examination extract. Avoid such answers as 'India, because it sounds just like something I heard in an Indian restaurant'. This may seem flippant, but has been seen several times on examination scripts. You need to explain that you have recognised the sitar or tabla, or whatever, **in the extract itself**. Remember that you are being tested on what you know, what you understand and what you can do – your answers must be completely relevant to the music.

The following is a question from the London 1998 Specimen Paper.

Question 2

   TWO sections from the same piece of Indian classical music will be played **twice**.

(a)   *Extract 1*
   Comment on this section with particular reference to speed/pulse, instrumentation, texture and structure.

   _____

   _____

   _____

   _____   *(4)*

   Extract 2
   Give four ways in which this section differs from the first.

(b)   (i)   _____

   (ii)   _____

(iii) _____

(iv) _____   *(4)*

(c) (i)   What is the name given to the rhythmic cycle in this music?

_____   *(1)*

(ii) Name one aspect of the way the melody instruments are played which give this music a distinctive Indian sound.

_____

_____   *(1)*

Chinese music

Orient music may sound strange to our ears at first, but here is a fascinating range of new tone colours for us to appreciate. Early Chinese music was used for court or ritualistic purposes, and it was believed that music should imitate the mystic harmony between heaven and earth. References to this date back at least 2500 years.

There are several types of scale in common use, but the pentatonic (five-note scale – see Chapter 13) is the best known. In fact five is a sacred number to the Chinese. They also discovered the so-called circle of fifths, C – G – D – A and so on, on which our Western scale system is based.

Chinese music does have notational systems. The oldest that can be understood today dates from about 500 AD, and was used for qin (zither) music. The qin (pronounce it 'chin') has seven silk strings stretched over a wooden soundboard. The erhu is the principal bowed instrument in China. Probably a thousand years old, this folk instrument has the horsehair of the bow located between the two strings; it is moved by the right-hand fingers to sound either of the two strings. The erhu is now becoming increasingly popular in the concert hall. The pipa is another very old stringed instrument, this time about 1500 years old! It has a pear-shaped body rather like a lute, with four strings, and is used for accompanying songs. You may also come across the sheng mouth organ, and the beautiful sounds of the 'moon' guitar.

Japanese music

The Japanese musical tradition owes much to the Chinese influence, and to some extent, to that of India. The koto derives from the Chinese qin. Over six feet long, it has thirteen silken strings that pass over movable bridges. The biwa (lute) derives from the Chinese pipa (see above), and the Sho mouth organ from the Chinese sheng. The samisen first appeared in China too. This is a three-stringed fretless instrument with a very long neck, and is plucked percussively with an axe-shaped plectrum that is very large in comparison with Western plectra.

Note: write down anything that will help you to remember the style of music that you listened to. Was it very different from the Chinese music? If so, why?

African music

To an ethno-musicologist (an expert in the musical culture of a particular group of people) there would be many different styles within the music of such a large continent. For our purposes, we can only generalise.

In many African tribes, percussive instruments are surrounded by taboo, and they are used in all the important rituals. Although harmonic structure is often not important, most African music is certainly very complex rhythmically. There is an infinite variety of drums, played singly, in pairs or in large groups. Besides their use in tribal ritual, drums are an important method of communicating – a sort of bush telephone service! Try to hear a recording of the so-called 'talking drums', or the Nigerian hour-glass drum, where tension in the drum heads is rapidly changed to vary the pitch of the drum.

Note: how different is African music from everything else that you have heard? What will you remember about it that will help you recognise further examples of it? How does African singing differ from Western-style singing?

This is a specimen question set by London for 1998.

You will hear an extract from a Paul Simon song, *Born At The Right Time*. The extract will be played **twice**.

Describe FOUR ways in which African music has influenced this composition.

(i) _____

(ii) _____

(iii) _____

(iv) _____ *(4)*

Note here how there is a link up between Western music and African music. You are not expected to be experts on ethnic music – just to respond to it musically and have a basic knowledge of the styles and instruments.

Indonesian music

The characteristic sounds of the gamelan orchestras of Bali and Java are unforgettable, and once heard you should have no difficulty in identifying them. A typical gamelan will consist of several different sized gongs (the bonang), metallophones with bronze keys (the saron), many different types of wooden xylophones, and metal and leather drums (including the kendang drum). The characteristic bell-like sound quality is created by the method of tuning; the instruments have the same note tuned slightly differently to set up a 'beat' between them. There may be any number from twelve to about thirty players in a gamelan and each village has its own version. Depending on locality there may be simple flutes or stringed instruments added. For example, the island of Bali has a musical sound that is distinct from that of Java, but for GCSE purposes you will simply need to recognise the overall Southeast Asian percussive sound.

Afro-Caribbean music

You will read a little about reggae, ska and rock steady in Chapter 14 (Black music). These popular dances and instrumental styles originated in Jamaica. But from Trinidad, just off the coast of South America, comes another type of folk music – the steelband. Apparently the Trinidad authorities had banned the use of bamboo instruments on the grounds of noise! It is said that someone thought up the idea of making steel drums in the process of mending his dustbin... What happens now is that oil drums are converted into steelpans. The top is sunk with a hammer and the positions of the notes worked out. The initial tuning is a careful process after the pan has been burnt to improve its tone. Steel drums are made in different sizes and played with rubber-ended sticks to produce the distinctive steelband sound.

Note: how do you tell the difference between gamelan music and steelpans? Find out and write it down!

▷ Listening and appraising

How you are tested

The Examining Groups all have different ways of testing your knowledge of and response to music. There may be multiple-choice questions, short one-word or line answers, or questions requiring longer and more detailed answers. Be sure to understand what each question is trying to test. Read each question, and listen to the cassette recording carefully to avoid misunderstanding.

Here is a checklist of topics or concepts that you should be familiar with to feel confident in this part of the examination. You can use the index and glossaries at the back to find further information as required, as most of these words are discussed in detail somewhere in this book. They are words that can be applied to many styles and trends of music.

sequence	ostinato/riff	simple/compound time
phrasing	development	tempo
form or structure	variation	dissonance/consonance
ornamentation	instrumentation	unison/polyphony/antiphony
dynamics	tonality	harmonic figuration
counterpoint	modality	harmonic movement
imitation	atonality	chromatic
modulation	texture	rubato
timbre	syncopation	Alberti bass

▷ **PRACTICE QUESTIONS**

Finally, here are some specimen questions to show the wide variety that may be asked. You cannot fill in the answers in this book, but you should read the questions several times, and ask yourself how you would go about answering them. Notice the number of marks that are available and gauge your response accordingly.

These few questions are intended to give some idea of what to expect in the Listening examination. All the Groups will test both general and particular listening skills (and set works, which are discussed in the next chapter). Your teacher will not be able to cover the whole range of world music – it is a vast subject – but will select appropriate examples for you to listen to throughout the course, bearing in mind the details of your syllabus. Remember with GCSE that the background factual content of music is less important than the discipline of listening.

▷ **Question 1**   You will hear an extract of rock music in three main sections. Write briefly on each section, mentioning the speed, mood and instrumentation.

Section 1 _____

_____

Section 2 _____

_____

Section 3 _____

_____   *(6)*

(**Note:** the question is very clear. It states that your answer must be brief, and tells you exactly what to write about.)

▷ **Question 2**   What are the two solo instruments in this extract?

(i) _____

(ii) _____   *(2)*

Is the extract taken from a symphony, an oratorio, an opera or a string quartet?

_____   *(2)*

What period does the extract come from: Renaissance, Baroque, Classical, Romantic or Modern?

_____   *(2)*

(**Note:** here you could possibly work out your answer by a process of elimination (knowing what it cannot be) or alternatively by being familiar with all the stated types of music or period styles.)

▷ **Question 3**   For WJEC you may be played a short melody with differences in pitch (and another with differences in rhythm) to your printed version. You may be asked to indicate where the mistakes occur, and state whether they were too high or too low.

Here is an example (WJEC 1995):

The melody you will hear played has been incorrectly written out below. It contains **four** errors in pitch. It will be played **four** times. The first three notes and the last three notes are correct.

Andantino

Fig. 3.2

(a) Put a circle around **each** of the notes which are incorrect.   *(2)*

(b) Indicate whether the notes you have circled are too **high** or too **low**.

The first note is circled is too _____

The second note circled is too _____

The third note circled is too _____

The fourth note circled is too _____   *(2)*

(c) On the staves below, write out the complete melody correcting the errors in pitch.   *(2)*

Andantino

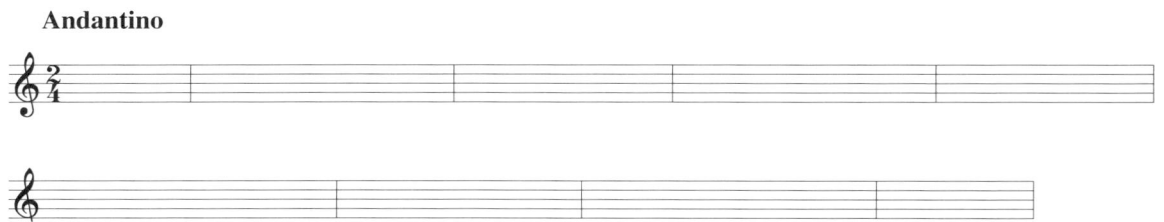

Fig. 3.3

▷ **Question 4**   For London in Part 2 (further Listening and World Music) Full Course candidates may be given a partial score of some music, and asked to answer some questions with several hearings on tape. You will be given time to digest all the questions thoroughly before the first hearing. Some of the questions may require straightforward factual answers that could be done without the tape. Organise your time carefully here, and don't mis-read the questions!

Here are some specimen questions on an imaginary extract of twenty-five bars:

(i) The key of this piece is B♭ major. Insert the key signature where necessary.   *(2)*
(ii) Name the instrument which first plays in bar 13.   *(3)*
(iii) Insert the following signs (Fig. 3.4) at appropriate places within bars 1–12.

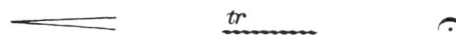

Fig. 3.4

(3) × (2)

(iv) Insert the missing accidental in bar 4.   *(2)*

(**Note:** (i) and (iii) are simple tests of music theory – you will need to learn this. In (ii) remember to count the bars throughout each hearing of the extract, for you cannot guess this sort of answer.)

▷ **Question 5**   *(Each excerpt played three times)*

You will hear **three** excerpts of dance music. Brief answers are required in Section A where you will hear each excerpt twice:

SECTION A Excerpt 1 (played twice)

(a)   time signature *or* type of dance _____

(b)   period of composition _____

(c)   possible composer _____

Excerpt 2 (played twice)

(a)   time signature *or* type of dance _____

(b)   period of composition _____

(c)   possible composer _____

Excerpt 3 (played twice)

(a)   time signature *or* type of dance _____

(b)   period of composition _____

(c)   possible composer _____ *(9)*

SECTION B (each excerpt played once)

Write about any features (such as instrumentation, structure and tempo) in these pieces which reflect the periods in which they were written:

_____

_____

_____

_____

_____

_____ *(6)*

(NEAB Specimen Paper 1998)

(**Note:** this question is clearly worded. In Section B answer the three points equally if you can, and the amount of space allowed for your answer gives you some idea of the detail required for maximum marks.)

▷ **Question 6**   The next extract is from a symphony. Name the instrument playing which is not usually heard in a work of this kind and indicate the word which best describes the closing section of the extract. The extract will be played twice.   *(2)*

Instrument _____

CANON / FUGUE / OSTINATO / OBBLIGATO / RONDO
(Underline your answer)   (WJEC 1991)

▷ **Question 7**   The verse of the song has four phrases. Which of the following best represents its structure?

AABB   ABAB   ABBA   ABBC   (IGCSE 1991)

▷ **Question 8**   You are going to hear two examples of folk music from different parts of the world. Each extract will be played *four* times with a pause between each playing.

Music A1
The diagram below represents Music A1.
Look at the diagram and read through questions 1 to 6.
Now listen to Music A1 and answer the questions.

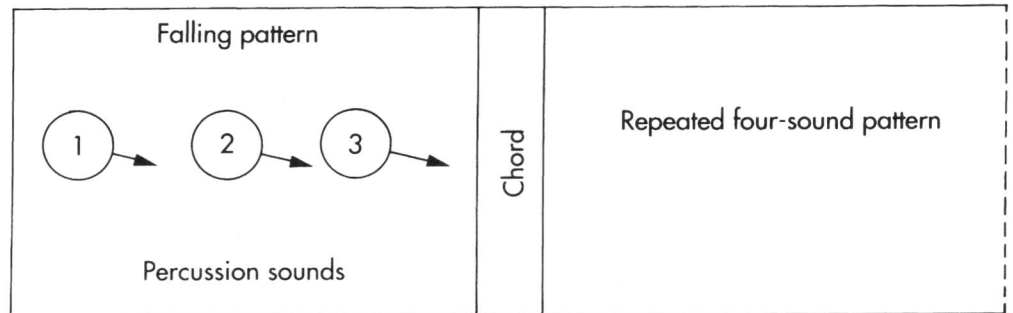

Fig. 3.5

1. Which pair of instruments is heard in this extract?

   ☐ banjos

   ☐ guitars

   ☐ harps

   ☐ violins   *(1)*

2. The second of this pair of instruments does not play at first. When does it enter?

   ☐ at the beginning of falling pattern 2

   ☐ during falling pattern 2

   ☐ at the beginning of falling pattern 3

   ☐ during falling pattern 3   *(1)*

3. Briefly comment on the rhythm of the percussion sounds.

   _____ *(1)*

4. Complete the following sentence, including *some* of the bracketed words in your answer:

   (notes, chords, discords, octaves, broken, rising, falling, by step, by leap, repeated)

   Each repeated four-sound pattern consists of _____

   _____ *(2)*

5. Which statement describes the complete repeated four-sound pattern section?

   ☐ It is all in the same key

   ☐ It has one change of key

   ☐ It is in several keys

   ☐ It is not in any key   *(1)*

6. Of which country or part of the world is this style of music typical?

   _____ *(1)*

                                                                                                           (IGCSE 1992)

▷ **Question 9**   This extract will be played THREE times.

'Prithee pretty maiden, will you marry me?
Hey but I'm hopeful – willow willow waly,
I may say at once I'm a man of propertee –

Hey willow waly O!
Money, I despise it, many people prize it,
Hey willow waly O!

Gentle Sir although to marry I design,
Hey but he's hopeful, willow willow waly –
As yet I do not know you and so I must decline,
Hey willow waly O!
To other maidens go you, as yet I do not know you –
Hey willow waly O!'

(i) In the first verse – which line repeats the music of line 1?

_____ (1)

(ii) There is an example of *sequence* in verse 1. Write out the words of the line where it appears.

_____

_____ (1)

(iii) Name the two types of voice in this duet.

_____ (2)

(iv) Give the number of a line where the two voices sing together.

_____ (1)

(v) Which of the voices sings this phrase in the second verse?

Fig. 3.6

_____ (1)

(vi) Name the cadence at the end of each verse.

_____ (1)

(NICCEA 1991)

▷ **Question 10** You will hear three examples taken from the same choral work. The examples will be played one after the other as a set, and you will hear the set twice. After a short pause the set will be played again and after another pause you will hear it for the fourth and final time.

(a) List *three* features which the examples have in common.

_____

_____

_____ (3)

(b) Is this music from an opera, a mass, a madrigal or a musical?

_____ (1)

(c) Ring *one* of the names given below as the composer of this music.

Gershwin   Haydn   Purcell   Rachmaninoff   Shostakovich   (1)

(d) Are the examples mainly in the major key, the minor key or a mixture of both?

_____ (1)

(e) Write a brief paragraph on *each* of the *three* examples.
Base your answer on the following:
forces used, both vocal and instrumental;
how many parts;
types of voices;
harmony, modulation;
musical devices such as ornamentation or sequence;
text;
comment on the way each example ends, e.g. in terms of a recognised cadence.

_____

_____

_____

_____

(18) (another whole page in addition to these lines was given)

(SEG 1991)

▷ **Question 11** *(Each excerpt played four times)*
You will hear **two** settings of these two words:

Kyrie eleison   *Lord have mercy*
Christe eleison   *Christ have mercy*

Setting A was composed in the Renaissance period.
Setting B was composed in the Classical period.

Identify the distinguishing musical features of each setting, relating each to the particular period of composition.
    How do these two pieces reflect continuity and change in the choral tradition?

Setting A *(played twice)*

_____

_____

_____

_____

(3)

Setting B *(played twice)*

_____

_____

_____

_____

(3)

Comment on how the two settings illustrate changes in choral traditions.
(Setting A, Setting B. Setting A, Setting B)

_____

_____

_____

_____

_____

_____

_____

(9)

(NEAB Specimen Paper 1998)

▷ **Question 12**   (*Played four times*)

You will have **one** minute to look through the music before the first playing.

This question is based on the opening section of the slow movement from Dvořák's Symphony *From the New World*. An incomplete score of the melody is printed below.

Write your answers in the spaces provided.

(4)

(3)

(2)

(1)

(3)

(13)

Fig. 3.7

(NEAB Specimen paper 1998)

▷ **Question 13**   You will hear **three** excerpts, A, B, and C. You will hear each excerpt **twice**, with a short pause between each playing.

You may find it helpful to tick the box each time you hear the excerpts.

A ☐ ☐   B ☐ ☐   C ☐ ☐

For each excerpt tick **three** features heard.
(Some features may appear more than once.   (*3 × 3 marks*)

	Excerpt A	Excerpt B	Excerpt C
Glockenspiel			
Harpsichord			
Marimba			
Recorder ensemble			
Saxophone			
Solo Violin			
Imitation			
Riff			
Walking Bass			
Glissando			
Pizzicato			

(SEG Specimen Paper 1998)

SUMMARY

▷   Become familiar with non-Western-European music. Listen to various styles and make notes about it.

▷   Use the practice questions above to be aware of the many different styles of Listening and Appraising questions. Note how many marks are available for each part of the question to gauge just how detailed your answer should be.

Chapter

4

Set works

▷ **GETTING STARTED**

To its devotees, music is the most fascinating and purposeful activity known to man. Many people are quite content to listen 'innocently' without bothering to think of the historical importance of a work, its structure or its instrumentation. Indeed, a great deal of pleasure is to be gained in this way, and people must be free to listen to music in any way they wish. But there are several different responses when listening to music – physical, emotional, imaginative, intellectual; of these, the intellectual response is the most sophisticated, and occurs when music is enjoyed and appreciated for its sheer beauty and the way the composer has manipulated musical form. Therefore the greater the knowledge of the way the music is constructed, the greater the response intellectually.

Naturally, it is possible to have several of these responses at the same time. With simple pop music even an untrained ear can respond immediately in a physical and emotional way. With GCSE we are aiming a little higher – the course aims to develop your capacity to respond to, and appreciate, all that is to be found in the music you play and hear.

Elsewhere in this book you will find explanations and examples of musical structure, technical terms and details of instruments which are mentioned in this chapter. Here some specimen analyses are given which should help you prepare and revise for your set work, even if yours is not included here. Remember that composers did not write their music so that exam candidates could analyse them – they are works of art that sometimes defy being put into categories. There is often more than one way to analyse a piece; you may even disagree with your teacher! Thinking out the different ways of explaining its construction will help you clarify your own thoughts on the work.

Please note that the seven analyses are not necessarily current set works, but you are well advised to study them as practice for your own. Consult you syllabus for specific information.

IGCSE	LONDON	MEG	NEAB	NICCEA	SEG	WJEC	TOPIC	STUDY	REVISION 1	REVISION 2
✓	✓			✓		✓	Analysis 1: Vivaldi			
✓	✓			✓		✓	Analysis 2: Handel			
✓	✓			✓		✓	Analysis 3: Haydn			
✓	✓			✓		✓	Analysis 4: Beethoven			
✓	✓			✓		✓	Analysis 5: Glinka			
✓	✓			✓		✓	Analysis 6: Debussy			
✓	✓			✓		✓	Analysis 7: Bartók			
✓	✓			✓		✓	Suggestions for study			
✓	✓			✓		✓	Summary			

> ## WHAT YOU NEED TO KNOW

Use the given analyses as 'models' for your own set work. The principles used in the analyses will help you approach any particular set work.

> ## Analysis1: Vivaldi

Vivaldi: 'Winter' from The Four Seasons Op. 8 no. 4

1. First of all make sure that you are using the correct edition of the work. The examining group will obviously base its questions on the stipulated publication; early works tend to differ substantially. (For this study we are using Edition Eulenberg No. 1223.)
2. Listen to and follow through the set work as many times as you can, improving your score-reading as you do so. With an orchestral score you may need to follow the melody lines first of all. You won't have time (in faster music) to read every note. Learn to scan – and if you count carefully, at least you should be in the right bar! Follow the shape of the melodies at first; it will certainly become easier with practice.

    'Winter' has many interpretations on record – you may like to listen to more than one. Some use original instruments and small orchestras; others modern instruments and perhaps a larger group.
3. Pencil Vivaldi's Sonnet into the relevant areas of the score (see the translation on p. VII of the score). It is assumed that the composer wrote these words himself, to explain the winter programme of his concerto. When you follow through now you will be able to see and hear more easily what Vivaldi is describing in sound.
4. Read about Vivaldi. When did he live and where did he work? How many Concertos in the style of 'Winter' did he produce? Listen to more concertos by him, especially the three other *Seasons*.
5. Be sure of the difference between a Baroque concerto such as this, and the eighteenth- and nineteenth-century Concerto with its elements of display.
6. Read up about Basso Continuo and the whole Baroque convention of figured bass.

You will often find helpful background notes in the score itself, as we do here in the Prefaces to 'Winter'. 'Winter' is the final concerto in the well-known set of four entitled *The Four Seasons* – for solo violin, strings and basso continuo. We are not sure when they were actually written but we know that they were published in 1725, by which time Antonio Vivaldi (c.1675–1741) was a mature composer. While he was music director at a girls' orphanage school in Venice, Vivaldi was composing prolifically for the orchestra there. In his lifetime he composed over 400 concertos, nearly forty operas and much church music (including the popular *Gloria*). Although he was ordained in 1703, a chronic chest complaint prevented him from entering the priesthood, but his nickname 'il prete rosso' (the red-haired priest) apparently stuck!

The Concerto is in F minor and cleverly depicts various winter activities and characteristics, such as 'chattering teeth' (see Fig. D in the score) which inspires an effective use of tremolando from the upper strings and soloist (Fig. 4.1).

solo violin

Fig. 4.1

'Stamping of feet to keep warm' (see Fig. C) employs a favourite Vivaldi device, the sequence shown in Fig. 4.2.

solo violin bars 23-24

Fig. 4.2

The opening 'shivering' orchestral build-up is produced by the simplest of means – trills in the solo part (Fig. 4.3).

Fig. 4.3

Notice the figures below the bass notes in this opening section. For example, bar 7 is labelled $^6_4$ (below the bass F) and the harpsichord player is required to add the chord (Fig. 4.4).

Fig. 4.4

This chord (B flat minor), can be played in an appropriate way at the discretion of the keyboard player – if it was not marked at all he would simply play an ordinary chord of F (minor) (Fig. 4.5). This is a straightforward and effective musical shorthand, and at the time saved composers a good deal of writing, especially with their lengthy operas!

Fig. 4.5

Notice in bar 3 the indication 'stacc. sim.' (staccato simile). This saves the repeated printing of the staccato notes as in bar 1, and it is easier on the eye not to see so many score markings.

The soloist makes a dramatic entry at Fig. B (bar 12) with a rapid demisemiquaver figure depicting the icy wind. The orchestral strings continue to punctuate this solo with references to their opening 'shivering' figure. This section has been in C minor. (Notice the necessary B naturals which confirm this key. Always look for these accidentals; they are usually new leading notes which affect the modulation into a new key for variety.)

At bar 19, the E natural brings us back to the tonic key of F minor for the strongly rhythmic 'foot-stamping' theme at Fig. C, already mentioned above. The solo violin embarks on more demisemiquavers and extends this figure with only basso continuo as accompaniment (bars 26–33). It remains in F minor throughout. The ripieno (backing strings) re-enter at bar 33 with a 'wind' figure of their own (♪ ♪ = another shorthand way of writing repeated demisemiquavers). Bars 34–5 are written in B flat major (A natural is the new leading note), and using a rising harmonic sequence to change key, Vivaldi goes to C minor at bars 35–6 (B natural is the leading note), then E flat major by means of the returned B flats in bars 36–7. So we finish this section and start the new one in E flat major (bar 38).

This next section is based on the opening material and feels slightly different, being in the major key this time. Notice the sequences again with full strings (41–44), and once more with the soloist (44–46). Fig. D, we have already discussed with its effective 'chattering' tremolando – an easy effect to produce for string players. This starts in C minor. Notice how Vivaldi gives tonal variety in this section by omitting the bass instruments altogether – the viola is the lowest instrument here. The movement is completed by a rousing return to F minor with the stamping figure first heard at Fig. C. Only 63 bars long altogether, the movement is a highly effective piece of descriptive string writing.

Think of the variety Vivaldi has achieved within his first movement – moments of drama (Fig. C) with a chance to shine for the harpsichordist; thinner textures where the soloist is accompanied only by continuo; and memorable harmonic figures throughout.

The delightful slow middle movement is only eighteen bars long! It is in the major key and calmly depicts someone resting peacefully by the fireside while outside it is pouring with rain. The composer establishes this restful contentment with an eight-bar solo violin melody which modulates to the dominant key of B flat major. The second half reiterates the melody and works back to the tonic, then adds two bars as a miniature coda. The rain is portrayed by simple means – pizzicato semiquavers in the 1st and 2nd violins (this also serves as a momentum to the music). The bass part throughout consists of repeated quavers (♪♪♪♪) and the viola is printed with a static line (marked 'con l'arco' – an instruction to use the bow, that is, not play pizzicato like the others). In some recordings this viola line is decorated and given more movement, and most effectively too.

The final movement, in 3/8 time, returns to F minor, and the programme is concerned with walking and slipping on ice which finally cracks and breaks. The winds blow furiously and bring the concerto to a furious dramatic conclusion.

The opening is for solo violin, with a tonic pedal sustained on continuo cello. (The words 'tasto solo' inform the harpsichord player not to fill in with chords; and 'arcate lunghe' simply means 'long bows' for the cellist.) This first melody is sometimes performed in a flexible rhythm to suggest the trepidation of someone walking on thin ice (Fig. 4.6).

Fig. 4.6

Notice how the pedal note changes to a dominant pedal (on C) at bar 21. The rhythm turns to quavers (♩♩♩) in the upper strings from Fig. G, then the downward scales at various speeds from Fig. H suggest a fall on the ice. The word 'tutti' at bar 48 implies that the harpsichord should play again from here. A staccato semiquaver figure commences at Fig I in the solo violin, depicting another attempt at walking on the ice – this time with more confidence (Fig. 4.7).

Fig. 4.7

Observe the tonic pedal notes this time are held in the 1st and 2nd violins (bars 51–60); the violas act as the bass part, while the basso continuo is silent. 'Tasto solo' is again indicated from bar 61–123 where the solo violin has most of the musical interest. Notice the soloist's strongly rhythmic figure at bar 73–9, its commencement is shown in Fig. 4.8.

Fig. 4.8

This section is built over the pedal note of G which is the dominant of C minor. Fig. L is where the ice cracks and breaks (Fig. 4.9).

Fig. 4.9

The Sirocco wind is depicted from Fig. M in C minor – a theme not dissimilar to Fig. G (although describing different things; Vivaldi is conscious of the need for a sense of musical repetition). Fig. M–N is hesitant at first, but the soloist interrupts at 120 with a rapidly scurrying scalic passage in E flat major. This is completely unaccompanied to begin with, then punctuated with tremolando demisemiquavers (♬♬♬ | ♪⁷) by the full orchestra every so often until 137 where the texture becomes thicker to the end. Bar 125 is back in F minor, and it remains in this key except for a brief transitory modulation at 131–134. This is a most exciting climax to the concerto.

Obviously, teachers will pick out different points when working through a score with pupils – some may emphasise the programmatic content (i. e. Vivaldi's sonnet), others may place more importance on chords, keys, themes and rhythms. The overall intention is for you to get to know the work very well and see how the composer has constructed it.

Here are some specimen questions on 'Winter'. When answering try to show your knowledge as clearly as possible – remember some of the questions are differentiated. In other words, you may be 'correct' with a minimum answer but try to give more detailed information if this is relevant. You can only expect good marks for a question if it is answered both fully and clearly.

A favourite, and obvious, question is to present the candidate with a page of the score and ask for it to be put into context: e.g. 'Where exactly in the work does this extract occur?'

Be precise! Supposing bars 9–13 of the slow movement (i.e. p. 16) were to be identified. A good answer would be: 'This extract comes from the slow middle movement (largo); it is from the second half where the solo violin presents the main theme in the dominant key of B flat major. The other strings continue as before and their individual pizzicato rhythms effectively depict the rainfall.' (A weak answer would simply state 'this comes from the slow movement'.) Obviously the detail required for a particular answer depends on the number of marks it carries. **Use your common sense!**

Specimen questions

Question 1
London (1989) gave bars 1–12 of the first movement of 'Winter' as a full printed extract. The following questions were asked. (Answers are not provided here; refer to the text above or glossaries at the back). Notice the amount of marks available for each question.

(a) Where exactly in the work does this extract occur?   (2)
(b) Name the key at the end of the extract.   (2)
(c) The bottom stave in each system is marked B.C. What does this mean,
     and which instruments would you expect to play in this part?   (2)
(d) Comment on the harmony of this extract.   (2)

Question 2
The second movement has one texture throughout. Describe this.   (8)

Question 3
Write a description of the third movement. You should refer to keys, texture, structure and any other matters which you consider would help a listener to understand this movement. You may if you wish give musical illustrations.   (14)

Practice questions and answers

Having carefully studied the notes on 'Winter' and using the glossaries at the back of this book, try to answer the following questions on 'Autumn' from The Four Seasons Op.8 no. 3.
(WJEC 1998)

Question 1
In the first movement, is the string writing mainly homophonic or contrapuntal?

Question 2
How important is this musical figure in the first movement?

Allegro

f

violin solo

Fig. 4.10

Question 3
We are told in Vivaldi's accompanying sonnet that, in this first movement, the peasants are celebrating their successful harvest with songs and dances. The movement ends with the peasants dropping off to sleep after too much wine. How does Vivaldi portray these two scenarios?

Question 4
How varied is the soloist's part in this first movement?

Question 5
The second movement represents a rest from the singing and dancing. How does Vivaldi create this feeling of relaxation?

Question 6
In what key is the third movement at (a) bars 1–8 and (b) bars 69–76?

Question 7
You will hear six different excerpts taken from throughout this Prepared Work. In each case give the name of the movement from which it has been taken, i.e. Movement 1, 2 or 3.

(a) _____

(b) _____

(c) _____

(d) _____

(e) _____

(f) _____

Answer 1
Homophonic; especially on the tutti sections.

Answer 2
Very important. As it is the main tutti theme it recurs several times throughout the movement: bars 1–6 (F major); 14–l9 (soloist – F major); 57–59 is a variant of the theme (G minor); 63–67 (D minor); 77–80 is another variant (C major); finally 106 to the end (F major).

Answer 3
The happy dancing mood is established immediately with the opening Allegro melody, which persists throughout (see A.2 above). The soloist also confirms this mood with his decorative episodes between the tutti sections. The drunken sleep mood is easily portrayed: a contrasting larghetto in a soft F minor provides instant contrast. For the first eight bars of section C, Vivaldi provides a reduced accompaniment of moving quavers to the solo melody of falling sevenths. At bar 97 the solo violin has only long held notes; violas enter in minims as a bass part, and the two violin parts have a punctuated *pp* middle part to the harmony.

Answer 4
The solo part is extremely varied. Once the soloist has played the main theme (bars 14–27 in double stopping), his part is mainly an embellishment to the contrasting episodes between the orchestral tutti sections. Bars 32–35 are semiquaver arpeggios; 36–38 are rapid descending scales; 39–40 are ascending semiquaver triplets; 41–43 further falling scales in demisemiquavers; 44–48 a mixture of expressive quavers and descending semiquaver triplets. From bars 49–56, the descending semiquaver triplets lead to rising crotchet trills, a rapid descending scale and punctuated single quavers. From bars 67–77 there is a mixture of arpeggio and scalic figures. The solo part at the larghetto (bars 89–105) is slow-moving and expressive.

Answer 5

By using slow-moving notes, played legato, in an adagio molto (very slow) tempo. The upper strings are marked sordini (muted). The volume decreases as the movement progresses. The harmony is constantly shifting and avoiding resolution.

Answer 6

(a) F major; (b) C major, the dominant.

▷ Analysis 2: Handel

Handel: Messiah (Nos 2–4 and 44 only)

Handel's oratorio 'Messiah' is a lengthy work containing 53 separate numbers divided into three Parts. The three extracts come from Part I which prophesies the coming of Jesus Christ (the Messiah); it tells of His birth, and sings of the joy which His nativity inspires.

The work is performed very regularly, although some numbers are sometimes cut because of its great length. Handel worked with amazing speed when composing this oratorio; it took him only twenty-four days in August 1741, and this was in the days before electricity – no light and no photocopiers! He used previously composed material for just four of the numbers, but everything else was new. *Messiah* was first performed the following year in Dublin.

The first three numbers considered here appear immediately after the Overture:

No. 2: Tenor recitative: 'Comfort ye my people'
No. 3: Tenor aria: 'Ev'ry valley shall be exalted'
No. 4: Chorus: 'And the glory of the Lord'

Practice questions and answers

The following questions and answers are designed to inform you on many aspects of the set extracts. You will not have so many questions on one work in the examination.

Question 1
What is an oratorio?

Question 2
Where do the words for *Messiah* come from?

Question 3
Give a general description of No. 2: 'Comfort ye my people'. *(12)*

Question 4
No. 3: 'Ev'ry valley shall be exalted' follows on from No. 2 with the same soloist. Comment on any similarities or differences between the two pieces. *(5)*

Question 5
Comment on Handel's use of word-painting in No. 3. *(5)*

Question 6
Write a general description of the Chorus: 'And the glory of the Lord'. You should comment on keys, structure, texture and anything else which you feel would help a listener to understand this extract. Use relevant musical illustrations if you wish. *(15)*

Question 7
Give an account of the 'Hallelujah' Chorus (No. 44), commenting especially on the differing styles of vocal writing. *(8)*

Answer 1
An oratorio is a musical setting of a Biblical story, for solo voices, chorus and orchestra.

Unlike an opera, there is no acting or costume, and performances today are usually in a church or concert hall rather than a theatre. Oratorios are constructed with seperate numbers, with a mixture of recitatives, arias, duets (and other solo combinations) and choruses. The orchestra accompanies the voices primarily, but there would usually be an Overture and some interludes for orchestra alone.

Answer 2

They come from different parts of the Bible and were compiled by Handel's friend, Charles Jennings.

Answer 3

This number employs two styles of recitative. The first, from the opening as far as figure C, is very lyrical with a gentle orchestral accompaniment. It is unusually tuneful for a recitative. The second style is in the last eight bars and is rather like 'recitativo secco' – dry, punctuated chords (although the strings are used here, not just harpsichord and cello as for true 'secco' style) with a dramatic vocal line in keeping with the words: 'Prepare ye the way of the Lord, make straight in the desert a highway for our God'. This piece ends with the customary perfect cadence, which, although written directly beneath the last words, is always delayed until the singer has finished. Another convention at this point is the singer's added passing-note, see Fig. 4.11.

Fig. 4.11

This is a very popular piece, and is frequently used by singers as a seperate solo item, together with the aria that follows.

It starts in E major, and the calm three-bar introduction not only sets the mood, but is used as a link throughout the piece (bars 14–15, 21–22, 27–29). This is common practice with Handel and other Baroque composers. Handel has two unaccompanied bars (8 and 20) where full attention is focused on the soloist. He starts to make the change to the more dramatic vocal style in bar 23: 'that her iniquity is pardon'd', where the solo line becomes more angular. There is a final statement of the introductory figure, this time in the dominant key of B major, before the final dramatic eight bars (ending in A major) which lead on to the companion aria.

Answer 4

Recitatives generally give information and set the scene with little or no repetition of words. They are often sung by a tenor voice as it carries well when there are so many words to hear and comprehend. Arias, on the other hand, are more reflective and the repetition of lines allows the listener to dwell on the meaning of the words. Arias are commonly preceded by recitatives, sung by the same singer.

The recitative in No. 2 has more repetition than normal and is unusually tuneful to begin with. The aria, also starting in E major, is very melodic and makes extensive use of melisma (many notes to one syllable) and word-painting, (see Answer 5 for more details on this.) Both pieces use the occasional unaccompanied bar which draws full attention to the solo line. There are similarities too in the use of the orchestra, as Handel gives it both a melodic and harmonic accompaniment role in the two pieces. The chords in bars 56–58 of No. 3 simply punctuate the singer's melodic line, which is similar to, but less dramatic than the final few bars of No. 2.

Answer 5

It is quite usual for composers in all periods to illustrate musically (or word-paint) the text that they are setting. Handel was no exception. Here he depicts a feeling of exaltation very effectively by using many notes (48 to be exact!) in a rising sequence in E major (bars 15–19). Similar treatments of the same word are used in bars 21–24 and 47–51. A simple portrayal of height and depth is given in bars 24–26 (Fig. 4.12).

and ev-'ry moun-tain and hill_____ made low

Fig. 4.12

Crookedness is given an angular melodic line in bars 33–34 (Fig. 4.13).

the crook – ed straight

Fig. 4.13

While in bars 29–32, and 36–41 he suggests a feeling of plainness by using a smoother melody (Fig. 4.14).

and the rough pla-ces plain _____

Fig. 4.14

Answer 6

The choruses in *Messiah* are one of the chief glories in the work, and are justly popular. Handel's long experience as an opera composer accounts for the dramatic verve and confidence to be found in his later sacred music. After the composer's death, choral societies up and down the land performed *Messiah* and some of his other oratorios with massed choirs and huge orchestras. Sheer size inevitably sacrificed much of the clarity and wit that has been re-discovered more recently, with the use of smaller forces in keeping with Handel's original conception.

'And the glory of the Lord' has a rich variety of choral styles: single line writing (as in the first alto statement); homophonic full choir (all parts moving rhythmically together); simple imitation ('shall be revealed'); dramatic doubling of parts ('for the mouth of the Lord hath spoken it' where tenors and basses sing powerfully together); two musical ideas sung simultaneously (bars 110–113 where the sopranos add the 'shall be revealed' figure to the lower parts 'and the glory' figure (Fig. 4.15). There is a dramatic silence near the end, followed by a grandiose adagio plagal cadence. Handel uses this type of ending frequently in his choral music.

shall   be   re – veal – – ed

shall be

and the glo – ry, the glo – ry of the Lord

Fig. 4.15

The chorus commences in A major, and passes through the dominant (E major) at bars 21–43; A major returns at 43 until bar 64 where the D#s bring back the dominant until that changes to its own dominant key, B major, with its A#s at bar 72 until bar 87. E major from bar 88 for the last time leads to a return of the tonic key at 102.

There are four melodic figures deployed throughout the chorus (Fig. 4.16). All four ideas are initially stated as a single line, then developed in various ways. There are passages in two-, three- or four-part harmony as well as single lines. Two ideas are used as orchestral interludes – bars 38–42 using (b), and bars 73–76 using (a); and there is invertible counterpoint (bars 129–134 invert bars 51–55), where the two lower parts singing figure (d) swap their lines with the two upper parts singing figure (c).

(a)

And the glo – ry, the glo-ry of the   Lord

Fig. 4.16

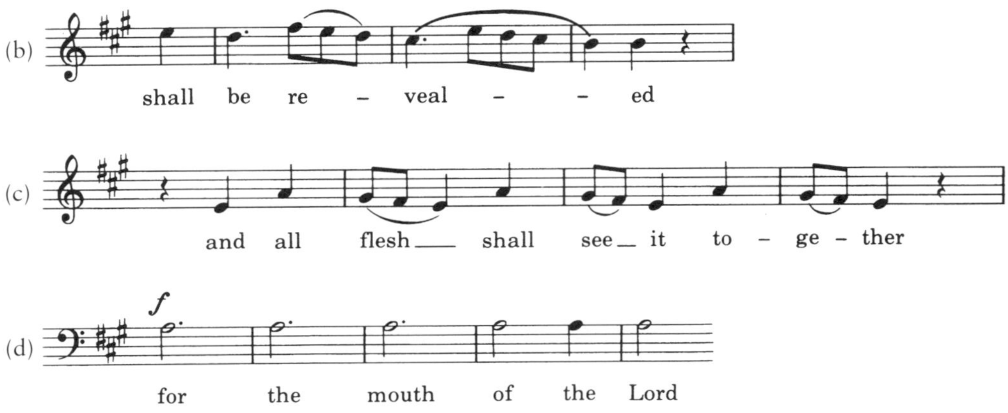

(b) shall be re – veal – – ed

(c) and all flesh —— shall see — it to – ge – ther

(d) for the mouth of the Lord

Fig. 4.16

These comments are but a sample of the wealth of Handel's ingenuity in this exciting first chorus from *Messiah*.

Answer 7

This rousing Chorus so moved King George II on first hearing it, that he rose to his feet and audiences have traditionally followed ever since! It is probably its simplicity that makes it so popular. Set in the triumphant key of D major it makes good use of trumpets and kettle-drums. After the short orchestral introduction the homophonic choral 'Hallelujahs' are sung in straightforward harmony based on primary triads. 'For the Lord God Omnipotent reigneth' is in unison with powerful octave leaps – a strong contrast before more chordal 'Hallelujahs'. At bar 22 the two ideas are combined – the Hallelujahs becoming a highly rhythmic accompaniment to whichever voice part is taking the 'Lord God Omnipotent' theme. The intricate counterpoint continues until an effective drop in volume at the words 'The kingdom of this world is become (suddenly loud) … the kingdom of our Lord'. Bars 41–51 are a complete fugal exposition to the words 'And He shall reign for ever and ever'. This breaks off with a most effective 'King of Kings and Lord of Lords' gradually rising in the sopranos, while the lower voices interject 'for ever' and 'Hallelujah'. The basses return to the fugal theme at bar 69 before the movement ends with a coda based on previous material culminating in a grand plagal cadence (see Chapter 13, page 144).

▷ **Analysis 3: Haydn**

Haydn: Trumpet Concerto

(London 1998 and 1999 Movements 1 and 2; IGCSE 1998 Movements 2 and 3)

This is a different type of concerto from Vivaldi's 'Winter'. Classical Concertos used a solo instrument which was contrasted with a larger backing symphony orchestra. Concertos were usually written in three movements – fast, slow, fast – and generally kept to the structural principles which had been evolved by the chief exponent, Mozart. Piano and violin tended to be the favourite solo instruments used by classical composers for their concertos – there are few existing trumpet concertos.

1. Check that you are using the correct edition of the score.
2. Follow the score through several times. Listen to the whole work, not just the stipulated movements, so that you get the full perspective. You may find the score reading a little harder than for Vivaldi's, but do persevere. The trumpet part should be easy to hear, although there are two other trumpets playing in the main orchestra. Be aware that the page divides into two! Look out for the // on the left-hand side of the page which denotes this split. Remember to count and you shouldn't get lost too often when following through. Score reading is something that improves with practice; remember to scan and not attempt to read all the notes.
3. Mark into your score any important points that you have been taught, or any that you find in the following analysis. This will help you to remember things as you become familiar with the score.
4. Read up on the life and works of Haydn. You should have a working knowledge of his background: humble beginnings – choir school in Vienna – the Esterhazy years– retirement and success with two London visits. There are many good books available

on Haydn. Ask your teacher to advise you on this. Be certain which instruments are required for the concerto, and find out all you can about the differences between the trumpet for which it was originally composed and its modern counterpart.

5. If you are unsure of any key signatures and scales when working out modulations, refer to the first section of Chapter 13.

Space permits only a concise analysis here, but it should be detailed enough for you to understand how Haydn constructed the three movements. You should work through these notes alongside the score several times to gain full benefit. It doesn't really matter if this is not your set work. It will be useful extra practice in helping you to think analytically.

Joseph Haydn composed his only trumpet concerto in 1796 for the Viennese court trumpeter Anton Weidinger. Weidinger performed on the newly invented keyed trumpet, and so for the first time could play all the notes of the chromatic scale. Before this time trumpeters had used the natural trumpet which could play only natural harmonics, rather like the bugle. This new instrument (although soon superseded by our modern valved instrument) allowed the composer the opportunity to write free chromatic movement for the first time (Fig. 4.17).

(2nd movt: bars 18-24)

Fig. 4.17

Although this is an enjoyable piece, scholars agree that the opening movement is not Haydn's most skillfully constructed work. There are probably too many themes, and they are not always put together well. As was usual, the exposition starts without the soloist, who does not play until bar 37. There are six themes in the first subject group:

(a) At bar 1 in the first violin, imitated by the wind at bar 4 (Fig. 4.18).

Fig. 4.18

(b) The rhythmic figure first heard in bar 8 (Fig. 4.19).

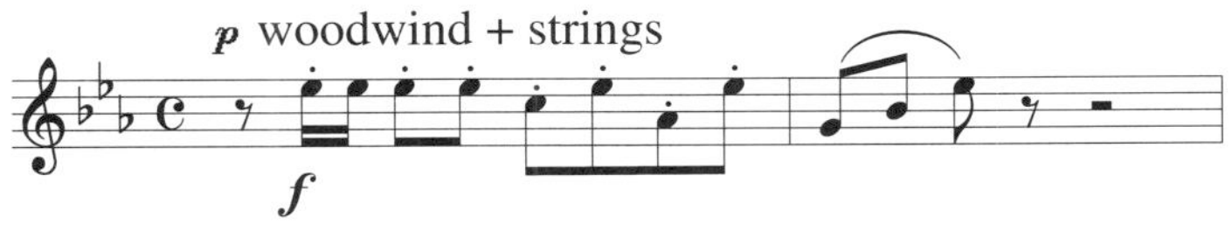

Fig. 4.19

(c) The first violin arpeggios in bar 12 (Fig. 4.20).

Fig. 4.20

(d) The bass part which falls in semitones from bars 14–19, repeated then in minims instead of quavers in bars 20–22. (Fig. 4.21)

cellos and basses

Fig. 4.21

(e)   A widely leaping figure in the first violin in bars 16–19. (Fig. 4.22)

vln I

Fig. 4.22

(f)   A semiquaver figure starting at bar 24 (Fig. 4.23).

Fig. 4.23

Space prevents a detailed analysis of the whole of this first movement. Instead, we shall look at one section in detail, and you can apply this analysis and study the remainder of the movement yourself. Here is a question from the London Specimen Paper for 1998.

Write a description of the section in the first movement, from where the solo trumpet enters (bar 37) to bar 92. Refer to themes, keys, instrumentation and any other important musical elements.   *(20)*

Examiner's answer
At bar 37 the soloist enters with a modified statement of the first subject in E flat major. Theme (a) appears first, followed by (b) at bar 44 and (c) at bar 48. Themes (d), (e) and (f) do not reappear. The bridge passage is short, starting at bar 52 with a new idea (g) passing through C minor to the second subject in B flat major played at bar 60 by the solo trumpet. This starts with a decorative version of (a) – Haydn was fond of monothematism (using the same theme for both first and second subjects). By the time we reach bar 66, however, he is using new material, theme (h), a chromatic, syncopated idea. At bar 73 figure (d) returns in the violins, imitated by the soloist. Bars 77–83 can be regarded as a short codetta to finish off the exposition. The development section, starting at bar 83, uses theme (f) in B flat major (A naturals) until at bar 88 a variant of the (g) motif appears, reaching an imperfect cadence (I–V) in C minor at bar 90. A fuller version of this same cadence follows in bars 91 and 92.

Most of the harmonic support is in the strings in this section. The wind gives some echo effects and extra colour without much real independence. The 'heavier' instruments, trumpets, horns and timpani give punctuated harmonic weight in the louder sections.

Second Movement
The overall key for the concerto is E flat major, but the middle, slow movement (Andante) is in the subdominant key of A flat major. It is constructed in ternary form, that is A + B + A. To begin with, theme A is played by the first violins, and then repeated at bar 9 by the solo trumpet (Fig. 4.24).

Fig. 4.24

This short opening section ends with a simple perfect cadence (chords V–I) at bar 16.

The B tune, initially played by first violins and flute, is handed over to the trumpet at bar 18. (See the first quotation above.) By bar 24 Haydn has modulated to the distant key of C flat major, and by bar 27 he is in D flat minor. A dominant of the original tonic is reached at bar 30, pulling the tonality back to A flat major for the second A section at bar 33. This time the trumpet plays first. The short coda, starting at bar 41, is based on the material from Section B.

Third Movement
The finale (third movement) is back in E flat major, and is built in Sonata-rondo form. This is a mixture of sonata form and rondo form (A–B–A–C–A), where the first episode (B) is initially in a key other than the tonic, but appears later in the tonic key (as the second subject would in true sonata form).

The first subject is presented by the upper strings only (bars 1–12) and then repeated tutti (by the full orchestra) at bar 13 (Fig. 4.25).

(vln.)

Fig. 4.25

The second subject is 'hinted at' in bar 27, but here it is still in the tonic, of course. The soloist enters at bar 45 after a stirring build-up. The exposition is re-stated and extended, this time with the trumpet accompanied by strings playing piano (*p*). A transition, or bridge passage, follows at 68–80. Notice the semiquaver imitation ( ) between the two violin parts at bars 71–75; as expected, these few bars are used to change the key towards B flat major, the dominant, for the second subject at bar 80 (Fig. 4.26).

Fig. 4.26

This starts with trumpet and violin imitating each other. Notice the tricky new trumpet motive at bar 86 (Fig 4.27)

Fig. 4.27

A second theme appears at bar 98 which is still part of the second subject (Fig. 4.28).

Fig. 4.28

And a third idea at bar 116 (Fig. 4.29).

Fig. 4.29

which provides a link back to the main theme in E flat major at bar 125. This time there is a canonic imitation from the flute at bar 127. This section 'A' starts as before, but changes at bar 141 by modulating into A flat major, the subdominant key. A freely-modulating section follows, which develops material from the first subject only, and passes through the following keys: F minor (bars 148–154); A flat major (155–156); F minor again (157–158) B flat minor (159–160); A flat major (161–162); F minor (163–167); C minor over a dominant pedal (168) and finally a reiterated dominant 7th chord (B♭ D F A♭) at 177–180 leads back to E flat major at bar 181.

The recapitulation (bar 181) is considerably shorter this time – 11 bars instead of the 68 in the exposition! In fact bars 181–191 could be compared with bars 57–67. The transition (at bar 192) is also shortened, changing at 196 by avoiding the previous imitation, and arriving at the second subject (in the tonic of course, this time) at bar 200. The new figure for the trumpet at bar 204 (Fig. 4.30) bears some resemblance to that in bar 86, but the second theme of the second subject is this time omitted. The third theme does appear however, at bar 220 in the first violins, repeated rather more fully in the woodwind at bar 224, then handed back to the strings at bar 232. This leads to a re-statement of the main 'A' theme by the trumpet at bar 238, but it disintegrates by merging into the coda. Notice the trumpet trills (see Chapter 13) at bars 249–253.

Fig. 4.30

A fortissimo tutti at bar 256, with tremolando ( ) in the lower strings to increase the tension, leads to an unexpected pianissimo B natural in all the strings, but E flat major is very soon reconfirmed (272). The pause mark ⌢ at 279 is an indication that a cadenza (solo 'display' passage) may be played, if required. This is left to the discretion of the soloist and conductor. At 280 there is a *pp* reference to the main theme, but the music quickly whips up to form a brilliant ending with typical Classical semiquaver configuration.

Practice questions

Now test yourself with the following questions. The answers are all in the text above, or in the glossaries.

Question 1
How many trumpet concertos did Haydn compose?

Question 2
Haydn used ternary form for the slow movement. What form did he use for the last movement?

The remaining questions are in IGCSE format. Refer to bars 13–25 of the second movement in the score (think of it as the printed extract – but you will not be told bar numbers). You would hear it in the exam TWICE. Questions 3–7 relate to the extract, and Question 8 relates to the last movement which is not included in the recording. Tick the box that has the correct answer.

Question 3
Which part of the extract is this taken from?

☐ The opening

☐ Very near the beginning

☐ The middle

☐ Near the end

Question 4
What key is used at the start of the extract?

☐ B♭ major

☐ A♭ major

☐ F minor

☐ E♭ major

Question 5
At what interval apart do the oboes play in bars 22–23?

☐ in thirds

☐ in fourths

☐ in unison

Question 6
In bars 19–21, what effect do the violas, cellos and basses produce?

☐ a glissando

☐ a ground bass

☐ a pedal

☐ a cadenza

Question 7
Which statement is true concerning the trumpet theme in bars 18–24?

☐ It comes from the opening of the second movement

☐ It first occurs just before the given extract

☐ This is the first occurrence

Question 8
(Last movement) When does the trumpet first play?

☐ Right at the beginning

☐ A few bars into the movement

☐ A long way into the movement

▷ **Analysis 4: Beethoven**

Beethoven: Symphony no. 5 in C Minor (Ist Movement)
(set by NICCEA for 1998)

Everyone knows the first eight notes of this piece! Many people, however, are unfamiliar with the remainder of this powerful movement. The so-called 'fate knocking on the door' opening is the germinal motif which is integrated wonderfully into a movement of over five hundred bars. Listen to the whole symphony several times before you begin to analyse the first movement. Feel the tremendous tension resolving later into a feeling of victory and remember that much of the work was written at Heiligenstadt, where Beethoven had seriously contemplated suicide.

Space does not permit a detailed analysis. From your study of the preceding pieces, and with a knowledge of sonata form (see Chapter 13, page 150, and Chapter 14, page 169, Things to do (No. 3)), work your way through the movement carefully. Question and Answer 5 below will help you with the basic structure.

Practice questions and answers

Question 1
What instruments are used in this movement?   *(3)*

Question 2
How does Beethoven treat the opening four-note figure throughout this movement?   *(5)*

Question 3
How is the second subject (from bar 59) contrasted to the first subject? *(4)*

Question 4
What is unusual about the coda (bars 374–502) in this movement? *(3)*

Question 5
Outline briefly the sonata form structure of the first movement. *(5)*

Answer 1
2 flutes, 2 oboes, 2 clarinets, 2 bassoons, 2 horns in E♭, 2 trumpets, timpani (C and G), and strings.

Answer 2
This famous motif (we can hardly call it a theme as such) is initially a falling sequence: a major third followed by a minor third. The aggressive rhythm of this motif is probably as important as the actual pitches used. Beethoven proceeds to vary the pitches enormously: it is played upside down (e.g. bars 386–7); it is used as an accompaniment to the second subject (e.g. bars 66–7); and it is even played on the same note (e.g. horns in bars 160–1 and in many other places).

Answer 3
It is mostly smoother, softer and more lyrical. It is in the major key (E flat) which contrasts with the more aggressive C minor opening. (Note that Beethoven uses the four-note figure as a punctuating bass part (bars 65–6, for instance).

Answer 4
For its time (first performance 22 December 1808 in Vienna) it was an extremely long coda. Beethoven treats it very much as a second development section – indeed the coda with 129 bars is the longest section of the movement (the exposition is 124 bars long, the development 123 bars, and the recapitulation 124 bars long).

Answer 5
First subject (bars 1–52) in C minor.
Transition (bars 52–58).
Second subject (bars 59–110) in E flat major.
Codetta (bars 110–124) in E flat major.
Development (bars 125–248).
Recapitulation (bars 248–372):
   [First subject (bars 248–296) in C minor;
   Transition (bars 296–302);
   Second subject (bars 303–372) in C major.]
Coda (bars 373–502).

Things to do

As a follow-up to this work on Beethoven, listen to some of Mozart's music. Can you tell the difference? Try some Mozart Piano Concertos – there are many to choose from.

1. Note the instrumentation used in the Concertos. Is it much the same as the Beethoven symphony? Is it different to the Haydn Trumpet Concerto? Are the instruments used in similar ways in both the concertos and the symphony?
2. How is the backing orchestra used in the concertos? Is it playing all the time, or does the piano have substantial stretches where it is allowed to play unaccompanied? How is the melodic content of each concerto shared between soloist and orchestra?
3. How does Mozart give variety in the sound that he creates? Is it accomplished through varying the orchestral texture, through volume changes, speed changes, thematic variety or mood changes?
4. Here is a specimen NICCEA question (as applied to another, now deleted, Set Work).
    You will hear TWO performances of (this concerto). Performance A followed by Performance B will be played TWICE. There will be a pause of 30 seconds between the first two performances of the music; the final playings will follow after a pause of one minute.

(i)   Write briefly about the differences between the two performances   *(8)*

(ii)   Which performance do you prefer and why?   *(2)*

With a question such as this, do not be frightened of stating the obvious. If you have noticed something relevant that is worth writing down, then do so! Part (i) is worth more marks, so make sure that you get down several different points – such as differences in speed, volume, size of the orchestra, pitch (one version might be slightly higher than the other), clarity of recording etc. In part (ii) the reason you give is probably the most important part of your answer. Justify your answer clearly!

▷ Analysis 5: Glinka

Glinka: Overture to Russlan and Ludmilla

(set by NICCEA for 1998)

For effective preparation of this set work you will need an orchestral score. Instead of studying this work in analytical detail, here it will be presented, again, as a series of questions and answers. The questions will be formatted along GCSE lines – ranging from straightforward one- or two-line answers to full paragraphs. There are far more questions than in the actual exam so that we can cover the work in suitable detail. Remember that you are rewarded for what you know; to merit top marks you must display a thorough acquaintance with the score.

Practice questions and answers

Question 1
How old was Glinka when he composed this work?   *(2)*

Question 2
For what occasion was it composed?   *(2)*

Question 3
What instrumentation does the work have?   *(5)*

Question 4
Give a brief account of Glinka's music.   *(8)*

Question 5
Outline the structure of this Overture.

Answer 1
He was about thirty-eight years old. Glinka (1804–57) wrote this overture in 1842.

Answer 2
It is the overture to his second opera, *Russlan and Ludmilla*, which was first performed at the Bolshoi Theatre in Moscow, 1842.

Answer 3
The overture is scored for a large nineteenth-century symphony orchestra: two flutes, two oboes, two clarinets, two bassoons, double bassoon, four horns, two trumpets, three trombones, three timpani, and strings (1st and 2nd violins, violas, cellos and double basses).

Answer 4
Glinka's first opera was *A Life for the Czar* (1836). He was the first Russian composer whose music was to win general acceptance outside Russia, so he is regarded as the 'father' of Russian music. He spent two years in Spain and some of his orchestral music is based on Spanish folk tunes. *Souvenir of a Night in Madrid* is an example. He wrote chamber music for wind and for strings, and many piano pieces and songs.

Answer 5
The overture to *Russlan and Ludmilla* is in sonata form.
   Speed: presto (very fast, $\downarrow$ =135).
   Introduction: bars 1–20, *ff*, D major.
   First subject: bars 21–58, *ff*, D major.

Bridge passage (transition): bars 59-80, *mf*.

Second subject: bars 81–119, *mf*, F major (an unrelated key), taken from Russlan's aria in Act II.

Codetta: bars 119–132, *p*, starting in A flat major (unrelated).

Development: bars 133–236, *mf*.

First subject: bars 237–274, *ff*, D major.

Bridge passage: bars 275–296 (but changes this time at bar 287).

Second subject: bar 297–end, *mf*, (in the dominant key; it is usually the tonic), codetta material starts at bar 335, but a true coda starts at bar 349 in the tonic key, D major.

▷ **Analysis 6:
Debussy**

Debussy: Children's Corner Suite for Piano

We are discussing here the following five of the six movements:

1. Doctor Gradus ad Parnassum.
2. Jimbo's Lullaby.
3. Serenade for the Doll.
4. The Snow is Dancing.
6. Golliwog's Cake-walk.

Debussy (1862–1918) possessed an incredible 'ear' for musical sound. If you examine his printed music you will find the utmost precision with notational detail. He won, as a student at the Paris Conservatoire, the coveted Prix de Rome (a chance to compose in Italy for three years), but he did not become well-known until after the first performance of his orchestral *Prélude à l'après-midi d'un faune* in 1894. He was a remarkable pianist, and composed much fine piano music in an individual style, using, for example, blocks of chords, the whole tone scale, the pentatonic scale, pedal and harmonic effects – in all a very original harmonic style.

This suite of six pieces, composed between 1906 and 1908, was dedicated to his daughter, 'To my dear little Chouchou, with her father's fond apologies for what follows'.

No.1 – 'Doctor Gradus ad Parnassum' is a humorous homage to the set of piano studies written in 1817 by Clementi. The Latin words mean 'Steps to Parnassus', and refer to the sacred mountain of the Muses who are supposed to inspire creative artists. It is a gentle parody of a child practising a piano study in C major. The child starts off confidently enough, but distraction soon sets in and as practice time approaches an end, the last few bars are hurried through and the piano-lid is slammed somewhat angrily!

Points to notice:

(a) The French words to indicate speed and expression.
(b) How this short piece has some substance, unlike many of the studies it satirises.
(c) The frequent key signature changes.
(d) The clefs are continually changing too, as the range of a piano is so wide.

Practice questions and answers

Question 1
Give the meaning of the following French terms encountered in this piece:

(a) modérément animé (bar 1)
(b) égal et sans sécheresse (bar 1)
(c) un peu retenu (bar 21)
(d) Animez un peu (bar 37)
(e) Très animé (bar 67).

Question 2
How does Debussy give a feeling of unity at the start of each section?

Question 3
No. 2 – 'Jimbo's Lullaby' is full of imagery for young children. We would call it 'Jumbo', of course – it is an elephant piece! Debussy uses the pentatonic scale some of the time to bring out the simplicity of mood. Notice the low, lumbering melody of the opening which depicts the slow, heavy creature. You can imagine that a stuffed elephant is being told a fairy tale by the child.

Name the key of the piece, and comment on the style of piano writing.

Question 4
No. 3 – 'Serenade for the Doll'. Debussy requests that the performer uses the soft pedal throughout the piece, even in the passages marked *f*. Some writers have commented on Debussy's psychological undertones in this seemingly innocent piece – how the child has authority over her doll with its fixed smile – but this is something we cannot explain for certain and must be left for the listener to decide. Again note the precision with detail, and how the melody is sometimes below the accompaniment. The overall key is E major.

Comment on the varying textures in the piano writing in this Serenade.

Question 5
No. 4 – 'The Snow is Dancing' seems to suggest a feeling of sadness in a child as he or she observes snow falling, perhaps for the first time.

Let us suppose for this piece that you are presented with the first page (say fifteen bars as in the Peters Edition No. 7252) and asked the following questions:

(a)   The key at the opening of this extract is ambiguous. Name the two possibilities.   *(2)*
(b)   Is there a melody in this extract?   *(2)*
(c)   How does Debussy continue the piece after this effect?   *(8)*

Questions 6
No. 6 – The final piece in 'Children's Corner' is the well-known 'Golliwog's Cake-walk'. Debussy, although trained extensively in the Central European classical tradition, was to develop a highly original composing style, comprising such wide-ranging interests as Balinese gamelan music, medieval plainchant and the then-contemporary ragtime from America, as in the 'Golliwog's Cake-walk'. We see the familiar ragtime syncopation (*ff* ♩♪ ♪♩♪) and the unexpected *ff* chords (bars 4, 12, 20, 24, 40 etc.). What is less well-known or understood is the rather impertinent satire towards Wagner, the nineteenth century musical giant whose harmony was much revered and emulated (but despised by others, of course). Here Debussy parodies the opening of Wagner's 'Tristan' opera of 1865 in the middle section, commencing at bar 61 until about bar 80 (Fig. 4.31).

avec une grande émotion (with much feeling)

Fig. 4. 31

This serious original melody is now given the undignified but harmless treatment of added staccato quavers with teasing acciaccaturas (♪), but Debussy would have to admit that Wagner at one time had been a temporary influence on him!

Comment on Debussy's use of rhythm in this piece.   *(2)*

Answer 1
(a)   moderately lively
(b)   evenly and not harshly
(c)   hold back a little
(d)   a little more lively
(e)   very lively.

Answer 2
He uses the same musical material so that bar 33 (in B flat major) is the same figure as at the opening, but now in quavers (augmentation), and similarly in bar 37 (in D flat major).

Answer 3
It is written in B flat major. Although the treble clef is used Debussy concentrates on the middle and lower registers of the piano to illustrate the physical character of 'Jimbo'. As

before, he is meticulous with compositional detail and the general dynamic level is extremely soft, there being one bar marked *mf*, but nothing louder. There is a prominent use throughout of chords using the interval of a major 2nd.

There are numerous French terms in this piece:

doux et un peu gauche (bar 1): gently and a little awkwardly; un peu en dehors (bar 21): as if outside (prominently); marqué (bar 34): marked, pronounced; un peu plus mouvementé (bar 39): a little more movement; sans retarder (bar 74): no slowing up.

Answer 4
Debussy was a master of pianistic expression. Besides requiring the soft pedal throughout the piece, there is a wealth of varied detail. The texture ranges from the effective silent bar (bar 65) to the single line writing, *pp* and staccato, (bars 61–2); two note chords (bars 66–68); ostinati figures (bars 1–2, 43–4 etc.); chordal writing in the treble clef only (bars 30–34); an Alberti bass effect (bars 106-114); common arpeggios (121–2); and arpeggiated chords (bars 90–96). These are only some of the piano textures in this delightful and artistic miniature.

Answer 5
(a) It is a mixture of F major and D minor.
(b) Not in the conventional sense of having a melody with separate accompaniment. The repeated semiquavers are drawn from the rising figure of bar 1, and there is a line of semibreves (bars 3–10) which may be treated as a melodic line. Much of the musical effect here is one of perpetual movement rather than a melody as such.
(c) There are sixteen more bars of perpetual semiquavers in similar style before it dissolves at bar 34 into a soft quaver-triplet counter-subject above the original rising four-note figure. Snowflakes dancing? The climax to this section is at bar 49 with heavy accents and repeated notes. There is a recapitulation of the first idea starting at bar 57 but Debussy omits the first six bars, (so it corresponds to bar 7). The final few bars mix the two ideas gently together (e.g. bar 68 treble clef = 40 bass clef) and it ends softly with a bare D minor chord with no third (F).

Answer 6
As is common with ragtime, the use of syncopation is paramount. There are also numerous accents on weak beats. The off-beat rhythms in the G flat major section (bar 47) are lightened further by acciaccaturas. The more legato movement in this section (when it mocks Wagner) is satirical partly by means of the added staccato and ornaments.

▷ **Analysis 7: Bartók**   *Bartók: Concerto for Orchestra (Movements 2 and 4 only)*

(set by IGCSE for 1998)

Béla Bartók (1881–1945) was commissioned by Serge Koussevitzky, the Conductor of the Boston Symphony Orchestra, to write a work for the orchestra in memory of his wife. Although Bartók was a sick man, dying, in fact, of leukaemia, he managed to complete this dazzling five-movement work – which shows off every instrument as a soloist in its own right, hence its unusual title – and it received its first performance at Carnegie Hall, New York in December, 1944.

Bartók had decided to emigrate to America when things had proved unacceptable to him in war-torn Hungary. He was an international pianist and authority on Hungarian folk-music; unfortunately these meant very little to America at the time and he had the unenviable prospect of building his reputation again from the beginning. But ill health dogged his work; recognition was slow, and he was forced to lighten his personal and intense style of composing to suit American tastes. He died in 1945.

No. 2 Gioco delle coppie ('Play of the Pairs')
This is a cleverly constructed movement in ternary form, where pairs of similar instruments are presented one after the other, each pair being harmonised in parallel fashion, a different interval apart.

After a side-drum introduction, played *mf* and without the snares, the order is as follows:

(a) bassoons in 6ths
(b) oboes in 3rds

(c) clarinets in 7ths

(d) flutes in 5ths

(e) trumpets (muted) in 2nds.

As a middle section and as a contrast, the brass instruments play a restrained chorale-like melody, followed by the four horns in similar mood. The side-drum is used intermittently as a quiet link at the ends of phrases. The upper woodwind imitate each other using the first three notes of the bassoon duet (from bar 8) as a way of returning to a recap of the first section.

The recap (bar 165) starts with exactly the same order of instruments, set at the same intervals apart as before. The main differences are as follows:

(a)   now has an extra bassoon added to the original pair

(b)   a pair of clarinets join the oboes

(c)   the two flutes join the clarinets

(d)   all the woodwind add to the original flute duet

(e)   the string writing which accompanies the pair of muted trumpets is more sophisticated; the tremolando is higher this time, and two harps playing glissando vary the texture still further.

The movement finishes the way it started with a quiet side-drum rhythm, which this time fades away to nothing.

Practice questions and answers

Question 1
Which instruments that Bartók used for the first movement are not required for the second movement?   *(3)*

Question 2
Describe some of the technical effects that Bartok demands of the string players in this movement.   *(5)*

Question 3
How does Bartók create a contrasting middle section in this ternary movement?   *(5)*

No. 4 Intermezzo Interrotto ('Interrupted Intermezzo')
It is said that Bartók heard a performance of Shostakovich's 'Leningrad' Symphony (No. 7) and, thinking little of its somewhat banal march tune, proceeded to denigrate it by subjecting it to musical ridicule in this movement. To be fair to Shostakovich, his war-time seventh symphony, written to help uplift the citizens of a besieged Leningrad, was itself parodying the goose-stepping Nazi enemy in the march tune. Bartók uses it as a somewhat forced interruption to his own inimitable music.

Question 4
Comment on the time signatures used in this movement.   *(2)*

Question 5
Disregarding the changes of time signatures, how does Bartók compose his opening statement in this movement?   *(3)*

Question 6
How does Bartók satirise Shostakovich in the 'Interrupted' section of this Intermezzo?   *(10)*

Question 7
How does Bartók produce a laughing effect in the 'Interrupted' section of this movement?

Answer 1
The 3rd flute (which doubles piccolo); the 3rd oboe (which doubles cor anglais); the 3rd clarinet (which doubles bass clarinet); the 3rd trumpet and bass trombone; bass drum, tam-tam, cymbals and triangle.

Answer 2
Throughout the 'Play of the Pairs' the string section is playing a subservient role to the duettists, but it is a most important background part. They set off the various duet themes

with their pizzicato chords; muted (con sord.) trills; tremolando (♩) and glissando (♪); harmonics (♪ where a string is touched lightly to produce a higher, weaker note); normal bowing and some playing at the point of the bow (punta d'arco); spiccato (bouncing the bow to produce short, crisp notes); and sul ponticello (bowing near the bridge), which produces an eerie sound.

Answer 3

Having used five different pairs of instruments one after the other, Bartók provides a more restrained middle section before the pairs return. This middle part is given to the brass without horns, who play a smooth *mf* chorale-like melody. The side-drum reminds us of its presence with quiet references to its opening rhythm at the end of each brass phrase. The four horns, aided by the tuba, enter with an imitative figure which remains undeveloped. The upper wind hint at the bassoons' theme with imitative 3-note figures (♫♪). This quieter section of music, with less emphasis on display, seems the perfect contrast before the return of the 'Play of the Pairs', which is even more intensified this time.

Answer 4

Bartók commences with a 2/4 time signature, but intersperses the opening theme with occasional 5/8 bars, which provide an infectious unpredictable rhythm. When the viola introduces the second idea (bar 42), there are bars of 6/8 3/4 5/8 7/8 and 2/4. The 'Shostakovich' interlude commences at bar 75 in 8/8, then changes to ¢ for the duration of the march. The viola theme (now rescored more fully) and the return of the opening theme (bar 135) retain their constantly changing time signatures as before.

Answer 5

He writes a four-bar string introduction: B A# E F#, then the oboe melody uses these notes as its sole material, and the accompaniment, too, consists predominantly of these same four notes.

Answer 6

He takes a fragment of Shostakovich's march tune from the 'Leningrad' Symphony, and proceeds to make it sound as 'corny' as possible. Bartók uses vamping (oompah) in the accompaniment, shrill mocking laughter in the woodwind, trombones blowing a 'raspberry' by means of loud glissandi; and an exaggerated (and later upside-down) version of the march theme itself. All these contribute to a satirical knock at Shostakovich.

Answer 7

This occurs three times. An initial discordant high woodwind trill gradually falls away, with different rhythms implying dying laughter. For example ♩♩♩ in the flutes fit against ♫♫ in the oboe and clarinets, producing an effective cross-rhythm. It is the mixture of these three elements: dischord, cross-rhythm and the callous trilling which produces music full of mockery.

▷ **Suggestions for study**

If you have read and carefully studied all the pieces discussed so far in this chapter, you should now be well acquainted with the thought processes that are required for this type of work. You probably now feel confident to undertake some study on your own. You know now what things to find out about, and most importantly, you have learnt what to listen for.

To conclude this chapter and by way of a summary, we shall now encourage you to study some more set works on your own.

Extracts from the ever popular musical *Phantom of the Opera* by Andrew Lloyd Webber have been set by NICCEA for 1998:

(a) 'Think of Me'
(b) 'All I Ask of You'

(From Polydor 831 563–2 *Highlights from Phantom of the Opera*.)

Working independently now, use the following points to make your own study of these extracts:

(1) Listen to the songs, thinking firstly of the emotional impact that each song makes on you. Did you like it? And if so what appealed to you in particular? Write down your initial reactions and feelings – you are studying a great deal of music and it is important to keep careful records of your work.

(2) Make notes as you research into the construction of the songs:

    (a) How important do you think the words are?

    (b) How does the melody relate to the words used?

    (c) What instruments are of importance in the song? What solos are played?

    (d) Does the mood stay the same throughout the song? If not, how does it change?

    (e) Can you work out the structure of the song? Think in terms of verse/chorus/solo etc. Sometimes it is helpful to use labels A + B + A and so on.

    (f) How important is the record production to the song itself? Would it exist satisfactorily in a less polished version?

    (g) Find out some background information on Andrew Lloyd Webber. Listen to other pieces by him to add to your familiarity with their style. You would enjoy *Variations*, which uses the well-known Paganini theme in a contemporary style.

Specimen questions

Here are some model questions which could be asked on any of the above songs. They are based on actual questions used by several Boards.

(a) Give the name of the song from which (this extract) is taken.

Name of song _____ ($\frac{1}{2}$)

(b) Name two instruments being played in the instrumental 'break' in (this extract).

Name of instruments _____ and _____ (1)

(c) Describe briefly the overall structure of the song from which (this extract) is taken. (2)

_____

_____

(d) Describe the song............ . Pay particular attention to the structure, and melodic, rhythmic and harmonic patterns. If you wish you may give musical illustrations.

_____

_____

(14)

▷ EXAMINATION QUESTION WITH STUDENT ANSWER

Here is a pupil's answer to question(d) above, with examiner comments. We have chosen to use the song 'Memory' from Lloyd Webber's *Cats* musical, but for extra practice you can apply the same suggestions yourself when answering the question with *Phantom of the Opera* songs.

'Good. An informative and interesting opening to an answer.'

'Good. Clear details of rhythmic structure.'

> Describe the song 'Memory'. Pay particular attention to structure, and melodic, rhythmic and harmonic patterns. If you wish you may give musical illustrations.
>
> *In this song Andrew Lloyd Webber does not use T.S. Eliot's words exactly. He asked Trevor Nunn to arrange them to make them more suitable for use as a song. It is a good song, well constructed, with a wide range of emotional power. Not surprisingly, it became the hit song from the Musical.*
>   *The character Grizabella sings the first two stanzas to the same tune. It is basically in 12/8 time with occasional bars of 10/8 and 6/8 to allow the words to fit satisfactorily. These changes of time signature are effective, breaking up a predictable four in a bar pattern.*
>
> *(continued)*

The next part of the tune ('Every street lamp...') has less movement. Lloyd Webber makes good use of sequence here, especially effective on the rhyme: 'mutters' and 'gutters'. The brightening effect of the keychange at this point is dispelled by a return to the original key and the first theme.

There is a complete change of key to the flattened sixth which lifts the mood of the song. This was a modulatory trait from the Romantic period. Here Lloyd Webber employs it well. He uses the orchestra alone for the first eight bars of the main theme, before the vocalist re-enters with the second idea, lower in the voice this time and more restrained, which underlines the sad and nostalgic quality of the song.

The climax occurs after an orchestral build-up to the main tune on the words 'touch me'. The song ends quietly with four bars for orchestra, using music from the introduction. The overall structure could be described as A A B A A B A.

Most of these questions are concerned with facts about the music, but any factual information about a work is only relevant if you can apply it intelligently to your emotional understanding. Any personal response to music must come from you. This book is designed to show you how to study effectively, and to give you a selection of Examination questions for each area of the syllabus – it does not set out to cover everything in detail for all seven Examining Groups.

SUMMARY

No one can make you enjoy a piece of music, but familiarity with it from the inside, through constructive analysis and repeated listening, will increase your appreciation of it. Overall, the prime reasons for musical analysis are these:

▷ To further your understanding of how music works, and to increase your enjoyment of it.

▷ To realise that no two works are alike.

▷ To develop further understanding of how composers adopt standard forms to suit their artistic purpose.

▷ To appreciate how a work belongs to its time and how contemporaries and forerunners influence the content of a composer's work.

▷ To encourage an intellectual and aesthetic advancement; to develop your experience of thoughts and feelings through sound.

You should be listening regularly to all styles of music – from all corners of the world – and you will gradually gain a rewarding insight into the rich and diverse world of musical sound.

Chapter

5

Solo performance

GETTING STARTED

Music is essentially a performing art, and the GCSE music exam aims to encourage people to become involved in as much music making as possible, either individually or in groups. The *solo performance* section encourages you to work hard at your instrument or voice throughout the course, perfecting technique, developing interpretative skills and allowing opportunity for performing in front of others. This area of the coursework will probably be left to you and your *instrumental teacher*. Your *class teacher*, once satisfied that you are aware of the requirements for solo performance, is likely to leave you to practise until just before the exam, as there are so many other things in the syllabus to be covered.

IGCSE	LONDON	MEG	NEAB	NICCEA	SEG	WJEC	TOPIC	STUDY	REVISION 1	REVISION 2
✓	✓	✓	✓	✓	✓	✓	Exam group requirements			
✓	✓	✓	✓	✓	✓	✓	What the examiner looks for			
✓	✓	✓	✓	✓	✓	✓	Hints to performers			
✓	✓	✓	✓	✓	✓	✓	Checklist for instruments			
✓	✓	✓	✓	✓	✓	✓	Summary			

▷ **WHAT YOU NEED TO KNOW**

▷ **Exam group requirements**

The exam groups vary in their requirements for this component. These can be summarised as follows:

IGCSE

To sing or play individually is a compulsory part of this Prepared Performance section. You also need to offer either an additional solo instrument (or voice), or singing or playing in an ensemble. Pieces are of your own choice, and can be accompanied as necessary. The full section should not exceed ten minutes. The individual performance may be either accompanied or unaccompanied.

London

This is a compulsory part of the Performing section. Your performance will be recorded and marked by your teacher, and then moderated externally. You are required to play one piece of your own choice up to five minutes in length. The standard of your performance and the level of difficulty will be taken into account during assessment.

If you wish to perform on a second instrument then this could be the option you choose for Paper 4 (you must choose one option). For this you play one piece of your own choice, and support this performance by immediately taking part in a viva (discussion) with your teacher. For 1–2 minutes, you must discuss your performance, covering any or all of the following points:

▷ Interpretation of performance instructions (e.g. dynamics, speed markings).
▷ Interpretation of any subjective or programmatic implications within the music.
▷ Any difficulties, or technical points (e.g. phrasing, tuning).
▷ Musical elements prominent in the music which require highlighting.
▷ The style of your performance relating it to the time of its composition.

Both the performance and the viva will be recorded and sent off for external marking. You must not play the same piece for this Paper 4 option as you did for the Paper 1 (Core Performing) section of the examination.

For the London Short Course, there are two choices for Solo Performing:

Option 1: Performing (30%) and Viva (10%) as for Paper 4 above.
Option 2: Performing (20%) your own composition for section A of this option.

MEG

Singing or playing a solo piece or solo part is a compulsory part of the Performing component. With your teacher's guidance, you should choose a piece or solo part which must be submitted on cassette. Accompaniment is permitted, provided that the solo is not consistently doubled.

NEAB

This is an option within the Performing section. You are required to sing or play one piece of your own choice, which may be accompanied or unaccompanied. An improvisation may be offered. The level of difficulty will be taken into account, and the performance must be recorded on cassette. It will be assessed by your teacher and moderated externally by the NEAB. Note that 'performing a solo part' (as it is described in the syllabus) may also be assessed in an ensemble performance.

NICCEA

This is a compulsory section of the Performing section. You are asked to present a programme which should last for up to five minutes, and you may offer an instrument, voice, instrument and voice or two instruments. You have free choice of music in any style, and solo music may be accompanied as appropriate. If you wish, you have the opportunity to play a significant solo part within a group performance. Solo performances may use music technology resources, such as pre-recorded backing tracks or MIDI techniques.

SEG

This is a compulsory part of the Performing section. You are required to sing or play at least one piece individually, demonstrating technical control, expression and suitable interpretation of the music. You should choose a piece which is long enough to demonstrate your ability. Ideally you should produce a score for the examiner, but failing that you should introduce the music in such a way that you clearly present its nature. Your performance will be recorded for assessment.

WJEC

This is a compulsory part of the Performing section. You are asked to sing or play a selection of music of your own choice which adequately displays the following skills:

(a) clarity and accuracy of rhythm and pitch;
(b) the use of appropriate tempo;
(c) effective use of dynamics;
(d) fluency of performance;
(e) sensitive balance of phrasing;
(f) stylistic awareness;
(g) technical control of the instrument;
(h) expression and suitable interpretation.

You may use one or two instruments for your performance, but you should not exceed five minutes in all.

Note

You are certain to practise your chosen pieces many times, but you possibly haven't thought of practising *performing*. Playing in front of an examiner (or an audience of course) is not the same as playing at home; and taking a practical examination is very different from having a lesson with your own instrumental teacher.

▷ **What the examiner looks for**

You have seen how the exam groups vary slightly in their requirements for this examination. Assume that whatever syllabus you take the examiners' approach will be much the same. Most examiners will have spent time themselves preparing students for examinations and know all the pitfalls. They will all be looking for the same thing: evidence of musicianship. A lower grade performance will gain credit for playing the correct notes in an acceptable tempo; a higher grade candidate will be rewarded for expressive fluency and a sensitive musical interpretation.

Examiners are sometimes faced with the difficult task of assessing a performance by a student who has chosen a far too ambitious programme. The examiner has to mark what he actually hears; he cannot give credit for the potential ability of a candidate. It is disappointing for a talented performer to be given low marks because the chosen programme was unsuitable for him at that time.

Before we go any further, it will be worthwhile to try to define the word *musicianship*, as it is much used in this book, and is that vital ingredient which examiners seek in any performance situation. In a nutshell, musicianship is that element of feeling in a performance which is intelligently added to the showing of technical skills. As stated elsewhere, it is more or less taken for granted that you will have mastered the correct notes and rhythms for your chosen programme.

Indeed, having said that, most examiners would prefer an expressive and sensitive performance of a piece that contained a few wrong notes to one that was clinically perfect in the technical sense, yet lifeless and unfeeling. **Feeling** must be added to a piece sensitively, however. There is much more to expression than 'loud' and 'soft'. **Light** and **shade** are continually varied in most pieces of music, and each phrase needs to be considered both individually and in the context of the whole before the piece is ready for public hearing. It is worth remembering that most pieces have a fair balance between a state of tension and relaxation. You should plan, in a longer piece, where the climaxes come; it is just as unsatisfactory for a performance to be perpetually 'laid back' as tense all the time. Think in terms of **climax** and **repose** and how you can shape these convincingly.

While emphasising the importance of the expressive content, it must also be stressed that a good technical facility is no less important; it is the successful combining of the two that leads to a satisfying, and moving performance. Singers and wind players will need to solve and master any breathing problems before they can hope to give a sensitive performance; similarly, string players will spend time considering their bowing, and the brass or wind player will need to concentrate on maintaining a good embouchure (mouth position on an instrument). The pianist will produce a satisfying tone only when a good sense of touch has been mastered

Hints to performers

Before we go further into detail for the different instruments, here are some general points of advice to performers.

- Choose your programme with great care. You need a piece or pieces that allow you to show what you can do, but don't try to impress the examiner by playing something that is beyond your technical and interpretative ability.
- If your syllabus allows you time to play more than one piece, aim to create a well balanced programme. Try to choose pieces of contrasting style, character or period so that you will be able to show different aspects of your performing personality.
- Certainly try to gain some experience of playing for other people, at a school concert perhaps, or by playing your pieces over to your family or friends. Listen carefully to any constructive comments they may have. You will probably find that nervousness affects you physically, so trial runs will help you learn how to overcome this. Remember a little nervousness can be a good thing – most people are at their best when 'psyched up'.
- Once you have mastered all the notes and basic details in your piece, give careful attention to the expressive qualities. If you require an accompanist make sure that you have adequate rehearsal time together. You need to get used to hearing the piano part, and then decide how best to interpret the piece as a whole. Think of the balance between the two of you. Sometimes the accompanist will have a share of the theme and you will need to play down. Always listen to the music so that you can form a constructive opinion on how each section should be played. The natural acoustics of the exam room are rather important, so certainly rehearse in there several times if you can. If it is a resonant room you may have to play slightly slower than you originally planned. Conversely, a 'dry' or more dead acoustic may persuade you to increase the tempo to keep the piece alive. This all takes careful listening and planning – don't leave it until the actual day!
- You will learn a lot about interpretation by discussing a piece with your instrumental teacher. Should it be cheerful or morose? Jumpy or smooth? You will find the understanding of Italian terms helpful here. Although they are daunting to learn, all experienced musicians instinctively know how to achieve a required mood when they see, for example, the word 'pomposo' in a Baroque piece, or 'nobilmente' in an Elgar composition. (It must be admitted that Elgar cheekily made up this word to sound Italian, but musicians understand the mood he means to set.)
- This may sound contradictory, but be careful not to over-interpret. The performance of a study which is essentially a technical exercise should not be 'expressive' for the sake of it. Similarly, ensure that your expression is suitable for the period of the composition. It would be considered bad taste, for example, to use excessive rubato (free tempo) in a Bach Prelude.
- The use of dynamics requires more thought than may at first seem likely. After all, if the music is written '*p*' then surely it is simply played softly. But how soft is soft? Dynamic markings such as this are bound to be relative – a pianissimo for a tuba will not be quite the same as one for a violin! Of course this goes without saying, but it is a necessary consideration when you start to think historically. Romantic composers had a different way of using dynamic markings to Classical composers, whereas Baroque composers tended not to use them very much at all. In early and Baroque music you have the added problem of deciding whether to follow the suggested editorial dynamics, which are often printed in parentheses, or to work out your own. Would it be suitable to add ornaments? Can you miss out some of the difficult trills which have been suggested? Should you vary the volume when you go back for a repeat? Would it be correct to slow down at the end?

    We have come back to the main point: you simply must use your ever-developing musical judgement, with the advice, of course, of your teachers. Try to listen to a recording of your chosen piece if at all possible. It may not be played in the way that you want to perform it, but it should give you some useful ideas for your own interpretation.

▶ The use of a metronome is a good way to set the composer's recommended tempo when you first come to study a piece, but it is not advisable to play along to the machine in a mechanical way. In fact composers often seem to contradict their own metronome markings when you listen to them conducting their own recordings. Again, trust your own musical judgement. The speed of a piece is right for you when you can play it convincingly in the chosen acoustic. The metronome marking should only be regarded as a guide.

▷ Checklist for instruments

The following criteria are intended as a summary of things to work at for a successful solo performance. They are not arranged in order of importance and they are by no means exhaustive – you will probably think of other important things to consider. Most of the points have already been mentioned above, but you should find this a helpful checklist for your particular instrument.

Woodwind
Accuracy of intonation
Good breath control and support
Good tone control
Good embouchure
Good technical control
Good fingering technique
Good articulation – legato and tonguing
Good interpretation
Good posture
Suitable phrasing and dynamics
Good use of specific techniques, e.g. flutter tonguing

Brass
Accuracy of intonation
Good breath control and support
Good tone control
Good embouchure
Appropriate use of mutes, glissando and 'en dehors'
Good slide or finger technique
Good hand and bell technique for horn players
Good articulation – legato and tonguing
Application of a wide dynamic range
Good interpretation
Good posture

Strings (bowed)
Accuracy of intonation
Good control of tone, with correct vibrato
Good posture: correct holding of instrument and appropriate control of the bow
Correct type of bowing (spiccato, staccato)
Appropriate fingering and use of positions
Good use of pizzicato, mutes etc.
Application of a varied dynamic range
Good interpretation

Percussion (untuned)
Good coordination of hand, fingers and feet
Correct use of various sticks and beaters
Good control of rhythm and tempi
Good response to dynamic changes
Production of effective tone and timbre
Correct setting up (e.g. snare drum tension)
Expressiveness

Percussion (tuned)
    (first read the list for untuned percussion)
    Good knowledge of keyboard
    Quick and accurate tuning of timpani (and re-tuning against other musical sounds)
    Use of single and double sticks
    Variation of touch
    Good balance of melodic line against accompaniment
    Accurate use of pedals
    Control of rolls and accents

Voice
    Accuracy of intonation
    Good breath control and support
    Good, clear diction
    A tonal balance throughout your range
    Equally clear vowels throughout your range
    Pleasing presentation
    Clear projection of your voice
    Good interpretation and phrasing
    Good posture
    Communication of the meaning of the words
    Suitable expression and good tone quality

Strings (plucked, e.g. guitar)
    Good intonation – careful tuning
    Good hand positions and coordination
    Good balance of melodic line against accompaniment
    Good plucking technique
    Good left-hand technique
    Pleasing tone
    Correct posture and footstool placing
    Wide dynamic range
    Control of special effects (tremolando, harmonics)
    For electric guitars – appropriate volume settings and control of effects
    Good interpretation
    For the harp – use of different positions and control of the pedals

Keyboards
    Good variety of touch (legato, staccato, accented)
    Good coordination of hands
    Good balance of melodic line against accompaniment
    A musical sense of phrasing and dynamics
    Appropriate and systematic fingering
    Appropriate and sympathetic use of pedals
    Good interpretation
    Good posture
    (For electronic organ – musical use of effects and pre-set buttons)
    (Harpsichord – control/choice of registration)

Pipe organ
    In addition to keyboard list as relevant:
    Appropriate choice/good control of registration
    Accurate use of the pedal board
    Good coordination of hands and feet
    Suitable phrasing as appropriate to the instrument
    Good interpretation

Electronic keyboard and synthesisers
    Good knowledge of the keyboard and effects
    Good control of rhythmic effects
    Understanding of synthesisers generally

Good imaginative/creative use of the instrument
Good interpretation

Folk and ethnic instruments
The criteria of the relevant instrumental group (above) should be used. In addition to this, you should consider the interpretative techniques and traditional styles appropriate to the chosen music.

A FINAL STATEMENT

The Subject Reports published by the exam groups after each examination session make interesting reading. In the Solo Performance section it is evident that a significant number of gifted candidates gave performances at a standard higher than 100% level. Likewise, a good number gave musical performances of simple music. It can be deduced from the wording in these reports that it is more sensible to offer pieces that you can perform to a good technical and musical standard, rather than risk a mediocre play-through of a piece that is technically too demanding. Also it is clear that offering a less good second piece may bring down your overall mark when the mark is an average of two. Potential candidates are reminded that their chosen pieces should not be too short, and that an accompaniment should be included where it is an integral part of the composition.

SUMMARY

▷ Choose the right piece for you – not too difficult, but not too simple.

▷ Do not play too much! One piece may be enough.

▷ Interpret the piece intelligently, sensitively, and, above all, *musically*.

▷ Play to an audience of friends before you make your recording or give your examination performance.

▷ **GETTING STARTED**

Music is a social activity. Making music with others can be highly rewarding – and not just financially! Singing or playing as part of a group brings that sense of teamwork as in any sport. Playing as a member of an *ensemble* should be one of the most enjoyable parts of GCSE music and, assuming it all goes well, you will feel a real sense of achievement.

This section of the examination aims to encourage that feeling of team spirit – a corporate activity to stimulate an interest that you may want to pursue for the rest of your life. For those of you not well-versed in French, the word *ensemble* literally means *together*, so that musically it implies a small group of players who are aiming to create an intimate and close musical performance. Smaller professional ensembles (such as string quartets) do not usually have a conductor; with all parts being treated as equal, they learn to work and play together without a director. It is very important to realise that each member of your ensemble must listen to the others carefully and respond accordingly.

In terms of the examination, an ensemble may usually be regarded as two or more members, but it is recommended that you try to choose music that will involve three or four or more. (Remember that your Solo Performance, of course, can include an accompanist and there is then no real difference between performing as a soloist and playing in an Ensemble of two). Many of you will play regularly in a rock band, wind band, orchestra, or sing in the school choir. As long as the part you take is readily identifiable (and for some Groups, not doubled by other people) and is a valuable contribution to a piece, then any combination of two or more performers is perfectly acceptable.

IGCSE	LONDON	MEG	NEAB	NICCEA	SEG	WJEC	TOPIC	STUDY	REVISION 1	REVISION 2
✓	✓	✓	✓	✓	✓	✓	Exam group requirements			
✓	✓	✓	✓	✓	✓	✓	Hints for ensemble playing			
✓	✓	✓	✓	✓	✓	✓	Interacting with others			
✓	✓	✓	✓	✓	✓	✓	Summary			

⟩ **WHAT YOU NEED TO KNOW**

⟩ **Exam group requirements**

The exam groups vary in their requirements for this item. They are summarised as follows.

IGCSE

This is an option within the Prepared Performance section. (Ensemble Performance is offered against Solo Performance on a second instrument – there is no Rehearsing/Directing of an ensemble for IGCSE). There should be three or more players in the ensemble, but the important distinction between 'solo' and 'ensemble' lies in the nature of the music. You may sing or use the same voice or instrument as in your Solo Performance, but your part must not be consistently doubled by anyone else. You have free choice of one piece or movement and your full performance section should not exceed ten minutes.

London

This is a compulsory part of the Performing section. Your performance will be recorded and marked by the teacher; it will then be moderated externally. You are required to submit a log of your participation in ensemble work throughout the course, which will be monitored by your teacher. It must include details of several performances involving other players, and at least three must have been observed by your teacher. These performances may be any musical event, not necessarily in the classroom. Your final assessment will take into account both the level of difficulty of the music played and the standard of the performance.

In addition to this log, you must submit either a tape recording of one occasion when you played or sang a solo part, or a recording (preferably on video) of you rehearsing and directing an ensemble (see Chapter 7).

There is no separate ensemble requirement for the London Short Course.

MEG

This is an option in the Performing (Coursework) section of the examination. There must be at least one person other than yourself playing live in the ensemble. Multi-tracked performances (including performance with a backing track) are acceptable, as long as you are still able to demonstrate true ensemble skills. Recorded accompaniments tend to limit the candidate's spontaneous response.

It is worth mentioning at this point that credit can be given where genuine performing ability can be demonstrated on a different instrument/voice. For this you will have to present and record a third piece in addition to your solo piece and your chosen option.

NEAB

This is an option within the Performing section. You may sing or play in the ensemble, and you are permitted to offer a different instrument from the individual performance. The ensemble should consist of at least two people, and your own part should not be doubled. You are required to prepare one piece. An improvisation may be offered, and the level of difficulty will be a factor in the assessment. The performance must be recorded on cassette. It will be assessed by your teacher and then moderated by the NEAB externally.

NICCEA

This is an option within the Performing section. You are required to offer a programme of up to five minutes duration, where your part is not doubled elsewhere in the ensemble. Members of the ensemble need not be examination candidates, and you may offer an accompanied performance (as in Solo Performing) but different pieces must be performed. Where music technology resources are used, it is important to make sure that the interactive skills of ensemble performance are demonstrated.

SEG

This is an option within the Performing section. You are required to sing or play in at least one ensemble piece of your own choice, where your part must not be doubled by other members of the group. There is no specified length for your piece or pieces, but choose something which shows your contribution adequately and to best advantage. You should try to produce a score for the examiner's use, but failing that, be prepared to explain the nature of your chosen piece. Your performance will be recorded, marked by your teacher, and sent to be moderated externally.

WJEC

This is an option within the Performing section. You are required to perform music of your own choice in an ensemble of at least two players (the other players need not be exam candidates). An accompanied performance would qualify for this section if the music were appropriate. Your part must not be doubled elsewhere in the ensemble. A pre-recorded backing is acceptable, but it may limit the way you can show musical empathy within an ensemble.

▷ **Hints for esemble playing**

The suggestions to be made in this chapter are doubtless duplicated elsewhere in this book, for performance standards for ensemble playing are not so very different from those for a soloist. (For more complete notes on performing technique, see Chapter 5.) The following ideas are common sense really, but must be stated.

▷ If you are requested to submit a copy of the score of your piece for the examiner to see during your performance, then every effort must be made to do so. A commentary is usually acceptable if you cannot provide a score, for example with a rock song where the group has not worked from printed music. Make sure that you explain fully to the examiner how the musical strands are employed throughout the piece. After all, you are probably performing a short two or three minute piece, and the examiner will need to see at a glance exactly what you are supposed to be playing.

▷ If you are performing 'live', be completely set up for the performance before the examiner arrives. Your teacher will have worked out a detailed schedule for the day so that time is not wasted. Have all your music ready, stands set up, amplifiers and speakers in place (with volume checked in advance!), and be fully warmed up and in tune with each other. Not only does this create a good impression and save time for all concerned, but it is, indeed, good performance practice.

▷ Thinking musically now, the question of balance is most important when playing with others. Once again, common sense should prevail here, but if you have a melodic instrument playing a tune, then your part should be more prominent than if you are supporting with an accompaniment figure. Taste and sensitivity – in other words, *musical judgement* – must be used at all times. There is far more to group playing than merely getting the correct notes. You must also be able to blend well with the others. Having said this, however, your chosen piece of ensemble music will probably be written in such a way that your part is a combination of melody and accompaniment, where each player takes a turn at the tune. For most people this is probably very obvious and would happen automatically, but it must be stated again: think carefully all the time about your part in relation to the other players. Should this section be more prominent? Is this an important theme or counter-melody, or is it merely a harmonic background? Music is often written as a sort of dialogue, where themes are handed from player to player in a conversational way. This sensitivity becomes second nature to experienced musicians eventually; the process may happen sub-consciously, but it certainly still goes on. No doubt your teacher will be available to advise you, or even direct rehearsals, but it will also require an intelligent contribution from you. Think musically, and listen critically to all the parts whenever you rehearse and perform.

▷ Once the ensemble music has been chosen, it is your responsibility to learn your individual part thoroughly. You will be sure to know when you are likely to rehearse the piece all together, so organise yourself so that you have sorted out any technical problems with notes in good time. When an ensemble is ready to start working at a finer interpretation of a piece there is nothing more infuriating, and time-wasting, than to find that one player is still struggling with his sharps and flats, bowing, phrasing or whatever.

Most GCSE candidates will be having instrumental lessons out of class, so it may be a good idea to take the music to that teacher for specialist help – he or she may well have helped to choose the piece in the first place and will therefore be more than willing to oblige. The more time that the ensemble can spend on achieving a balance of sound, sensitive phrasing and agreed general interpretation, so much the better.

▶ Regarding the choice of ensemble pieces, it is impossible here to give actual titles of pieces that you might play, for every combination of instruments and abilities is quite different. It can only be suggested that you **spend time** carefully choosing a piece where each player is adequately involved, without his or her part being too difficult. It is better, surely, to perform a slightly easier part well than to take on a more showy part, only to spoil it in the examination where you have only one chance.

▶ If the ensemble has decided to use a conductor (your teacher, perhaps, or a musical classmate), make sure that you keep an eye on him or her. Remember that a conductor is there to express the music as well as to keep a steady beat. The alternative is for one of the ensemble players to be appointed as leader or director. Rehearse thoroughly so that he or she is well prepared for the difficult task of starting and finishing the piece with just an up-bow, a breath or a nod. A polished opening and ending, with chords sounded perfectly together, is vital to the success of your performance.

▷ Interacting with others

It was stated above how important it is musically to blend well with others. Similarly, you should endeavour to blend well socially when working with other musicians. In a small group such as this, everyone has the right to offer their views and opinions to help improve the standard of the piece. However, there may come a time when a particular member has to eat humble pie and accept the judgement of the majority, or your rehearsing will never achieve a satisfactory performance. It is surely an important part of the experience to learn to interact with others. You may be the only player of your instrument and therefore know best its technical limitations or characteristics but the final interpretation in an ensemble should be the result of a mixture of opinions.

Your teacher, of course, may decide to direct the piece in all rehearsals and the final performance. In this case you will need to behave as if you are in a professional orchestra – the conductor is the maestro, and is entirely responsible for interpretation. Your responsibility is to play your instrument in a way which responds accurately to the conductor's directives.

These are two very different ways of contributing musically and you must accept your teacher's method of working. Both methods have their place and can be very satisfying. Nothing will be achieved satisfactorily in a group unless you all show some initiative and cooperation. Having suggested that no one member should dominate an ensemble, the other danger is that no-one will take any responsibility! Try to be helpful in an unselfish, yet contributory way.

▷ A FINAL STATEMENT

The reassuring thing to remember about GCSE is that any candidate may be part of an ensemble, even with the most modest performing skills. Do not assume that you have to be a brilliant performer. The exam groups take into account the difficulty of your individual part by using a difficulty multiplier in the marking scheme. Your chosen pieces are divided into categories – very easy, intermediate difficulty and reasonable difficulty – and you are assessed accordingly. Examiners are also well aware that some instruments are more demanding technically than others, and this, too, is taken into account.

SUMMARY

Before rehearsing with your ensemble you will find it helpful to check the following points:

▷   Am I totally accurate – in pitch, rhythm, and intonation?

▷   Are details such as breathing/tonguing/bowing/fingering/pedalling all sorted out?

▷   Have I mastered the expressive aspects of the music – phrasing, dynamics, expression marks?

▷   Am I able to play my part fluently in the correct tempo?

▷   Am I playing it the 'correct' way stylistically?

▷   Have I thought out the problem of page turning?

▷   Have I really chosen the best piece to demonstrate my ability to the best advantage – where I feel confident and secure?

Before performing in the examination, or submitting the recording, consider these points:

▷   Am I properly tuned up? (This is particularly important where more than one guitar, or other string instrument, is being used).

▷   Is the ensemble piece correctly balanced, with the melody line prominent and the accompaniment more in the background?

▷   Have I chosen the best place, acoustically, for the performance or recording?

Rehearsing and directing an ensemble

▷ **GETTING STARTED**

Rehearsing and directing an ensemble is less likely to be chosen as a Prepared Option by many candidates. It is good that most GCSE groups offer this option, but it will probably be chosen only by those candidates with an interest and an ability to conduct, who have good aural skills and the confidence to go with it.

Before you finally decide on your options for Prepared Performance read this short chapter through carefully and consider what is involved – there is more to it than standing up in front and beating time!

IGCSE	LONDON	MEG	NEAB	NICCEA	SEG	WJEC	TOPIC	STUDY	REVISION 1	REVISION 2
	✓	✓	✓	✓	✓	✓	Exam group requirements			
	✓	✓	✓	✓	✓	✓	Useful hints and techniques			
	✓	✓	✓	✓	✓	✓	Conducting technique			
	✓	✓	✓	✓	✓	✓	Layout of ensemble			
	✓	✓	✓	✓	✓	✓	Recording progress			
	✓	✓	✓	✓	✓	✓	Summary			

▶ WHAT YOU NEED TO KNOW

▷ **Exam groups requirements**

The exam groups have slightly different requirements for this item, which can be summarised as follows:

London

This is an option within the Performing section. In order to authenticate your contribution to this ensemble work, you are required to submit a recording (preferably on video), in which you are seen rehearsing and directing an ensemble of singers and/or players in the performance of one piece of your own choice. If you wish, you may include on your recording a selection of performances in which you rehearse and direct, but you must ensure that they are of your highest standard. (The alternative to rehearsing and directing is a recording of one occasion where you are playing or singing an individual part.)

For the London Short Course, Rehearsing and Directing is a choice with Option 2, and is worth 20% of the total marks. You are required to organise, rehearse and direct a performance of the composition(s) that you have submitted for Section A of this Short Course. This could involve managing a group of singers and/or players, making sure that the music is available as required, or it could simply involve giving clear directions to a player. The recording will be marked by the teacher, and will be moderated by the Council.

MEG

This is an option within the Performing Coursework section of the examination, and you may choose this instead of playing or singing as a part of an ensemble. You must submit a video recording of a rehearsal and the performance – an audio cassette is not acceptable as it cannot provide sufficient evidence of the candidate at work. For assessment of your rehearsal and performance tape, the moderator will consider these criteria:

(a)   technical control through appropriate rehearsal procedures
(b)   a suitable sense of ensemble through the use of musical elements in directing a performance.

NEAB

This is an option within the Performing section. You are required to offer an audio or video cassette recording of at least one rehearsal and the final performance of one piece of music. A written report should be submitted, in which you explain your choice of music, your preparation, the schedule of rehearsals over an extended period, and comment on progress made.

Candidates should be encouraged to choose music and an ensemble which are both capable of development throughout the allotted time. Marks are awarded according to the following criteria:

(a)   realisation of appropriate music for the ensemble;
(b)   understanding and direction of the voices and/or instruments in rehearsal;
(c)   direction of a performance of some of the music rehearsed.

There must be no fewer than three performers.

NICCEA

This is an option within the Performing section. Candidates are expected to direct rehearsals of various pieces over the two year course. The visiting examiner will then need to observe you working on another piece, previously unrehearsed but which the performers will have an opportunity to prepare in advance. You will have 10 to 15 minutes for the rehearsal, and you should provide either orally or in writing an overall plan and a plan for the assessment rehearsal. You will be assessed on Planning (20%), Content (40%) and Communication (40%).

SEG

This is an option within the Performing section. You are required to rehearse and direct an ensemble of more than two performers, but this need not be the first rehearsal of the ensemble. While it is understood that you may not achieve performance standard during this rehearsal you will be expected to work with the group as if towards an eventual performance. The rehearsal should last for 10 to 20 minutes. Marks are awarded for your effectiveness as a musical leader rather than for the perfection you manage to achieve. Your work must be recorded onto cassette or ideally a video recording, as these are useful aids to the moderator.

WJEC

This is an option within the Performing section. It is expected that candidates will direct rehearsals of several pieces during the course, and the examiner will need to observe a further rehearsal of one or more of these pieces, lasting up to 10 minutes. Marks are awarded for your organisation, and qualities of musical direction. You should also be prepared to discuss any aspect of the rehearsal with the examiner afterwards. Before the examination rehearsal you should give a score (or outline) of the music to him. If a score is not available you should give an oral description of the piece. The members of your rehearsal group need not be exam candidates.

▷ **Useful hints and techniques**

If you do choose this option, remember that the examination 'rehearsal' is 15 to 20 minutes long for some exam groups. You will need to choose your music with care, plan the rehearsal thoughtfully and decide on the standard of performance that you are aiming for.

Here are some thoughts for guidance which are relevant for all the syllabuses that include this option.

▶ First of all, prepare an **overall plan**.

Choose music within your own ability, so that it is not too difficult for you to detect any mistakes and inaccuracies. Also take into account the ability of the group you are to direct. If you choose a piece that is too demanding you will probably not have time to move beyond correcting basic technical errors; conversely, if it is too easy for them there will be little opportunity for you to display your skills of direction.

Bear in mind the instrumentation and balance of your ensemble, and if you are preparing more than one piece aim for some variety or contrast.

Give careful consideration to your score and decide what your priorities will be. Prepare it very thoroughly yourself so that you form a clear idea of the composer's intentions, and can more quickly recognise problems as they arise. Try to anticipate sections in the music where things are most likely to go wrong, or which you feel will need particular attention in the rehearsal.

▶ Make a **rehearsal plan**.

What are you aiming to achieve in your rehearsal? A perfect performance is unlikely, of course, given such a limited time – what emphasis will you place on correct notes and reasonable tuning, as against the more expressive considerations? Remember, this all depends on the abilities of your players and the relative difficulty of your chosen music but you must consider what standards you intend to achieve.

▶ Think of the **content** of your rehearsal.

You will need to be able to recognise basic errors such as wrong notes and poor tuning, for example, and simultaneously give attention to aspects of rhythm, phrasing, dynamics, blending and ensemble. (By ensemble, we mean synchronised chording, especially at stops and starts, and a sense of 'togetherness' generally.)

Aim to develop an ability to work on particular weak spots rather than try to cover too much. In a timed exercise such as this it is better to 'perfect' a shorter section than just play through a larger section. Should the melody be more expressive here? Was someone not watching you hold that pause? Was the accompaniment figure too prominent? Your performers are probably reading from a single line and will look to you for clear direction, both spoken and through meaningful conducting.

▶ As the person in charge of the ensemble you will need to develop and demonstrate a sense of **musical leadership**.

You must convince the examiner (and the players, ultimately) of your competence in musical interpretation. Perhaps the most important skill for this option is the ability to communicate exactly what you want to your players.

You must establish a good relationship with the group. Control of people does not mean you must be unfriendly! Think of yourself as first among equals. Aim to make decisions quickly, and try not to change your mind, which may confuse the players – they must always know where they are.

▶ The **presentation** of your rehearsal is important.

Were the methods you employed the correct ones? Were they suitable to achieve your required aim?

Alter the pace when rehearsing to give variety. Although people won't get bored in your short rehearsal, sustain their interest by varying your voice occasionally to avoid monotony and keep things moving along.

Could people understand what you were saying? Were you loud and clear? Be articulate without talking too much. Good conductors communicate with musical actions more than their voices.

Did you involve everyone satisfactorily in the rehearsal? Or were you so intent on one particular section that the poor trumpeter was almost forgotten and only played three notes?

▶ What **overall impression** do you think you gave?

Did you sense the group enjoyed it all and felt a sense of shared achievement? Did you manage to interpret the music according to the composer's intentions? You may have achieved the right notes but were the tempo, dynamics and phrasing appropriate?

▷ Conducting technique

Beating time is just one aspect of being a conductor, but a vital one. You can practice giving a good, clear beat on your own in front of a mirror at home – you could even conduct your own records! Assuming that you are likely to work with a fairly small group, it is not necessary to use a baton. Bare hands can be perfectly clear and sometimes more expressive than using a stick. Try both ways during practice and use whichever is the most comfortable for you.

Your down beat is the most important, and must be very clear; see Fig. 7.1

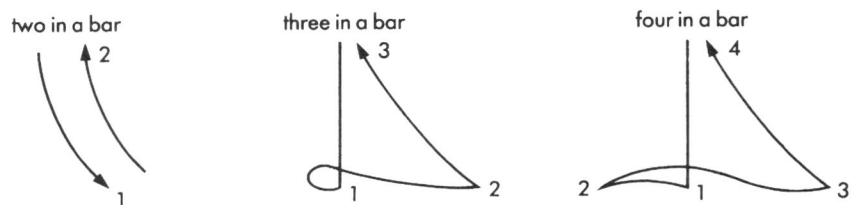

Fig. 7.1

The diagrams in Fig. 7.1 are for right-handed people; reverse the direction of beats 2, 3 and 4 if you are left-handed. Notice the curved beats; this is rather more graceful than robotic straight lines. After all, you are trying to express the feeling of the music as well as keep a clear and steady beat. Your other hand will not move around so much, but is used for further expression: softness, loudness, tenderness, anger.

Don't overdo the hand movements – aim for clarity; you are not giving a gymnastic display! Use your face, and especially your eyes to maintain a rapport with your players. Whereas words can help you explain your musical intentions in a rehearsal, in a performance you are totally dependent on gesture – body language, in fact. To an experienced player, even a slightly raised eyebrow can be a clear signal as to how the music is to be played. A smile or frown from you will be obvious enough. Of course, the sort of gesture you give will depend on the music and your personality. There are many ways to interpret music physically, and in the end you will have to work out your own salvation. Whatever you do, be clear – don't try to be a showman on this particular occasion!

▷ Layout of ensemble

Finally, one or two suggestions concerning the layout for your ensemble. Again, this is common sense really, but worth stating. Plan out how you want your players to sit. If there are only a few, then a semi-circle is the obvious setting. With more players, you may have to use ranks making sure that all the players can see you and that you have eye-contact with them. Problems of balancing a group of players musically, can be partly solved by careful placing. You would not have a percussionist too close to the front, for example.

Also check that the music stands are placed at a sensible height: too low and the players play down to the floor; too high and they can't see you over the top! If you are directing a group of singers, arrange it so that they are grouped fairly close together in a way that they can hear each other, but also ensure that they can all see you for clear direction. You may well have to experiment (well in advance of the examination) with placing of voices or instruments. Some rooms have 'dead' spots where the sound is particularly poor. Remember that carpets and curtains absorb sound; it may be a good idea to open curtains to increase the resonance and 'flatter' the sound.

▷ **Recording progress**

NEAB requires a written and/or taped record of your progress in rehearsals. Use the following points to help you consider what you say in this commentary:

(a) Why did you choose your particular pieces?
(b) How often did you rehearse and how long for?
(c) How did you organise your rehearsals?
(d) What musical difficulties did you encounter?
(e) Did you feel a sense of progress during the rehearsals?

The examination boards vary in their requirements for the preparation of the examination rehearsal. With NICCEA you are not permitted to rehearse the actual examination piece in advance. This is perfectly reasonable, for it can so easily become staged – a rehearsed rehearsal. Whatever syllabus you work from, make sure that you get plenty of experience by working with several different pieces so that you feel fully confident on the day.

A FINAL STATEMENT

Good luck with your directing! Remember that for top marks the examiner is looking for confident and clear direction leading to a well thought out and well controlled performance.

SUMMARY

▷ Choose the piece very carefully.

▷ Plan out how you are going to work in rehearsal.

▷ What is your overall *aim* in that rehearsal?

▷ Learn how to conduct clearly. Decide how you will present yourself as a leader.

▷ Carefully plan the layout of your rehearsal room.

8

Sight-reading

> ## GETTING STARTED

This is not a favourite activity for most music students, but it is a necessary exercise if you are to become fluent in reading music. Only two groups include sight-reading as an option, so you may not be obliged to tackle this section. A specified preparation time is allowed for each test, under supervision. If you wish to sing the tests, don't worry too much about the quality of your voice as long as you can sing in tune. In fact, tests using voice may be sung, whistled or hummed at the candidate's choice, and will be transposed where necessary.

IGCSE	LONDON	MEG	NEAB	NICCEA	SEG	WJEC	TOPIC	STUDY	REVISION I	REVISION 2
✓		✓					Exam group requirements			
✓		✓					The key signature			
✓		✓					The time signature			
✓		✓					Scanning			
✓		✓					Counting			
✓		✓					Speed			
✓		✓					Looking ahead			
✓		✓					Expression			
✓		✓					Sight-reading tests			
✓		✓					Summary			

▶ **WHAT YOU NEED TO KNOW**

▷ **Exam group requirements**

IGCSE

For this option, you sing or play two graded tests from a choice that is selected by your teacher – and unseen by you! You are allowed ten minutes preparation time with your instrument, but vocalists are not allowed any instrumental help. Each of the tests will have expression marks which you should observe. Both of the chosen pieces will be assessed and the better mark of the two awarded. (For extra practice here, you could work from the Sight Reading Tests published by the Associated Board of the Royal Schools of Music or by Trinity College, London, where Grade 1 = Test 1 and Grade 4 = Test 2.)

MEG

Sight-reading is one of the Terminal Task options within the Unprepared Performing section. Three tests will be set. The first two will be for a solo instrument, but the third will be for two instruments playing as an ensemble. You are expected to demonstrate expression, technical control, and a suitable sense of ensemble.

Test 1:   Up to 8 bars in 3/4 or 4/4 time.
Test 2:   Up to 16 bars, in 2/4, 3/4, 4/4 or 6/8 time.
Test 3:   Up to 20 bars, but the standard will be equivalent to that of Test 2. The second part of this ensemble test will be played by the teacher-assessor or another competent person. The candidate's part will start the test and will include rests. Both parts will be printed on the candidate's sheet.

▷ **The key signature**

The key signature is the first thing to check carefully when you play a new piece. You should know, by glancing at the number of sharps or flats at the beginning of the line, exactly what key you are in (see Chapter 13 if you need to refresh your memory). You must keep this in your mind throughout the exercise. Remember that an accidental lasts a whole bar, so that:

for example, contains two B naturals because they are both within the same bar. These are more likely to appear in the more advanced tests.

▷ **The time signature**

The next thing to look at is the number of beats in a bar. Candidates usually take more note of this than the key signature, but be careful in particular with your counting in 6/8 time which can be rather tricky. Remember that you can either count the six quavers individually; or count in two main beats, where the quavers are grouped into threes. For example

count 1 2 3 4 5 6 for a slower speed, or 1____ 2____ for a quicker tempo.

In Chapter 13 the section 'Rests and Note Values', explains this in more detail. The easier tests are likely to be in 3/4 or 4/4 where the counting is more straightforward.

▷ **Scanning**

The preparation time may not be long enough to 'play' the tune through mentally at the intended speed. Try to **scan** through the line of music, noticing key signature and time signature as already suggested, and then observing any difficult areas – an accidental to remember, perhaps, or a tricky rhythm that requires careful counting. Make a mental note of what it is and where it occurs.

▷ **Counting**

This should go without saying really, but some candidates do seem to forget all about counting. Correct rhythm is fundamental in all music, and accuracy can only be guaranteed by counting each beat quietly to yourself. Besides helping the rhythm it will keep you in a strict time.

Here are some of the problem areas in sight-reading rhythm:

(a)   The difference between ♩. ♪♩ and ♩. ♪♪

If you rely on 'feel' and don't know the piece (as in any sight-reading) you can so easily mix up these two rhythms; but when you count, there is no excuse for error:

example (i) 3/4 ♩. ♪♩ ♩   example (ii) 3/4 ♩. ♪♪

In example (i) the dotted quaver + semiquaver both fit into the first beat, and in example (ii) you must count 'one – two' before you play the quaver. Mentally say the word 'and' (as shown above) to be sure of getting it right. If you are still unsure on this ask your teacher to help you further, and give examples for you to practice. This is a very common error in all music examinations.

(b)   The triplet ♩♩♩ sometimes catches people out. In a ♩ beat it fits into one beat: 4/4 ♪♪♪♩ ♩ it must be played as three equal notes. Very often it is inaccurately performed as ♩ ♪♪ because, generally speaking, people rush the triplet. **Remember** a triplet is three notes played equally in the time of two of the same kind.

(c)   Be sure to take rests into account. Do count them carefully! It is easy to mix up minim and semibreve rests: ▬ = a semibreve (4 crotchet beats) and

▬ = a minim rest (2 crotchet beats).

Also take care when you see this sort of rhythm: 4/4 ﹅ ♪♪♪ ♩
1 and 2 and 3 – 4

Here you should count the quaver rest as 'one' then play immediately, fitting the single quaver in before the second beat.

(d)   Simple syncopation may be included in an advanced test: 4/4 ♪♩ ♪♩
1   2   3 – 4

– the notes do not fit on the beats as you can see the numbers underneath, producing a characterisitic jazzy rhythm. Practise this one carefully. (You may find this easier if you count it as: 4/4 ♪♪♪♪ ♩)
1 and 2 and 3 – 4

▷ **Speed**   Err on the side of safety. An examiner will forgive a rather slow speed if the performance is fluent and accurate within that speed. It is harder to give credit for a rushed, yet hesitant and unmusical rendition. Choose your overall speed by looking at the most difficult fragment. It is no good slowing down when it gets difficult and then changing gear for the easier bits!

▷ **Looking ahead**   You must be mentally ahead of the notes that you are playing, to give yourself time to perceive the information, process it and then perform it correctly. Don't stare at a long note while you are playing it; by all means count its value, but at the same time be solving the next immediate problem or your music will sound hesitant and disjointed.

▷ **Expression**   Some tests may contain phrasing and expression marks. You should make every effort to apply these. Obviously you are going to concentrate mainly on notes and rhythm, but all music has a wealth of added detail to indicate how it should be played. In a normal practice session you would probably work at these fine points after mastering all the notes, but here (in a simple test) you should aim to incorporate as much as you can straight away. All music – even simple exercises – consists of more than the printed notes. Try to be expressive, even if there are no markings indicated.

▷ **Sight-reading tests**   Figs. 8.1 and 8.2 are some sight-reading tests for you to look at. They are to help you gauge the standard required as well as provide extra material for practice. These exercises are graded from A to D in order of difficulty. Figs. 8.3 and 8.4 are actual examination questions. Have a go!

A.
VOICE (transpose as necessary)
La la etc.
A. Moderato
FLUTE
mf
A.
TRUMPET
A.
OBOE or FLUTE
mf
poco rit.
A.
CLARINET or TRUMPET
f
mp
B. Allegretto
VIOLIN
mf
B.
PITCHED PERCUSSION
B. (rhythm)
GUITAR (chords and rhythm)
chords D G Em – A7 D A7 D
B.
VOICE (transpose as necessary)
mf
La la etc.
f
B.
VIOLA
mf
C.
CELLO and DOUBLE BASS
C.
OBOE or SAXOPHONE
C.
BRASS BASSES

Fig. 8.1

CLARINET or FLUTE or OBOE or TRUMPET

C.

CELLO and DOUBLE BASS

C.

CLARINET

D.

SIDE DRUM

D.

MONO ORGAN + chords

D.

FLUTE or VIOLIN

D.

SIDE DRUM

D.

Fig. 8.1 continued

PIANO AND ELECTRONIC ORGAN

A.

B.

C.

Fig. 8.2

D.

Fig. 8.2 continued

DESCANT/
TENOR
RECORDER

(ULEAC 1992)

A.

TIMPANI/

· (ULEAC 1992)

B. Yaman in dadra

SITAR/
HARMONIUM/
INDIAN FLUTE/
SINGING/

(ULEAC 1992)

B.

FRENCH HORN

(ULEAC 1992)

C.

VIOLA

(ULEAC 1992)

C.

DRUM KIT

(suspended cymbal, snare drum,)
high-hat cymbals, bass drum)

(ULEAC 1992)

D.

VOICE

(ULEAC 1992)

D.

STEEL PANS

(Soprano/Ping Pong
(High or Low))

G F   E F   E D E   D C A G   C   E   D C B D   C

(ULEAC 1992)

Fig. 8.3

Here are some 1991 SEG sight-reading tests for you to practise:

Preforming at sight – all candidates must attempt Test (a). You may have up to one minute to prepare before you begin.

Test (a), tap or clap the following rhythm.   *(3)*

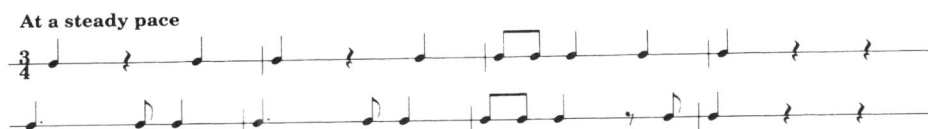

At a steady pace

Fig. 8.4

All candidates must attempt Test (b). Candidate should choose a pitch and clef suitable for their instrument or voice. Candidates chooosing voice must be given the first note. You may have one minute to prepare before you begin.

Test (b)

(3)

Fig. 8.5

Test (c) CLASSICAL GUITAR: play the following passage.

(5)

Fig. 8.6

Test (d) TRUMPET/CORNET (suitable for B flat, C, D or E flat)
BRASS BAND INSTRUMENTS (suitable for B flat cornet, B flat flugelhorn, E flat soprano cornet)

(9)

Fig. 8.7

> ## A FINAL STATEMENT

You are advised not to leave this element of the syllabus until the last moment. For those of you who receive instrumental tuition outside of class, you can always ask your teacher to give a short test as part of your lesson. Courses for Grade exams should have included this anyway, although sight-reading practice is often sadly neglected. If you don't have private lessons then your class teacher will be pleased to find you some tests of a suitable standard. Do discipline yourself to practise sight-reading 'little and often' throughout the course; it cannot be crammed – it demands regular practice. Sight-reading may not be the most exciting part of music-making, but it does pay dividends. Before long you will be reading much faster and more accurately.

SUMMARY

▷   'Practice makes perfect' – don't leave this activity too late!

▷   Scan quickly through a test. Look at the key signature and the time signature.

▷   When you play through the test, count carefully and choose a safe speed, so you can cope with the most difficult part.

▷   Be expressive while you are playing, and try to stick to dynamic markings when they are given.

▷   Look ahead!

Memory tests

GETTING STARTED

A good musical memory is a considerable asset to a musician. If you are a singer, you will obviously learn your songs or choral parts much quicker; if you work in the pop field, and don't normally use written music, you will progress much faster with a good memory. Some people will find this part of the course quite easy – singing a short tune back will be quite natural to them, especially if they had plenty of singing experience in their Infant and Junior schools. Others, perhaps with little or no use of singing voice behind them, will feel embarrassed at having to sing. Boys especially seem to feel vulnerable, with their recently lowered voices, when it comes to having to pitch a note. With practice, and increasing confidence, most people manage these tests rather well in the end. Also, many candidates will have had experience of memory tests in their Grade exams. Either way, don't worry – it is relatively painless!

IGCSE	LONDON	MEG	NEAB	NICCEA	SEG	WJEC	TOPIC	STUDY	REVISION 1	REVISION 2
✓							Exam group requirements			
✓							Useful techniques			
✓							Memory test exercises			
✓							Summary			

▷ WHAT YOU NEED TO KNOW

▷ **Exam group requirements**

IGCSE

This is a compulsory test in the Unprepared Performance section. All candidates are required to clap or tap a rhythm after hearing it played twice on the piano. After a further hearing candidates must then sing or play the same phrase.

▷ **Useful techniques**

This is obviously not an area of work that you can revise for at last minute. Memory work needs continual practice, especially for the longer exercises. Although you are given the option to use your instrument it is usually recommended that you sing these tests, unless you have an exceptionally fine ear and memory.

Regular practice with any form of aural tests is far better for you than last minute cramming. You will find after a while that your memory will gradually improve, as you start to feel the patterns within a given melody. Most short tunes are based on scalic figures or arpeggios, and sequences (repeated patterns at a higher or lower pitch) are not uncommon. Try to hear groups of notes, or a whole phrase, rather than single ones. After all, when we listen to someone speaking we don't hear single words at a time – we take in a whole sentence.

Don't try to tackle the advanced tests until you are capable of regular success with the easier ones. In fact, any practice that you can do with singing will add to your increasing confidence; even singing well known melodies quietly to yourself will improve your memory skills.

However, for boys whose voices have recently changed, the problem is not so much remembering the tune, but in finding the pitch of the first note within the new voice range. You can often overcome what amounts to a loss of vocal confidence by testing yourself at a keyboard with single notes. Usually boys who have not used their singing voice for a few years will automatically attempt to sing at their lowest pitch, which is frequently an octave too low. This does not really matter at first, for the important thing is to make that low note in tune. Try doing this several times – you should easily manage on your own, even if you are not a keyboard player – or you can ask a friend to work with you. Soon you should graduate to two- or three-note tests, but make sure that you keep it at a comfortable pitch. When you are achieving success with this every time, extend it to a two-bar phrase and so on. You will obviously need someone else at this point to play the tunes for you, and do insist on a pitch range that suits your voice! Until you are well used to singing again, you will probably sing too low and out of tune so that if the test is set too high for you, you are back where you started.

You may be able to persuade your class teacher to give you some singing-back practice on your own. Experience has shown that boys who normally sing very little lose all confidence when confronted with the prospect of singing in front of their class-mates. To cover their embarrassment, notes are often grunted back with little or no sensitivity or attention to rhythmic detail. You will almost certainly be more confident on your own at first, and when you feel more able to do it well you will probably not worry so much about the audience. You will have to sort this out for yourself.

▷ **Memory test exercises**

Space permits the printing of only a few exercises; ask a friend (who is musically reliable!) to play these over to you, then sing them back according to the requirements of your Examining Group. Once you have become used to the style and length of these exercises, you will be able to find others for someone to help you with. (Aural books for the Associated Board or Trinity College of Music exams can be useful here).

The exercises are included for you to see the standard that is required. But for extra practice you should tackle, throughout the course, some that are outside your actual syllabus. Move on to the more difficult ones when you feel ready. It all helps.

Each time you are given a memory test, either in practice or in the examination, concentrate intently and sing it back immediately before you lose it. Don't forget that there is more to music than mere notes – for full marks you will need to be perfectly in tune, and also completely accurate in relation to rhythm and tempo.

Practice exercises

The tests in Fig. 9.1 may be transposed for the appropriate voice. The practice exercises are graded from A to C in order of difficulty. Hum, sing or whistle the following:

Fig. 9.1

Fig. 9.2 gives two actual tests for you to use. Test A (London 1991) is suitable for Soprano voice, Tenor voice, Descant recorder, Tenor recorder, tuned Classroom Instruments and Guitar.

Test B (London 1992) is suitable for Bass voice, Cello and Bassoon.

Fig. 9.2

Fig. 9.2 continued

▷ **A FINAL STATEMENT**

If you stop to think, we all have incredible powers of memory. Thinking musically, everyone can remember hundreds of songs, both melodies and words. We learn these without trying; when we enjoy hearing a song many times, somehow it all stays in the memory, often for years after having last heard it. This is all the more amazing when you consider how similar tunes can be. Bearing this in mind, it should not be too daunting a task for you to sing back a short phrase with no words. Do practise regularly, however, and don't leave it until it is too late!

SUMMARY

▷ Practise regularly – don't leave this until the end of the course.

▷ Concentrate fully, both when listening to and repeating the test.

▷ Be as expressive as you can, but don't worry too much about the quality of your voice – just be in tune!

10 Improvisation

GETTING STARTED

Improvisation is **instant composition** – an impromptu expression of musical thought. Students tend to be wary of demonstrating this 'subconscious music' at first, feeling that it is insufficiently prepared. A written composition demands considerable effort, whereas an improvisation is spontaneous music; hence the initial attempts tend to be extremely short. As confidence is gained, so the length increases – sometimes too much so, making pruning necessary!

As with any other music, a framework is necessary upon which to build your improvisation. Using a particular chord scheme as a structure will help to give this 'instant music' some suitable repetition and a sense of shape. The examiner will be looking for three main things:

(a) a fluency within the given style or theme, or an adherence to the chosen topic;
(b) evidence of development in melody, rhythm or harmony;
(c) an overall structure or form.

Even if you are not being assessed on Improvisation as a topic in itself, you may to wish to improvise as part of your Solo Performing. You should also find this chapter helpful towards your Composition work.

IGCSE	LONDON	MEG	NEAB	NICCEA	SEG	WJEC	TOPIC	STUDY	REVISION I	REVISION 2
✓	✓	✓	✓	✓	✓		Exam group requirements			
✓	✓	✓					Chord schemes			
✓	✓	✓					Improvisation on a given rhythm			
✓	✓	✓					Improvisation and melodic motif: single line instruments			
	✓						Improvisation on a given pitch with free rhythm			
✓	✓						Improvisation and melodic motif: keyboard instruments			
		✓					Improvisation on a given topic			
✓		✓					Improvisation to a given verse			
	✓						Improvisation on a given texture			
✓	✓	✓	✓	✓	✓		Summary			

> ### WHAT YOU NEED TO KNOW

▷ **Exam group requirements**

Once again, the Groups vary in their requirements.

IGCSE

This is an option within the Unprepared Performance section. You are asked to choose one idea from a list of three given to you 10 minutes before the examination, and then improvise on that idea for no more than three minutes. There will be a rhythm, a note pattern and a sequence of chords (Jazz instrumentalists may improvise to a chord progession played by another person.) They will be written out in staff notation and played twice to you if required. Vocal candidates have 10 minutes in which to prepare a melody in any suitable style from a choice of two sets of words: folk song, hymn, classical, modern, pop etc. You may add an accompaniment if you wish.

London

This is an option for both the Full and Short Courses. The candidate is required to improvise one piece, either instrumentally or vocally, and the marks are worth 10% of the whole examination. After being given the necessary instructions you will have up to 10 minutes to prepare before the actual test. A choice of tests will be offered, including musical motifs, rhythmic patterns and chord sequences. If you wish, the teacher will play any or all of the test stimuli twice before you make your choice.

MEG

This is an option (as a Terminal Task) within the Composing section. You will be given up to 20 minutes to prepare a composition after which time you are asked to record a performance of your work. You may compose in any style using a stimulus in one of the following formats:

(a) a short rhythmic pattern in standard notation;
(b) a short note pattern in traditional notation with letter names;
(c) a short melody in staff notation;
(d) a short chord sequence with a bass part in staff notation and roman numerals (III, V, VI etc.);
(e) a short chord sequence using letter names (G Em D7 etc.) and tablature (for guitars);
(f) some words to choose from a selection of styles.

The teacher will play your chosen stimulus twice if required, and you are permitted to use instruments, voice and recording equipment during the preparation time. You may make notes which can be submitted as part of the final composition if you wish. A maximum of about two minutes is sufficient, but it is accepted that many pieces will be shorter than this. The duration of your piece in no way reflects attainment.

NEAB

Strictly speaking, this is not a separate option, but NEAB allows both solo performing and the ensemble performance to be offered as an improvisation. This is especially useful for jazz players.

NICCEA

This is a part of the Solo Performing section, and is not a separate option. Any opportunity for the performer to play a significant part is defined as a solo, thus jazz players are given the chance to improvise a solo if they wish.

SEG

This is not an option as such, but is incorporated into the Solo Performing section. SEG defines a solo part as one which enables the performer to play a significant part. This gives an opportunity for jazz players to improvise if they so wish.

Before we consider actual examination questions, or suitable topics for you to practise full-length improvisations, there is a more fundamental question to answer. Which instrument will you use? Bear in mind that it is extremely difficult to improvise on given topics with a trombone or similar melodic instrument. You have far more scope with a piano, electronic keyboard or a guitar. No offence to trombonist or the like, but they would be more sensible to choose a melodic motif, unless they have a fairly advanced and versatile technical skill. Do consider the practicality of your main instrument now that you have read through the examination boards' requirements above. For many of the categories it is assumed that a chordal instrument is being used.

▷ **Chord schemes**   Let us examine chord schemes first. This is really improvisation from the bottom upwards – a concentration on harmony where any melody used is worked as an afterthought. For this work you will need to have a basic keyboard proficiency, where you are able to think about chords quickly and change them smoothly. You might find suitable chord sequences in any simple pop song.

Practice question and answers

Improvise for approximately one minute on this chord sequence:

C   Am   Em   F   Dm   F   G   C.

Example answer 1
Play the chords over with a repeated pop rhythm as in Fig. 10.1

Fig. 10.1

or by giving four beats to each chord (Fig. 10.2).

Fig. 10.2

Does this appeal to you as an eight-bar sentence? Perhaps it can be enhanced by changing some of the rhythm; see Fig. 10.3.

Fig. 10.3

Example answer 2
Although it has now been shortened to a six-bar line, the rather predictable 8 × four-bar pattern has been broken up, giving a slight 'kick' to the rhythm. Bar 5 has a similarity to bar 3 which gives a sense of unity. Always try to think musically, even when you are working with simple material. If you play music in a monotonous way it is bound to sound boring; by playing it expressively you will start to bring it alive. Of course you can also vary the dynamics quite substantially to make it more interesting.

These eight or six bars could well be repeated, then you will probably want to change the chords. How can you extend it?

The obvious structure for immediate extension is a ternary, (A + B + A) where you return to your given chord scheme (A) after a new contrasting section (B).

What chords would you choose for your middle section (B)? We could change to the subdominant key for variety, using a shorter pattern:

Example answer 3

$$\text{F} \text{ / Am } \text{/} \left| \text{B}\flat \text{ / Gm C} \right| \text{F / Am / } \left| \text{B}\flat \text{ / Gm F } \right.\|$$

Fig. 10.4

This has two good points about it. First of all, there is some similarity in chord progression: B♭ – Gm in the middle has the same interval (that is, a minor 3rd apart) as the opening C – Am in the first pattern. This may seem unimportant, but it gives further unity. Secondly, the placing of a chord on the fourth beat in bars 2 and 4 gives a new rhythmic interest. You might prefer to continue with the rhythm from Example 1 rather than change it just yet.

Fig. 10.5

The first chord pattern can then be played once more, making the standard A A B B A structure with at least twenty-six bars, or as many as forty bars depending on how you used the A section, and how you plan your repeats.

So far so good, but it is rather ordinary. How can you develop it further? Two ways spring to mind:

(i)   carry on using the material we already have, perhaps with some variation: A + B + A + B2 (varied) +A; or

(ii) introduce a new episode (C).

You could even use a combination of both.

(i)   First, then, the development of the B section (B$_2$).
      If you vary the moving quavers in an upward direction it can be made to sound melodic and more positive (Fig. 10.6).

Fig. 10.6

or as in Fig. 10.7 (which is even stronger):

Fig. 10.7

(ii) You can balance the shorter B section by making the new C section longer as in Fig. 10.8.

Example answer 4

$$(\text{Section C}) \quad \text{Am / G /} \left| \text{F / G / } \right| \text{Am / Dm / } \left| \text{Em / / / } \right|$$

$$\text{Am / G /} \left| \text{F / B}\flat \text{ / } \right| \text{Dm / F / } \left| \text{G / / / } \right.\|$$

Fig. 10.8

This is a minor mode, which can add a new dimension without changing the mood. The end of the second half has been contrived to end on a brighter sounding G major chord the dominant of our original C major. You could make the second four bars of this section the climax of the improvisation by building up strongly to the return of Section A.

With this new material the overall plan could now be played as in Fig. 10.9.

Example answer 5

A (12)   B (8)   A (12)   B2 (8)   A (6)   C (16)   A (12)

Fig. 10.9

You may decide to miss out some of the repeats on the A section (as above, after B2) to avoid predictability. The model above has approximately seventy-four bars, which is a perfectly acceptable length for this sort of exercise.

Experiment

The secret is for you to spend as much spare time as you can 'doodling' at the keyboard or guitar, experimenting with chords and rhythms in many different ways and keys. This is the best way to discover new ideas. You will start to evolve your own style and chord clichés before long, and given this sort of chord progression in the examination, you will find you have several musical tricks up your sleeve which you can turn to good use. Fig. 10.10 and Fig. 10.11 give you two further examples to practise. They are printed as they first appeared.

(i)   C   F   Am   D7   G7   C   MEG 1988

Fig. 10.10

(ii)   G   Em   Am   D   WJEC Specimen Test
       I   vi   ii   V

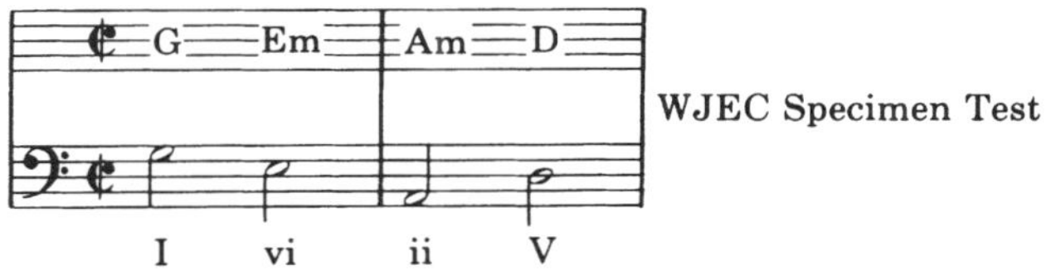

Fig. 10.11

Improvision on a a given rhythm

If you are a drummer/percussionist, or have a particularly strong sense of rhythm, you may choose to improvise on a given rhythm, rather than a melody or chord scheme. Make sure that you hear or read the printed rhythm correctly; your improvisation must relate to it closely.

How do you develop the given two or three bars? The secret is to decide which is the main characteristic within the fragment. For example, supposing you were given the motif in Fig. 10.12.

(London 1989)

Fig. 10.12

You could exploit either the dotted quavers [♪. ♪ ♪. ♪ | ♩] or the semiquavers [♩ ♪♪♪♪ ♩], or preferably both. In other words, having played the printed figure, extend it by concentrating on the two elements. The piece should contain dynamic interest to compensate for its lack of melody or harmony. You might decide to work within an arch shape with a climax at the centre as illustrated in Fig. 10.13.

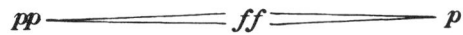

pp ——————— *ff* ——————— *p*

Fig. 10.13

alternatively, with a climax at the end (Fig. 10.14).

p ——————— *ff*

Fig. 10.14

The choice is yours, but remember not to play all at the same level, for this would be considered weak.

Fig. 10.15 gives you some more rhythmic figures to work at. The brackets refer to suggested fragments which you might develop.

(i)  🎵 (London 1989)

(ii)  🎵 (WJEC Specimen Tests)

(iii)  🎵 (London Specimen Tests)

(iv)  🎵 (MEG Specimen Tests)
(Make a feature of the crotchet rest here)

(v) 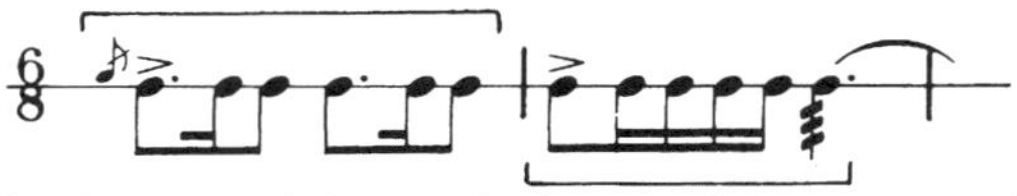 🎵 (EEG Specimen Tests)
(Make features of the crushed note, the accents and the roll at the end)

Fig. 10.15

Your teacher will be able to give you plenty of examples for practice. In many ways this option goes hand in hand with sight-reading, for it is so important to read the given rhythm correctly.

▷ **Improvisation and melodic motif: single line instruments**

Here we look at improvisation based on a melodic motif, for single-line instruments. Your way of working here is not dissimilar to that for rhythmic improvisation, except that you have to think melodically at the same time! Extract your fragment for development in the same way, concentrating, besides rhythm, on particular intervals that characterise the motif. One safety tip to ensure fluency in case you dry up in the middle: have an ending worked out so that you can conclude the improvisation convincingly. Your ability to read the given motif must be good; be especially careful with 6/8 examples, where people so often tend to go wrong.

Sequence

The use of sequence, if not overworked, is a common device in melodic extension. Let us presume that you have been presented with the motif in Fig. 10.16.

Fig. 10.16

First of all, establish the key. It must be in E minor, rather than G major, because of the D#. (It would be calamitous if you played the whole thing in a major key, although you are allowed to transpose).

Secondly, identify the melodic and rhythmic characteristics worthy of development. Melodically, a good choice would be:

⌐a⌐ with its semitonal rise and fall back down again;

and ⌐b⌐ which is a simple scalic figure. Rhymically, the two dotted fragments are the same, and equally important.

Now, how do you extend it? We need an answering phrase to the opening: Fig. 10.17 gives an example of an original phrase/answering phrase.

Fig. 10.17

In this example the rhythm has been repeated exactly to balance the two phrases. In fact ⌐a_1⌐ is an inversion of ⌐a⌐ and ⌐b⌐ has stayed almost the same. By creating this answering phrase we now have three figures to develop: ⌐a⌐, ⌐a_1⌐, and ⌐b⌐.

From now on, you must think quickly! Keep the music flowing with its gentle 6/8 lilt. Instead of coming to rest on a dotted crotchet too often, turn it into ♩ ♪ occasionally, so that you keep a feeling of forward motion. Avoid too many two-bar and four-bar phrases, as we have at the moment, as it can rapidly become predictable. (You can read more about melodic extension in Chapter 11.)

Sequences are useful, as we have said; **repeating patterns** at a **higher** or **lower pitch** is a good method of extension. In Fig. 10.18 you can see a sequence based on the ⌐b⌐ figure.

Fig. 10.18

The second bar is a rising sequence of bar 1, changed at the end to produce a new figure, a perfect 5th, which we can call ⌐c⌐. The answering two bars then contain three more references. Perhaps this is beginning to sound very contrived, and more like a written composition where you have the time to think in this way. But actually with practice and applied musicianship you will start to do these things automatically.

In the preparation time before the examination, you could think out material for use as a **contrasting section**. You might take yet another fragment from the given motif, which we will call ⌐d⌐ and ⌐d_1⌐ (see Figs. 10.16 and 10.17). In Fig. 10.19 we see this interval of a third used profitably.

Fig. 10.19

Although we are concentrating on ⌐d⌐ notice that ⌐b₁⌐ and ⌐b⌐ have been used as well, creating a real unity. You can extend this middle section in a similar manner, and then return to a version of your first section.

Here are some further melodic examples for you to work at.

(London 1988)

Fig. 10.20

In Fig. 10.20 there are two motifs of interest: at ⌐a⌐ the falling semitones, and at ⌐b⌐ an angular figure with a steep rise and immediate fall. This example would, therefore, give a good opportunity to create an improvisation based on contrasts between smoothness and angularity.

(WJEC Specimen Tests)

Fig. 10.21

In Fig. 10.21 notice that there are three figures for development. At ⌐a⌐ a falling fourth, at ⌐b⌐ a dotted scalic figure (which could be used in either direction), and at ⌐c⌐ a syncopated ♪♩ ♪♩ jazzy figure. You should be able to find plenty of scope for extension in this example, even if you choose to use only two of the motifs; it is up to you.

(London Specimen Tests)

Fig. 10.22

A third example in Fig. 10.22 is a phrase for bass instruments. It is fairly straightforward, with a descending scalic line in C major ⌐a⌐ and a final rising 4th⌐c⌐. The F# – G ⌐b⌐ is an inessential chromatic note – in other words it is 'extra' to the key. Any or all of these fragments could be developed as above.

▷ **Improvisation on a given pitch with free rhythm**

Here you are free to create your own rhythm, but the shape of a melodic line is given. This appears to give you freedom, but for a musical result, try to remember your initial rhythm so that you can refer back to it. Be sure to make it an interesting rhythm, too; there is a great temptation, when you see notes without a rhythm, to play them as if they are all equal. Look at Fig. 10.23.

[MEG 1988 Specimen Tests] (Syllabus B)

Fig. 10.23

In this example you could exploit the rising arpeggio ⌐a⌐ at the beginning, and/or the falling sequence of thirds at ⌐b⌐.

[MEG 1988] (Syllabus B)

Fig. 10.24

In the second example (Fig. 10. 24) there is a falling sequence ⌐a⌐ based on the interval of a 4th, and an octave figure ⌐b⌐. Both are well worth developing. You can easily make up your own examples for further practice.

▷ Improvisation and melodic motif: keyboard instruments

Here we look at improvisation based on a melodic motif, for keyboard instruments. The thought processes here are much the same as for single-line instruments, with the added problem of providing an appropriate harmonisation to the melody. Assuming you have a reasonable keyboard proficiency, it should be easier to produce a fluent result than on a single-line instrument. The piano's sustaining pedal will 'hold' for you, and your chords will also give an effect of fullness. With electronic keyboards your chosen sound quality will add novelty value, but don't rely totally on this. It's the musical content that counts!

Firstly, do not assume that everything has to be harmonised. It is quite acceptable for a keyboard to improvise on a single-line if you want to or need to. Work in your own style to the best of your ability. It is a mistake to think that harmonised is 'better' than unaccompanied. This part of the performance section is assessing your musicianship, not your technical prowess on a keyboard.

However, if you wish to add the 'correct' chords to your extended melody, the safest thing to do is to limit yourself to chords I, IV and V (that is tonic, subdominant and dominant), until you become really proficient. Most ordinary pieces and songs can be harmonised with these three chords, but for variety and a minor 'flavour' chords II and VI might be added.

Let us work in G major first of all:

    chord I   = G B D
    chord IV   = C E G and
    chord V7   = D F# A C

Be totally familiar with finding these chords in this key (and eventually all keys up to two or three flats and sharps – although you can choose your own key in the examination). Fig. 10.25 gives you a starting melody for extension.

Fig. 10.25

Select your chords by deciding which of the three listed above fits the melody most suitably. **Don't attempt to harmonise every note** – this is most important.

The first bar in Fig. 10.25 contains G B D B so the obvious harmony chord is chord I. In bar 2 we treat the middle note of as unimportant – the C and A belong to chord V7 (D F# A C), and the note B simply runs between them; it is a passing note and does not affect the harmony. Likewise with the quavers in bar 3 , the A and F# belong to chord V7, and the G passes between them.

The six changes of chord so far are basic harmony, which could be made more interesting by the introduction of other chords, but for the time being be patient! Master the three primary chords perhaps by playing long notes in the left hand at first, until you feel confident enough to vary it.

Fig. 10.26

In the example in Fig. 10.26 we have used the bare minimum of harmony. We have followed the thought process of choosing the appropriate chords, and decided to write them in the simplest way.

The next step (Fig. 10.27) is to find a way of decorating the basic material so that it has more movement. A simple **Alberti bass** would be suitable:

Fig. 10.27

It will take many weeks of regular practice to become adept at choosing chords immediately, and using a suitable broken-chord accompaniment with them. The ear is the ultimate judge with this work, not the textbook; if you find a sound or style pleasing to you, then work away at it until you are satisfied. You will gradually evolve your own style. Working with chords in this way will be beneficial to your composition work and aural skills, as well as your keyboard facility, so it is a very worthwhile exercise. You will probably enjoy **doodling** at the keyboard for its own sake anyway – it is a form of discovery for you.

When you feel ready to move on, the task becomes even more demanding. It is necessary to extend the given fragment of melody and harmonise it at the same time. It would be useful to read the section in this chapter on single-line improvisation once more, to refresh your memory. Your improvisation needs to continue in the given style, and you must not let the process of chord-finding hold you back. The melody must be most prominent. **Remember** – a simple melody that is harmonised effectively with basic chords, and developed musically, is preferable to a more flamboyant piece that is incoherent and unmusical.

▷ Improvisation on a given topic

Here you are expected to improvise freely, creating sounds that suggest the overall mood of the topic you choose. It is a good idea to prepare for this by having a store of musical ideas up your sleeve to help you on the day. For example, if you practise mood painting for water, the countryside, a thunderstorm or the supernatural, you will probably find that something rather similar will turn up!

Keyboard players can produce some lovely effects by using the sustaining pedal – atmospheric effects that are evocative of water or the supernatural. Silences can be very effective too, so there need not be sound all the time. But you should avoid too much effect and too little music: try to give your improvisation some substance, by using repetition and structure. If possible, use the whole range of your instrument and be creative with dynamics, phrasing and tone quality, and aim to make music that is satisfying and charged with feeling. Here are some actual exam questions for you to work on:

(a) Growth   (London 1989)
(b) Supernatural   (London 1989)
(c) The river   (London 1989)
(d) Thunderstorm   (London 1988)
(e) Busking   (London 1988)

(f) In a field	(London 1988)
(g) Carnival	(London 1991)
(h) Departure	(London 1991)
(i) Kaleidoscope (changing patterns)	(London 1991)
(j) Darkness	(London 1992)
(k) Early Morning	(London 1992)
(l) Flying	(London 1992)
(m) A depiction of flowers using a rising scale	(London 1994 syllabus)
(n) A Chinese festival	(London 1998 Specimen Paper)

Improvisation to a given verse

You will have probably decided which style of verse you want to improvise to before the examination. Read the extract through slowly and carefully. Look for important words that help to set the mood, in the same way as the motifs or fragments were selected in the musical examples above. Find any imagery that could be *translated* musically, and quickly decide on the style that you are going to use.

This type of improvisation is likely to be quite short, as you are unlikely to repeat too many words. Make sure that your melody is appropriate to the style of the chosen words and that it feels finished at the end of the verse. Repetition may be difficult with a single verse, but more possible, perhaps, in the pop style.

Here is a selection of verses for you to practise:

(a) *Traditional*
O look in the mirror
Set here in my heart
And see that your image
Of me is a part –
Of me is a part.

(b) *Hymn*
Thou art my Father.
Thou art my Mother.
Thou art my Saviour.
Thou art my Friend.
In all places Thou art my Saviour.
What should I fear and why should I repine?

(c) *Poem*
Down in the street there comes the hurdy gurdy man
Cold his fingers, still he plays as best he can.
Shuffling in the snow, he moves with painful gait.
Not a penny piece is laid upon his plate.
Not a penny piece is laid upon his plate.

(d) *Pop*
I was walking down the street
Singin' my melody
Singin' my song to the rhythm in my feet
Rhythm in my feet just
Walkin' singin', rhythm swingin'
Sing along swing along – rhythm in my feet.

(MEG)

Improvisation on a given texture

For this option you are free to interpret the graphic notation as you think appropriate. Fig. 10.28 is an example from a specimen paper.

(MEG Specimen Paper)

Fig. 10.28

In this example (Fig. 10.28) volume and pitch are fairly easy to interpret; notice the relative gaps in respect of silence. Silence is often forgotten in improvisation; it can be a most effective part of your piece. Don't forget to have some repetition, and aim for a satisfying structure. You should think out your musical strategy by isolating fragments, in just the same way as in the sections on improvising on a rhythm or melodic motif.

When you have experimented with musical ideas responding to the notation in the given example, decide which fragments you would develop.

A FINAL STATEMENT

In summary, the Improvisation section of unprepared performance needs to be thoroughly prepared! Although you will not know the actual test question until the day, you can spend much time during the course working in different styles, to evolve an individual style of your own. We have stressed the importance of form and structure, but perhaps fluency is even more important – **keep it going!** Remember that you are giving a performance, however short. There must be a feeling of climax and a sense of direction to maintain the listener's interest. Think of your improvisation as if you were performing printed music and learn to value your developing skills in *instant composition*.

SUMMARY

▷   When improvising – don't stop! Make a 'mistake' part of your performance.

▷   Be thoroughly prepared by practising this activity regularly.

▷   Be expressive even though you are thinking about what notes to play.

▷   Don't be too long – it may ramble.

Composing 1: Traditional notation

GETTING STARTED

All candidates are required to *compose or arrange music in a traditional or in a contemporary idiom* (National Criteria 3.3). To some students, the thought of composing a piece of one's own is quite frightening. It seems to conjure up an image of solitary confinement for months on end in some freezing attic before dying in your early thirties! Take courage – composing can be a very satisfying activity once you have mastered some basic techniques and gained some confidence in yourself.

This section of the examination encourages you to achieve the satisfaction of making something of your own – a piano piece, a song, or some incidental music for a play perhaps – the satisfaction of discovering something you can say, no matter how modest it may sound. To have invented and moulded musical phrases where none existed before: to select and reject harmonies for a particular context: to agonise over which note should come next: these are all important experiences which can help to shape your musical development and stimulate further creative thinking.

You are probably using this book at the start of an actual GCSE music course, but will undoubtedly have been making up simple tunes, or more extended pieces, for some time. How did you work? Did you compose straightforward melodies and write them down immediately, or did you have a tape recorder handy, so that you could listen critically to a play-back and improve things before committing ideas to paper? Perhaps you are able to hear musical ideas in your head without having to use an instrument to help you, or maybe you prefer to strum a guitar or 'doodle' on a keyboard to stimulate an idea.

IGCSE	LONDON	MEG	NEAB	NICCEA	SEG	WJEC	TOPIC	STUDY	REVISION 1	REVISION 2
✓	✓	✓	✓	✓	✓	✓	Harmonic extension from a simple chord scheme			
✓	✓	✓	✓	✓	✓	✓	Tuned percussion (or keyboard): four players			
✓	✓	✓	✓	✓	✓	✓	Three model compositions			
✓	✓	✓	✓	✓	✓	✓	Examples of student compositions			
✓	✓	✓	✓	✓	✓	✓	Summary			

> ## WHAT YOU NEED TO KNOW

There is, of course, no correct way to create music. Composing is a process of organising sounds into a form that is aesthetically pleasing. How you choose to work is entirely up to you, but to progress you must be actively involved in the whole process of creating and be very self-critical with regard to any performance of your work. **Imagination** is the secret. Composing helps to train a musician's creative thinking and, of course, most important, it trains the art of listening. A person that once took sound for granted can be shaken from their complacency by this activity, as it demands the continual making of active choices.

The examining groups vary in their requirements for the submission of pieces and their assessment, and you can read about this in more detail in Chapter 2. The material in this chapter, however, is relevant to all Boards. A fundamental point to remember with GCSE is that composing is encouraged as a course activity, and that the final assessment is on a selection of work produced throughout the course.

Composing includes pastiche and experimental work, free composition, melody writing, harmony, part-writing and arranging (National Criteria 4.3). Notice that the activity is quite clearly referred to as Composing, not Composition. In other words, you have the freedom to work with the process of compiling sounds in your own individual way, unhindered by the traditional rules of harmony and counterpoint demanded in music examinations in the days before GCSE. You must be sure to design each of your pieces for a specified medium – for example, solo voice/instrument, vocal/instrumental ensembles. Also remember that cassette recording (if required) together with the musical scores and/or commentaries must be available for external moderation by about the end of the Spring Term of the examination year.

In this chapter, we are going to suggest ways of composing using standard musical notation. Four ideas for a composition are given and then seven student compositions are presented and commented on for you to see how others have worked. You can read in Chapter 2, in the section on composing, the actual requirements as to the number and duration of compositions for the different examining groups. Assume, generally, that it is fully acceptable for your teacher to provide you with any initial material, e.g. a tune for you to harmonise, or a poem for you to set to music. After that, you are expected to continue on your own, and if your teacher makes suggestions during the process of composing, details of this help must be made available to the examiner.

For candidates who have little or no experience of composing, the worst problem can be plucking up the courage to show your teacher your first piece. Most students spend a good deal of time improvising at a keyboard or on a guitar, and this is a valuable way of experimenting with ideas – but do have the confidence to think of your 'doodling' as being worthy of an idea and then you are on the right track. This chapter does not pretend to be a full-scale guide to composition, it presupposes good instruction in school or college and can serve only to stimulate or refine ideas. Space permits only bare guidelines with some of the ideas that follow. They are intended to help you get started on your own pieces not necessarily for you to work at them as actual examples.

> **Harmonic extension from a simple chord scheme**

Idea 1

Using keyboard or guitar, take a relatively simple chord scheme: C Dm7 F G (Fig. 11.1) and improvise rhythmically by playing it over and over again in a straightforward pop rhythm.

Fig. 11.1

What springs to your mind? Do you wish to add a vocal line? Or an instrumental melody? Or simply extend the rhythmic effect with other chords? For the sake of illustration, let us assume that you decide to extend this initial idea into an instrumental piece by adding on another sequence of chords (Fig. 11.2). Maintain a similar rhythm to your opening:

A   B
$\frac{4}{4}$ C Dm7 F G :‖: Am Em Dm G :‖

Fig. 11.2

The second (B) section has more of a minor feel to it through having mainly minor chords but ends with a (dominant) G chord implying a return to C major. Should this new section be repeated exactly or should it be varied in some way?

Already we can think of the top line as being quite suitable as a melody. If you are not too keen on it, simply change the shape of the chords so that you have a different note from the chord at the top. Perhaps, now, our second section could be rearranged as in Fig. 11.3, in place of a straight repeat.

Am   Em   Dm   G   Am   Em   Dm   G

Fig. 11.3

So far our structure can be thought of as:

A1   A1   B1   B2

We can think of the ♪♩ ♪♩ rhythm as being the important part of our **hook**, or the catchy bit that sticks in the mind. It now seems right to bring back the first idea so as to reinforce it. You might consider it necessary to decorate the return of A at this point. It breaks up any feeling of monotony, yet we still feel it as the original idea. There are countless ways that you could use these chord schemes; just carry on improvising in your own style until you are completely satisfied. You will know when it is right.

So far our overall structure works out as a ternary form (A + B + A):

A1   A1   B1   B2   A2   A2

This is perfectly satisfactory, but rather short. You may well feel that the A1 and B1 sections could be repeated several more times (perhaps with some variation) to give an expanded ternary form, and perhaps a third idea (C) could then be brought in as shown in Fig. 11.4.

F   B♭   C   G

Fig. 11.4

Once again, a simple four-chord pattern has been deliberately concocted so as to finish with the chord of G, the dominant of our original C major. It would then make sense to bring back the original idea straight away, thereby producing a simple rondo structure (A + B + A + C + A), or in our case:

A1   A1   B1   B2   A2   A2   C1   C1   A1   A2

You can have enormous fun experimenting with chords, and in time you will find that certain combinations of chords will become particular favourites. This simple piece could easily be turned into a song; your lyrics need not be at all complicated. Alternatively you could arrange it for various instruments or even program it into a music computer. The simplest of ideas can be made to sound exciting when you choose an attractive sound on your synthesizer. **Experiment** – and have the courage of your convictions!

If you are not able to write your piece out using traditional notation you will need to provide a commentary instead. Let us assume that a candidate has decided not to extend the piece further and has found some difficulty in notating it. He has recorded it as an instrumental piece using the school synthesizer and music computer, and has written the following commentary to accompany the recording of the piece.

Model commentary

Reluctant rondo

This piece was given this rather humorous because I did not really set out to compose a rondo as such. My composition is the result of improvising at the keyboard until I found chords that I felt satisfied with. The overall structure (A B A C A) happens, by chance, to be the same as a traditional rondo, hence the unusual title!

I took a straightforward sequence of four chords: C Dm7 F G and experimented with it until I found a satisfying rhythm.

I was keen for the syncopation ♪♩ ♪♩ to be a strong feature of the piece, so this appears in each of the three main sections. My B section is a minor version of the A section, and answers it in a complementary way. I thought that the minor chords would act as a varied flavour to the strongly major A section.

The final section (C) gives the impression at first of modulating away from the home key, but soon twists itself back so that the original C major is never far away:
F B flat C G (dominant).

The final return of the opening section is played strongly with a slight rallentando so that we know the end is near; it is a mixture of A1 + A2 to make a strong ending. Throughout, I was aiming at simplicity.

Once I had composed the rondo (using a Yamaha PSR-36 keyboard) I wanted to record my piece using more sophisticated sounds. This I was able to do by using an Atari 1040 ST Music Computer (with C Lab Notator software) and a Kawai K1 synthesiser. I like the strong bass sound (called 'kick bass' on Single 1 D-1) on the K1 synth. I decided not to change this sound at all until I got to section C when I used the contrasting sound 'Reflection' on Single 1 C-5. With careful mixing I arrived at the final version and although it's rather short, I feel quite pleased with it.

This commentary shows fairly clearly how the imaginary candidate has worked – developing and refining the final structure from the basic material of four simple chords. It is written in a clear and unpretentious way, and communicates a feeling of enthusiasm for the task! The technical detail that is included to explain how the piece was recorded is not just waffle to fill up space. It shows that the candidate considered the sounds very carefully (again, with experimentation on the computer) until he arrived at something he felt satisfied with. A point to note here is that the recording is as important as the composing process, for if you select rather ordinary sounds the piece may not succeed. It is rather like a professional composer who writes a good piece and then arranges it in an uninteresting way for orchestra. You really need to be imaginative with both aspects of the task.

You will find Chapter 10 on Improvisation (especially the section on chord schemes) helpful as well. It deals with much the same work and may be worth re-reading at this point.

▷ Tuned percussion (or keyboard): four players

Idea 2

This second idea is for four players, but you could easily add more. It limits itself to the notes of the pentatonic scale. The suggested instruments are tuned percussion or keyboards, but you should feel free to use anything available, bearing in mind that instruments must have parts that are suitable for them, in register, movement and duration.

Take care to remember this when you are composing or scoring out your first pieces; gradually it will become automatic. For example, bass parts tend to be slower moving than higher melodies and have fewer notes. Do experiment – if it works, and you feel satisfied with it, then it is right!

Let us call the four parts A B C and D rather than specify actual instruments and let us write in the treble clef for now, it can always be adjusted. Our pentatonic scale will be based on the tonic of C, so the notes we shall be working with are C D E G A. Ostinati can be very useful in a piece of this nature; experiment with short repeated patterns to achieve this sort of scoring (Fig. 11.5). In this case A and B each have a two-bar ostinato and C and D have a one-bar ostinato. There are many sorts of scale throughout the world. We have chosen the pentatonic as it is a practical one to use for tuned percussion, but you could quite well use a harmonic minor scale, the whole tone scale, or even a 'home-made' one. Experiment with different scales and see what you can come up with. The pentatonic can easily sound Japanese, Chinese or Scottish depending on how you use it – it doesn't really matter as long as you like the way it turns out.

Fig. 11.5

You could then be rather clever by trying to organise a dialogue between A and B by staggering their entries. The original A part has been dropped; A now plays the same music as B – but two beats later, as a simple canon. Perhaps you could also create more interesting C/D parts as in Fig. 11.6

Fig. 11.6

You may decide to score your quartet without a prominent melody, in which case the character of the piece will depend on the perpetual movement of the ostinati and the timbres of the chosen instruments. If you work this way, make sure that you concentrate on the other musical ingredients – *dynamics, tempo, nuance* etc. – to compensate for the lack of melody in the traditional sense. Be musical about it, don't just work away thinking that the right notes in the right place make a good performance! Aim for subtlety: perhaps a very quiet beginning, building to the loudest part in the middle and fading out at the end. This arch-shape is a common and satisfying way of building a piece.

Extending the piece

How can this sort of idea be extended? After all, ostinati can only be played so many times before they become monotonous. Listen to some music by Steve Reich, Philip Glass or John Adams. These minimalist composers (so-called because they exploit a minimal amount of musical material) are expert in their use of ostinati, and can make pieces lasting half an hour sound interesting, by subtle and almost imperceptible changes every now and again. These composers are cited as masters of ostinati, but you may want to try creating some minimalist music yourself. If composers such as Glass have written pieces as long as opera using minimalist techniques, it is obviously possible at GCSE level to use simple instruments for very short pieces. (For example, listen to Steve Reich's *Music for Pieces of Wood*, or his *Clapping Music* – they are both very effective.)

If you find this subtle changing of ostinati too difficult (and it is a skill that needs a lot of practice), try to make a piece in ternary or rondo form. Your episodes could be in a different pentatonic key, perhaps based on G (G A B D E), or F (F G A C D). You might find a motif (a short rhythmic or melodic figure) from your opening section which can become the basis of your new episode. This will help to give some unity, avoiding the prospect of separate sections all tacked on to one another.

How about making the ending of your piece a round? This could be done either by rewriting your first section, or producing an entirely new section as a coda. Here is a suggested round which is based on the original material from Fig. 11.5.

Fig. 11.7

The asterisks indicate the point of entry for each of the four instruments. The first bar of the round derives from the C part of Fig. 11.5. The rhythm has been simplified and the octave jump is inverted. Notice how the quaver rhythm in bar 3 of the round occurs again at the end of bar 7; this will sound effective when all four parts are playing.

Some general considerations

Here are some musical considerations which you should apply to all your composition work:

▷ It is generally accepted as good practice not to make your melodies too angular and jumpy. Don't be frightened of repetition in melody writing. With beautiful tone and a well chosen accompaniment a melody can have surprisingly few notes. Sibelius in his second symphony has an oboe melody that commences with nine repetitions of the same note, B flat, before it actually moves. It is in a lento tempo marking, and it sounds marvellous! Having said that, of course, there are obvious exceptions. The serialist composers (Schoenberg and Webern being the more 'severe' exponents of this genre) deliberately set out to compose their 'melodies' with no repetition at all until all twelve notes of the chromatic scale had been used once.

▷ Music is usually written in even numbers of bars – phrases of four, six and eight bars are the most common. This gives a balance between phrases, and helps to give shape to melodies.

▷ You may find it easier at this stage to commence and finish your melodies on the home note, or certainly one of the notes from the tonic chord (chord I of the scale). Also a long note at the end of a melody or piece gives a satisfying sense of finality.

These three points are a summary of average practice, but there are always exceptions. We have mentioned the serialist composers who avoided repetition and smoothness: similarly, modern jazz is often very angular and irregular. Even Haydn in the eighteenth century was fond of using a five-bar phrase to avoid any sense of squareness.

> ## Model composition I

Idea 3

You may like to compose a song by setting some well known words to music. Shakespeare has always been a favourite, as his words are so versatile; they withstand a variety of musical styles. 'Under the Greenwood Tree' is from Act II scene V of *As You Like It*. This idea is presented as a **model** composition to demonstrate two very different ways of treating the same melody:

(a) in a simple rock style;
(b) in a more traditional style as an art song.

Here is an outline of some of the thought processes involved.

First of all, you must read through the chosen text several times. It is necessary to become familiar with the rhythm of the words and absorb the style, noticing any imagery or repetition:

Under the greenwood tree,	Who doth ambition shun,	If it do come to pass
Who loves to lie with me,	And loves to live i' the sun	That any man turn ass,
And turn his merry note	Seeking the food he eats.	Leaving his wealth and ease,
Unto the sweet bird's throat,	And pleas'd with what he gets	A stubborn will to please,
Come hither, come hither,	Come hither, come hither,	Ducdame, ducdame, ducdame,
come hither:	come hither:	Here shall he see
Here shall he see	Here shall he see	Gross fools as he,
No enemy,	No enemy,	And if he will come to me.
But winter and rough weather.	But winter and rough weather.	

'Greenwood tree' and 'lie with me' suggest a Pastoral (countryside) and somewhat lazy mood. It is also a good idea to read the play to gauge the mood in context. The extract is sung by the character Amiens, so we should preferably use a male voice. Our choice of key is purely arbitrary, but a major key seems more appropriate. We'll use G major.

Space prevents us from describing every step involved; Fig. 11.8 is the resulting melody which, with some contrivance, will fit the other verses as well.

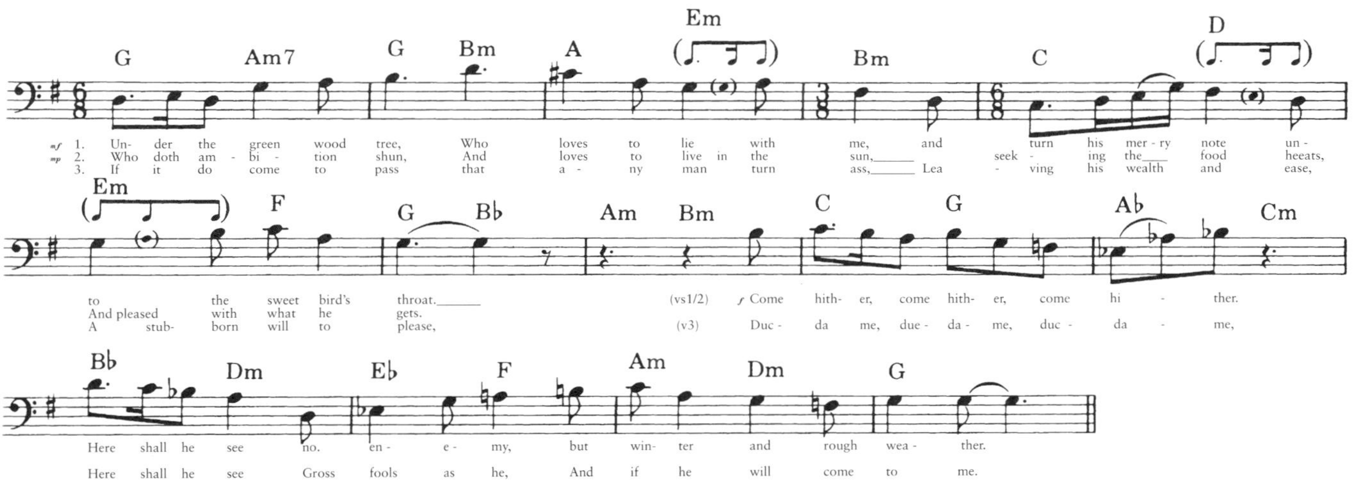

Fig. 11.8

The 3/8 bar is really only half a bar of 6/8 time. This was dictated by the rhythm of the words: it would be rather weak to wait on the word 'me' for a full bar, and the 3/8 provides rhythmic interest in itself. The 'come hither' harmonies, which veer sharply away from G major, provide harmonic variety before the return to the tonic key. The F natural on 'rough weather' is a mild concession to sixteenth century modality as the flattened leading-note gives a period flavour.

Having composed the melody, here are two ways of presenting it:

(a) The simple rock style uses the straightforward chords as in Fig. 11.8. You will need to provide an interesting introduction, where the colour is provided by an unusual progression of chords which returns between the two verses. This is shown in Fig. 11.9

Fig. 11.9

(b) The second version, Fig. 11.10, uses a piano accompaniment to create an art song. Here the piano part is more than a harmonic accompaniment – its music derives from and enhances the melody itself. The harmony chosen is deliberately simple, with a few mild dischords to add flavour, and the accompaniment aims to capture the lilting character of the melody. The quick notes of 'turn his merry note' have been 'borrowed' in bar 1 of the introduction. The piano part is built over a tonic pedal (drone) in bars 5–10. Notice how the gap after 'sweet bird's throat' hints at the introductory figure. The 'come hither' accompaniment doubles the melody in the bass with simple chords above. The introduction for verse 2 is identical to the opening, and also serves as a short postlude (closing section) to finish the song. You are not expected to copy either version of this; it is included as an example and serves to show what different results can be achieved by using different styles. Both versions are equally successful. You will probably want to work in a different way, but try to make your accompaniment as interesting as your melody, especially with a piano part.

Here are some famous Shakespeare songs that you may like to set in your own style:

1. Oh, mistress mine, where are you roaming? (see *Twelfth-Night* Act II scene III)
2. It was a lover and his lass. (see *As You Like It* Act V scene III)
3. Blow, blow, thou winter wind. (see *As You Like It* Act II scene VII)

Under the Greenwood Tree

R. J. LAMBERT

Fig. 11.10 *Under the Greenwood Tree*

Fig. 11.10 continued

▷ **Model composition II**

Idea 4

This piece is submitted by the author as a 'model' composition. The objective in composing it was to write a lively piece for flute and piano and illustrate many of the points that have been mentioned earlier in this chapter. The musical intention was to use a light-hearted 'vamping' piano style, and a jig-like melody for flute (redolent of an Irish piper). The piece is quoted in full in Fig. 11.11 and a commentary is given as a further example for you to absorb. It is by no means an easy piece, and would require an excellent flautist and no mean pianist to perform it.

Abigail's Jig

R. J. LAMBERT

Fig. 11.11 *Abigail's Jig* – for flute and piano

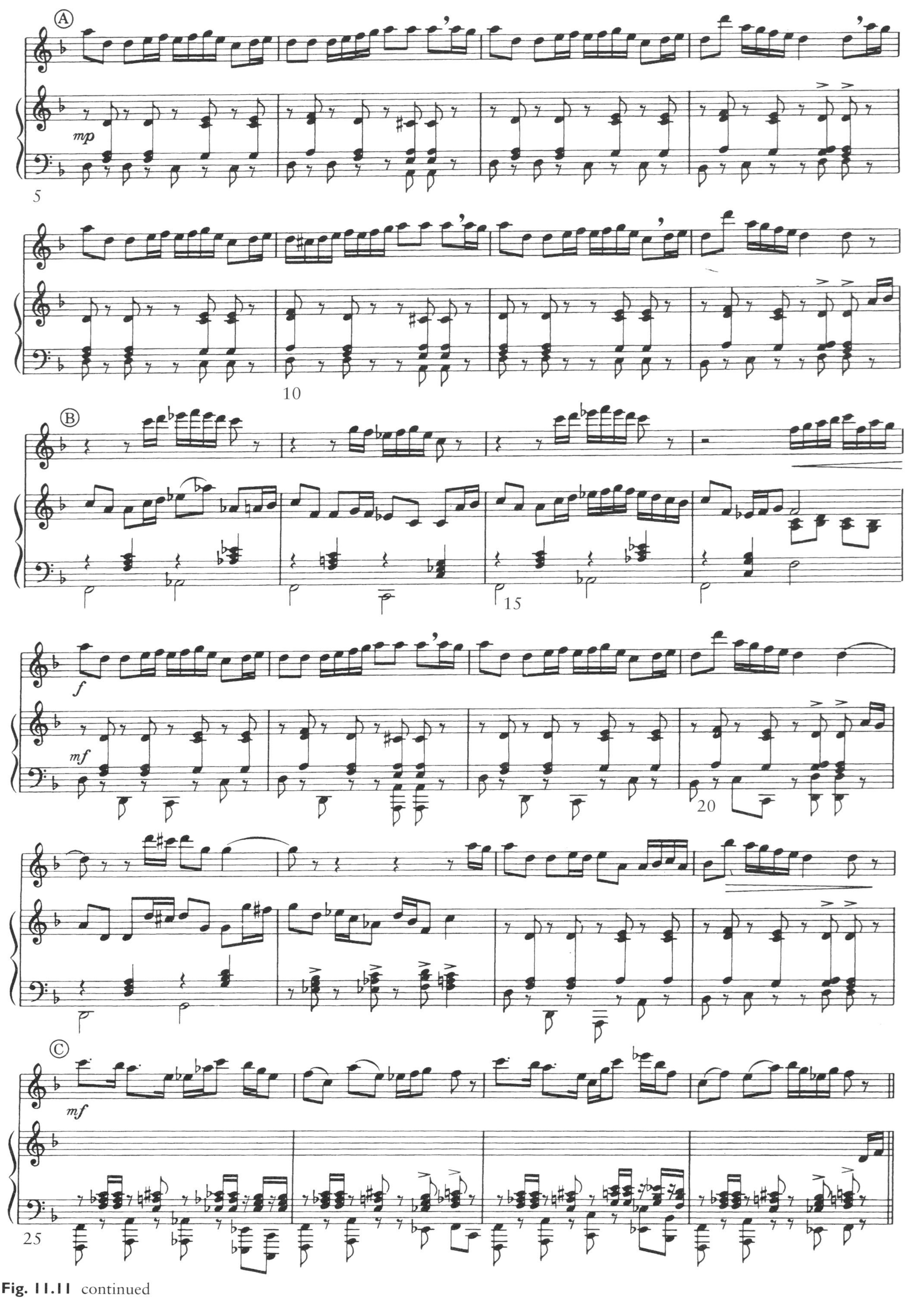

Fig. 11.11 continued

Fig. 11.11 continued

Fig. 11.11 continued

70

Fig. 11.11 continued

Model student commentary

> ### ABIGAIL'S JIG
>
> This piece was especially written for the school flute teacher. It was recorded by him and the Director of Music as both parts are too difficult for any of the pupils to play! I tried to capture the atmosphere of an Irish jig as played by a piper, with a harmonically straight-forward piano part using a mixture of 'vamping' and melodic imitation of the flute part.
>
> The introduction is intended to be humorous and rather musically misleading. It starts in F minor but is immediately contradicted by the chords of A, A flat, E flat and Cm7. It openly parodies the 'cowboy' music of Aaron Copland, and uses flattened leading note chords (instead of a dominant) throughout. This modal harmony helps to create the mood of pseudo-folk music.
>
> The main theme starts in the flute in the unexpected key of D minor. The piano has simple vamping chords until figure B, where it has an answering theme in F major interrupted at regular intervals by the flute. The main theme returns, forte this time, with a similar answering theme in the piano four bars later.
>
> At figure C the introductory figure returns, but for variety a flute counter-melody is added this time. This four-bar phrase serves as a link into the second main theme which is presented by the piano.
>
> This theme is also in D minor and is based largely on arpeggios and scales. Two or three bars before figure D the harmony modulates sequentially and builds up in volume to a key change to E minor at figure D. I decided to suddenly drop the volume on the actual key change in keeping with the humour of the piece. The main theme is played by the flute but within four bars the second theme appears, as before, in the piano with flute interjections. The climax of the piece is at figure E where the flute plays decorative triplets against a strong statement of the main theme which is played in augmentation (in this case, double value). The last two bars of the piece are a fortissimo statement of the introduction with the added flute counter-melody. The piece finishes with a demisemi-quaver rush up the scale on the flute.
>
> The piece took me about a week to complete from the initial keyboard improvising to the completion of the scoring, and I thoroughly enjoyed working at it. My teacher suggested the key change to a higher key to raise the tension a little, but the actual notes are all my own work.

Teacher assessment

This commentary is deliberately detailed as an example of the sort of analytical information you could include. Do make it all relevant and avoid unnecessary waffle. This particular commentary was included as an example, but a commentary for a piece that has been so carefully notated is probably superfluous. If you wish to include a brief explanation of how your piece came about that will be quite sufficient.

Analysing compositional technique

The rest of this section describes the piece in greater detail, this time with the purpose of analysing compositional technique. It may help to trigger off some thoughts for your compositions, and it also provides extra practice in analysis as required for some Set Works. It must be emphasised that this music stemmed from doodling at the keyboard.

Improvisation is a pleasurable activity in itself. Even though much of what you play at this stage will probably be scrapped, the time spent is never wasted; improvisation is really a sort of unwritten composition and the technique you develop in working at it can be drawn upon later.

The opening four-bar phrase sets the mood of the whole piece. Its rhythm is as important as the deliberate 'wrong' chords. It took a fair bit of time at the keyboard before the unusual sequence of (normally) unrelated chords arrived:

Fm A A♭ E♭ Cm7 | Fm A E♭ Fm | Fm A C E♭ B♭ | Fm A E♭ F(major) |

Notice how bars 2 and 4 are similar – this cadence is deliberately strong because the other bars are so unusual. Bar 3 has a repeated rise of a similar interval (a third).

You may like to experiment with these unusual groupings of chords: decide on your tonic key and juxtapose this with chords that are not closely related. For example, still in F major you might try: F – D – A♭ – E♭ – F. Notice how the two final chords here and in the Jig make the same cadence, E♭ – F. The E♭ major chord (the flattened seventh chord) acts as a substitute for the more usual C – F, and the effect is very similar to a perfect cadence. It therefore has the power to bring the short sequence back to the original tonic.

Once the tune arrives the accompaniment is kept extremely simple, to give full attention to the flute melody. The overall key of D minor is not so very far away from the F minor/major of the introduction – it is part of the humour of the composition to use a different key for the introduction. The tune is played twice but notice small differences in the flute part this time, and that the piano part changes its rhythm slightly to avoid predictability and to add interest.

Figure B grows naturally out of figure A. It centres around the tonic of F, and has some connections with the chord sequence of the introduction: (F A♭ | F Cm | F A♭ | F Cm7 F) but this is a subconscious choice – it was not planned. It allows the pianist the opportunity for some dialogue, although the flute does its best to join in whenever it can. Because the basic melody is rather four-square, every opportunity to 'seal over the cracks' is taken. Here the flute interrupts at bar 16 with a semiquaver run into a return of the main theme. A variant is offered at 21–24 to break up the obvious pattern of repeated tunes. It is based on the falling 5th motto (as at the beginning of bar 5), but develops into a harmonic reference (in bar 22) to the introduction.

Figure C again uses the same chord sequence as the introduction, but this time the flute joins in with a counter-melody. This tune is partly determined by the underlying chords but dotted rhythms are introduced to give something new after the smooth-running semiquavers. This brief reference to the rather strange opening serves as a link to the second theme which the piano introduces five bars after figure C. In many respects it is a similar melody to the first theme, and was in fact designed not to change the mood. It is presented by the piano, but the flute enters with the arpeggio figure (see bar 33). We can see that the opening of the second theme is an inverted version of the first (Fig. 11.12):

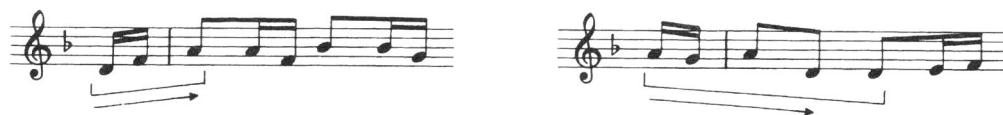

Fig. 11.12

(It could be argued that this sort of detail is either over-contrived or purely coincidental; however, it is considered to be good compositional style when there is a unity of ideas, themes and figures. Don't always attempt to produce a completely new idea for its own sake – endeavour to draw out a secondary idea from the preceding material.)

The end of this section is a modulatory passage leading to a new key at section D. One of the easiest ways of changing key is by means of a sequence (a repeated pattern of notes or chords) F . . . (down 4th) . . . C; Gm . . . (down 4th) . . . D (see bars 43–44). Above this the flute is decorating somewhat fussily to create a feeling of climax.

The upward key change is a common cliché in a short piece of this nature. Instead of developing the material further, or introducing new ideas, it is not unusual to repeat the main theme and end the piece in a higher key – higher of course, to increase the effect of brightness or tension. In this particular case the approach to the change of key is quite a dramatic build-up, but when the E minor arrives at figure D the volume drops immediately; the sense of humour is still there! The main melody is played only once (four bars) before the second idea is brought in – emphasising the compatibility of the material. Four bars later, however, the 'correct' theme (corresponding to that at letter B) is brought in but with 'wrong' harmony, similar to the introduction:

G (tonic) B♭ | Am Dm | Bm B♭ | G B♭ G |

Figure E is the loudest and most dramatic part of the piece: the flute is playing decorative semiquaver triplets arranged sequentially (in a similar pattern) against the main theme played at a lower register in the piano part, while a feeling of breadth is created by an octave-rolling bass beneath. The tune is written here in double the original note values (augmentation), which is another fairly common and useful compositional 'trick'. At the same time the flute semiquavers give a feeling of decoration by using the opposite effect of half values. The short coda, four bars from the end, uses two ideas: firstly the arpeggio figure (from bar 33), now still in augmentation in the piano, and finally, at figure F, the original introductory figure with added flute counter-melody which rounds the piece off with a lively scalic flourish. The final chord is E major, a conventional minor – major ending where the G# has a brightening effect. This is called a *Tierce da Picardie* (Picardy Third) and is a device which has been used by composers for hundreds of years!

Model composition III

This is another piece for flute and piano submitted by the author as a 'model' composition. Play it over, or try to hear it through and this time, instead of discussing it bar by bar or writing a model commentary on it, answer the following four questions.

Cantilena
for
flute and piano

RICHARD LAMBERT
Op IIc

Fig. 11.13

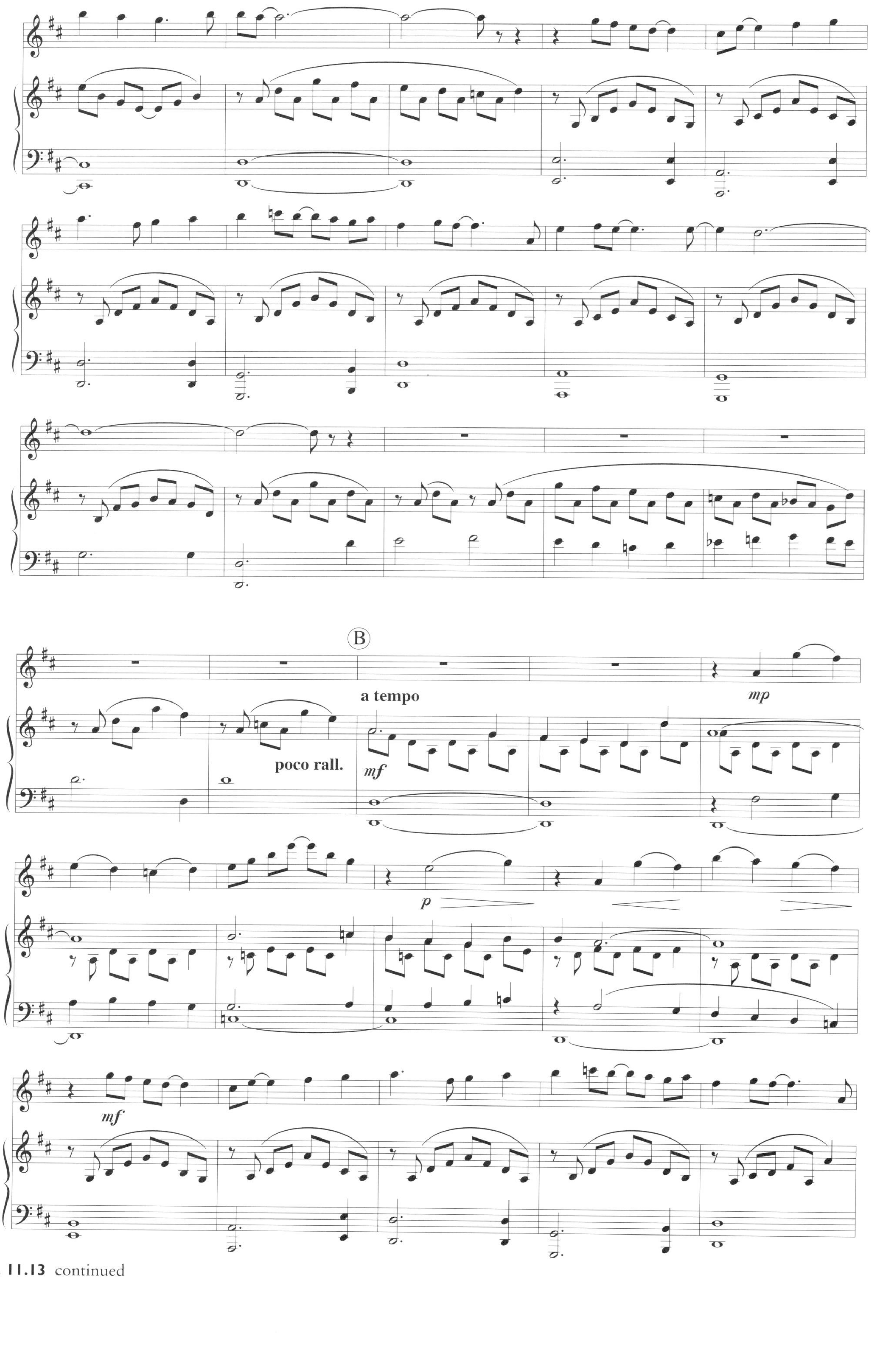

Fig. 11.13 continued

Fig. 11.13 continued

Fig. 11.13 continued

Fig. 11.13 continued

Practice questions and answers

Question 1
Despite its 'classical' appearance, the composer has tried to capture a popular flavour in this piece. How has this been achieved?

Question 2
Comment on the use of repetition in this piece.

Question 3
How are dynamics employed?

Question 4
How does the composer start and finish the piece?

Answer 1
▷ Primary and secondary chords in arpeggiated (Alberti) figures in the piano part (as mainstream pop ballads might do).
▷ By using pedal notes (held notes) especially on the tonic note.
▷ The 'bluesy' style in the third main theme (at figure D, for example, and certainly at the eleventh bar after figure E where the F natural 'clashes' in the same bar with an F#).
▷ By using syncopated rhythms (for example in the seventh bar after figure E in the flute part).
▷ The mood at figure C is a pseudo-rock style.

Answer 2
Rhythmically there is much repetition, especially in the arch-shape arpeggio figures that predominate the accompaniment. Melodically speaking, themes are repeated (as you would expect), but are varied to avoid monotony. For example, the melody from figure A is restated in the piano part at figure B, but handed back to the flute after eight bars. The contrasting theme (figure C) occurs twice during the piece, and the third theme is sounded twice (figure D in the piano, and again at figure E in the flute).

Answer 3
The piece is mostly marked *mf* or *mp*, in keeping with the songlike mood. The climax, at figure C, is marked *f* (loud) and for just two bars *ff*. The piece ends quietly, right down to *pp* (very soft) in the last bar.

Answer 4
The introduction consists of a five-bar figure (in the form of a three-bar phrase and two one-bar phrases). This is designed to break up a four-square feeling. The key is D major, but this introduction has an ambiguous tonality (C naturals and E♭s confuse the feeling of D major). The coda is also five bars, but mirrored this time with two one-bar phrases and then a three-bar phrase. The tonality is now finally D major.

Now you try to write a piece with straightforward arpeggio patterns, or with slightly varying themes and counter melodies. Good luck!

▷ **Examples of student compositions**

To conclude this chapter here are seven examples of student compositions, all of which were submitted for examination. It is a pity that you can only see the pieces and not hear them; music often comes alive when played well even if it sometimes looks uninteresting on paper. Three of these compositions had commentaries attached which are also included here for you to think about. These compositions have not been selected on grounds of merit, although they certainly contain some creditable ideas; they are presented with examiner's comments with the following aims in mind:

(a) to improve your own standard of presentation and accuracy of notation;
(b) to see how others develop their initial ideas;
(c) to consider the importance of commentaries when added to a score.

March for Trumpet and Piano

Candidate's score
The *March for Trumpet and Piano* is reproduced as Fig. 11.14. The piece itself is only 24 bars long.

Fig. 11.14 *March for Trumpet and Piano*

Candidate's commentary (submitted with the composition)

> As I used to play the trumpet and now play the piano, I had a fairly good idea what a march for trumpet and piano should sound like. I decided to write it in ternary form and in the key of C major (the trumpet being transposed up to D major).
>
> Firstly, I wrote the trumpet's tune and then I composed the piano accompaniment. I did not directly record the tune, but programmed it into a Yamaha CX5 Music Computer. I used a trumpet sound and an electric piano sound. When I finished programming it into the computer, I played it back, recording it onto a cassette.

Examiner's comments

This short piece works quite well, and is cast in an effective ternary form. The melody for trumpet is satisfactory, although more use might have been made of the triplet figure which appears only once. There is no real sense of climax to the piece; this might have been achieved with a higher range of trumpet notes towards the end, instead of repeating the first section exactly. The use of dynamics is rather unimaginative: the piano part is simply marked *mf* all the way through, and the instructions for trumpet are only marginally more interesting. The ⟨⟨ ⟩⟩ marking in bar 10 is likely to produce a strange 'ballooning' effect, and should be reconsidered.

The candidate is perfectly correct in stating that the B♭ trumpet is a transposing instrument, but there is no need to provide both C and B♭ parts here. A score normally contains one or the other, and it proves confusing to see both. Apart from that, the notation is very clear with only minor inaccuracies (in bar 1 the piano quavers should not be under the minim but on the fourth beat and in bar 11 the C trumpet part has the semiquaver indication missing).

The commentary is perfectly adequate considering that it is in addition to, not a substitute for, a notated score. It gives a clear explanation of how the candidate went about creating and recording the piece.

Scherzo for Piano

Candidate's score
The *Scherzo for Piano* is reproduced as Fig. 11.15

Fig. 11.15 *Scherzo for Piano*

Fig. 11.15 continued

Examiner's comments

This is an effective piano miniature. I am not sure that *Scherzo* is the right title for this piece – apart from the fact that historically, composers wrote their Scherzos in a quick 3/4 time with one beat to a bar, it actually implies something light-hearted; literally a 'joke', which is not the case in this piece. Perhaps the title could be reconsidered.

The piano writing is well thought out in both hands, with effective imitation as in bar 2. The piece is interesting rhythmically, and the semiquaver figure ( ) helps to give the piece some movement. The sequence in bars 9 – 12 is treated well: bar 12 has a sense of forward motion instead of waiting, as in bar 10.

A + B + B is an unusual structure for a piece. Is this satisfying as it stands? Should the A theme return to finish off the piece? Details of phrasing are good at the beginning but seem to dry up after bar 10, and it must be admitted, too, that the dynamics are rather uninspired. The notation itself is clear, but care should be taken to align the beats accurately between the hands. Avoid placing a ♪ above a ♩ as in (bar 12). (The quaver being shorter should be moved along.)

Five more minutes spent on notation to check the final details and markings would have improved this written score considerably.

Puck's Lullaby

Candidate's score
Puck's Lullaby is reproduced as Fig 11.16.

Fig. 11.16 *Puck's Lullaby*

Fig. 11.16 continued

Candidate's commentary (submitted with the composition)

The school did a production of A Midsummer Night's Dream *and we were asked to compose the incidental music for it . This piece is written for Puck, end of Act Three Scene Two . The play was set in the 60s, mini skirts and hippies all the fashion, so the music had to be appropriate. It is written for keyboard synthesiser with drum beat, flute and voice in the style of a 60s pop song . I chose C minor as the key to give the piece a dramatic and eerie quality because Puck is, in fact, casting a spell .*

(continued)

I wrote the accompaniment first It is very simple chords with slow quaver repetition in the right hand. The melodic range was restricted by the singer (a non-trained fourth former). The phrases can be sung in short breaths again as dictated by the singer and Shakespeare's metrical verse. For variety in the texture I placed a flute above the main melody which is sometimes imitative.

Its function in the play is to put right the mischievous antics of Puck. I tried to put this across in the music and the tension is maintained until the last two bars . I wanted an unusual cadence and used the minor version of the leading note as a variant on the dominant .

Puck has been playing with the emotions of the four lovers throughout the play and only now is putting things right, Lysander, Hermia, Demetrius and Helena falling in love with the right people. During the piece there is a slight use of dissonance but always resolving harmonically.

Examiner's comments

This was submitted in beautifully clear notation; it is a very well written piece and there is a clear explanation as to its construction. This is a good example of how a piece can grow from its improvised accompaniment. The rather narrow-ranging vocal line is understandable when one reads the commentary. There is a sensitive imitation between flute and voice in bars 10–11; this is treated very musically, for the vocal line does not copy it exactly, and the flute goes on to another figure, so avoiding predictability. The dynamics are used sensibly throughout.

The candidate mentions the use of dissonance in the commentary – is bar 6 correctly notated with the E flat in the vocal line against E natural in the accompaniment? This does work perfectly well; or is it a simple error?

One small point: the low flute B natural in bar 2 is not possible on a real flute (middle C is its lowest note). Be careful with instrumental ranges when you are using synthesisers to help you.

A Movement for Clarinet Trio

Candidate's score
A *Movement for Clarinet Trio* is reproduced as Fig. 11.17.

Fig. 11.17 *Movement for Clarinet Trio*

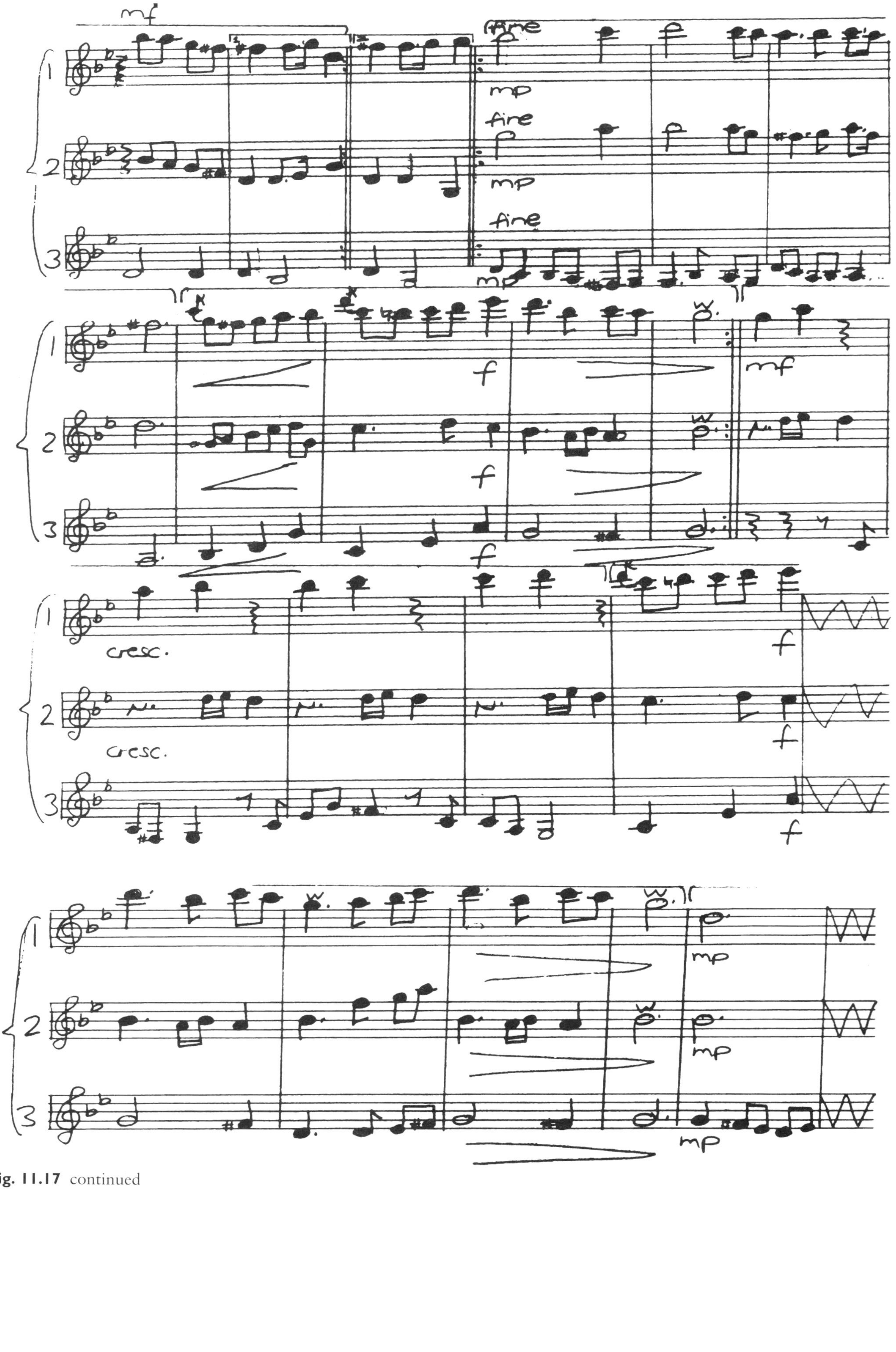

Fig. 11.17 continued

Fig. 11.17 continued

Examiner's comments

This is an example of a piece that looks rather dull on paper, but comes to life with a good performance. It uses the full range of the clarinet well between the three players, and the dynamics are employed intelligently, providing a good contrast within the movement. The second clarinet figure (commencing at bar 18) subtly grows from the ornamental figure in bar 16. This may be subconscious, but is good compositional technique. Perhaps a modulation (key change) somewhere would have added more colour.

Are those phrase marks written over the tops of the bars? If so, it would be better to indicate a legato mood with an instruction at the top of the piece, rather than use these markings which imply slurring, instead of tonguing for wind players.

Do you mean F# – E♭ in bars 27/29/31/33 etc? It is by no means wrong, but many pieces avoid this interval from the harmonic minor scale and use F# – E natural or F – E♭ instead. It may be useful to indicate both notes with accidentals to clarify this.

Psalm 134

Candidate's score
Psalm 134 for four-part choir is reproduced as Fig. 11.18.

Fig. 11.18 *Psalm 134*

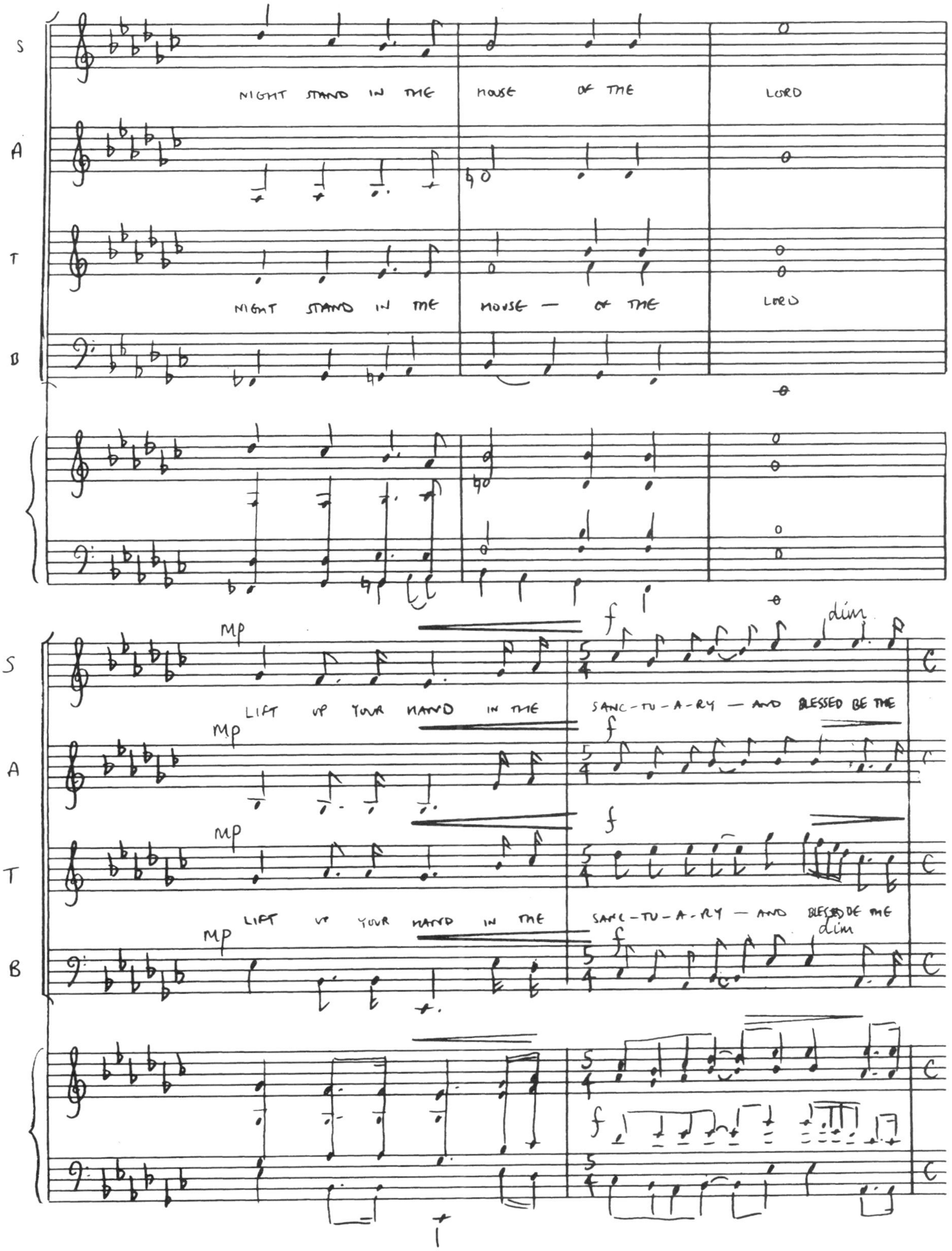

Fig. 11.18 continued

Fig. 11.18 continued

Examiner's comments

This candidate, who openly expresses a love for the choral music of Rachmaninov, achieves here a fine pastiche of the dark Russian vocal style. The Psalm is one of a set of three, all of the same high standard of musical thought and clarity of notation. The candidate thoughtfully includes a piano part which would prove invaluable in rehearsal, as the vocal lines are difficult to score-read. The use of E♭ minor and the deep bass notes add to the lugubrious atmosphere. This piece requires a very good choir to give the fine performance it deserves. The score is beautifully clear and written in conventional vocal style with separated quavers.

Chinese Robot

Candidate's score

An extract only: the opening of a computer-generated piece is reproduced as Fig. 11.19.

Chinese Robot

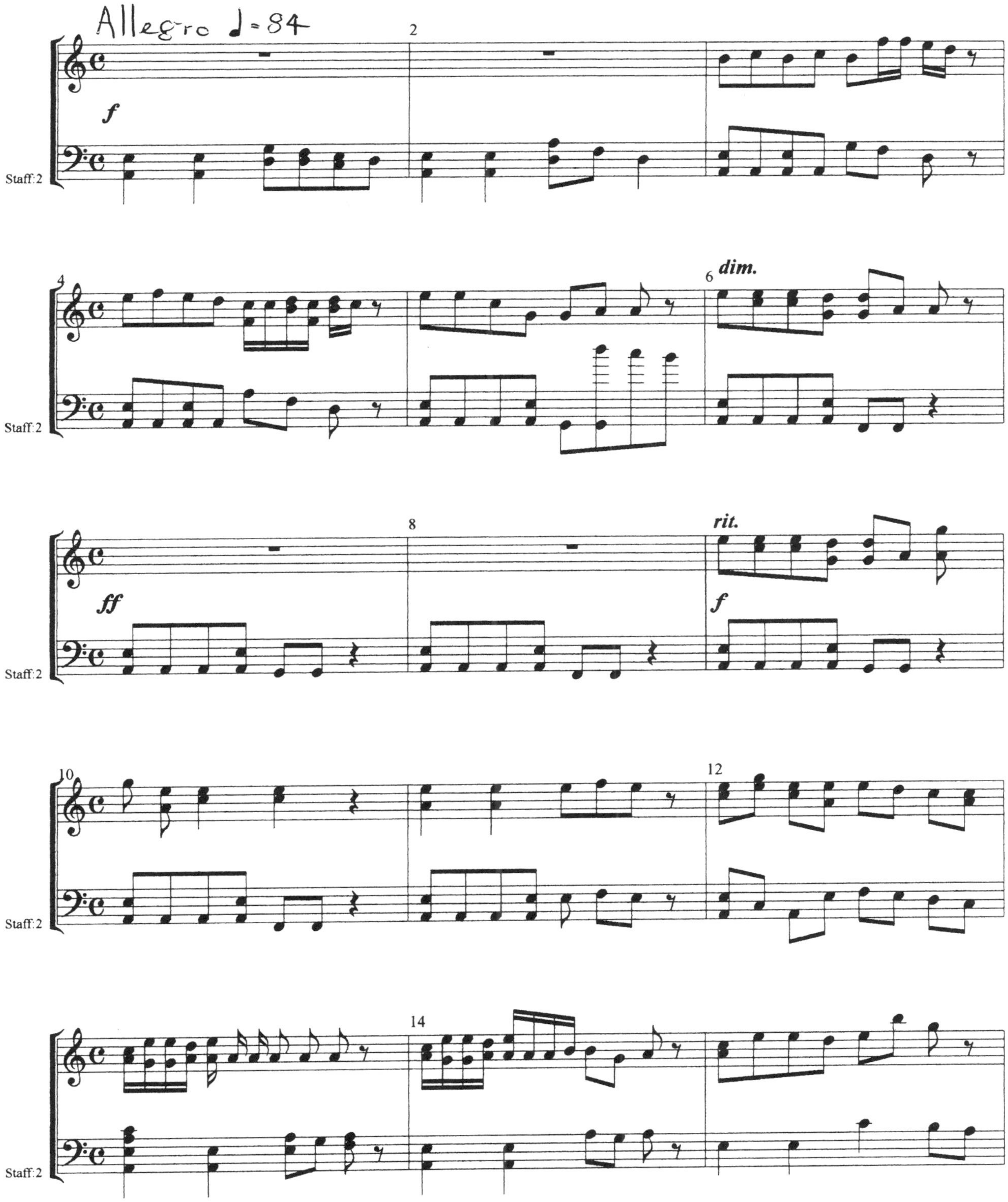

Fig. 11.19 *Chinese Robot*

Candidate's commentary (submitted with the composition)

> *I composed this piece of music inspired by a small mechanical toy robot I have, that looks Chinese. This composition has a very simple tune that is mostly scales and arpeggios with more notes laid on top to decorate it, I tried to achieve a Chinese effect by utilising allot of two note chords climbing and falling in scales.*
>
> *To perform the drum beat I used a synthesis drum pad and I also used this to perform all the sound effects, i.e. the whoosh sound as the intro. and outro, and also the mechanical noises. During the piece the drum beat stops and starts at places this is to give some variation and to highlight the melody.*

Examiner's comments

This is another example of a piece that appears rather ordinary on paper but improves with the tone colours and percussive effects that a computer can easily provide. If this was performed on a piano it would probably be uninteresting and ordinary; this candidate added computer percussion to the recording rather than rock-style drumming. It was mechanical and humorous, in keeping with the title. Only the opening fifteen bars are shown here – the whole piece is over fifty bars long.

The strange harmonies in bar 12 (parallel sevenths) appear to betray a lack of traditional harmony, but the computer sounds that the candidate chose gloss over this and it does not stand out as an error (as it would on the piano, for instance). Computer notation usually looks better than written music, but errors can easily creep in if you are not careful. The semiquavers in bar 13 should all be grouped into fours (as in bar 14); the vertical alignment in that bar is not good and the top rest is incorrect. This may all seem pedantic or fussy, but we are aiming for the highest standard! The indication to slow down in bar 9 (*rit*) is a mistake; the recording did not slow at all, and there is no return to the original tempo. The accompaniment is given a dynamic marking in bar 1, but the melody (bar 3) does not have one. Do we infer that both strands are the same volume? It is always best to make things like this clear. It would have been clearer to put the very high notes in the lower part of bar 5 in the melody, because that is how it actually sounds. This was probably a 'blip' on the computer.

As far as the commentary is concerned, more detail as to the computer equipment would have been welcome, and basic information on how long the piece took to complete is always useful to the moderator. The English is not perfect either! Despite these comments the piece was a successful and enjoyable composition.

Music, When Soft Voices Die

(P.B. Shelley) for voice and piano

The final student composition was submitted by a strong singer who was only an averagely competent pianist. This beautiful setting of Shelley's short poem helped to earn the candidate her starred A grade. It is included here primarily to give one more example of a student's work, but it might also be useful for you to answer some questions on it.

Fig. 11.20 *Music, When Soft Voices Die*

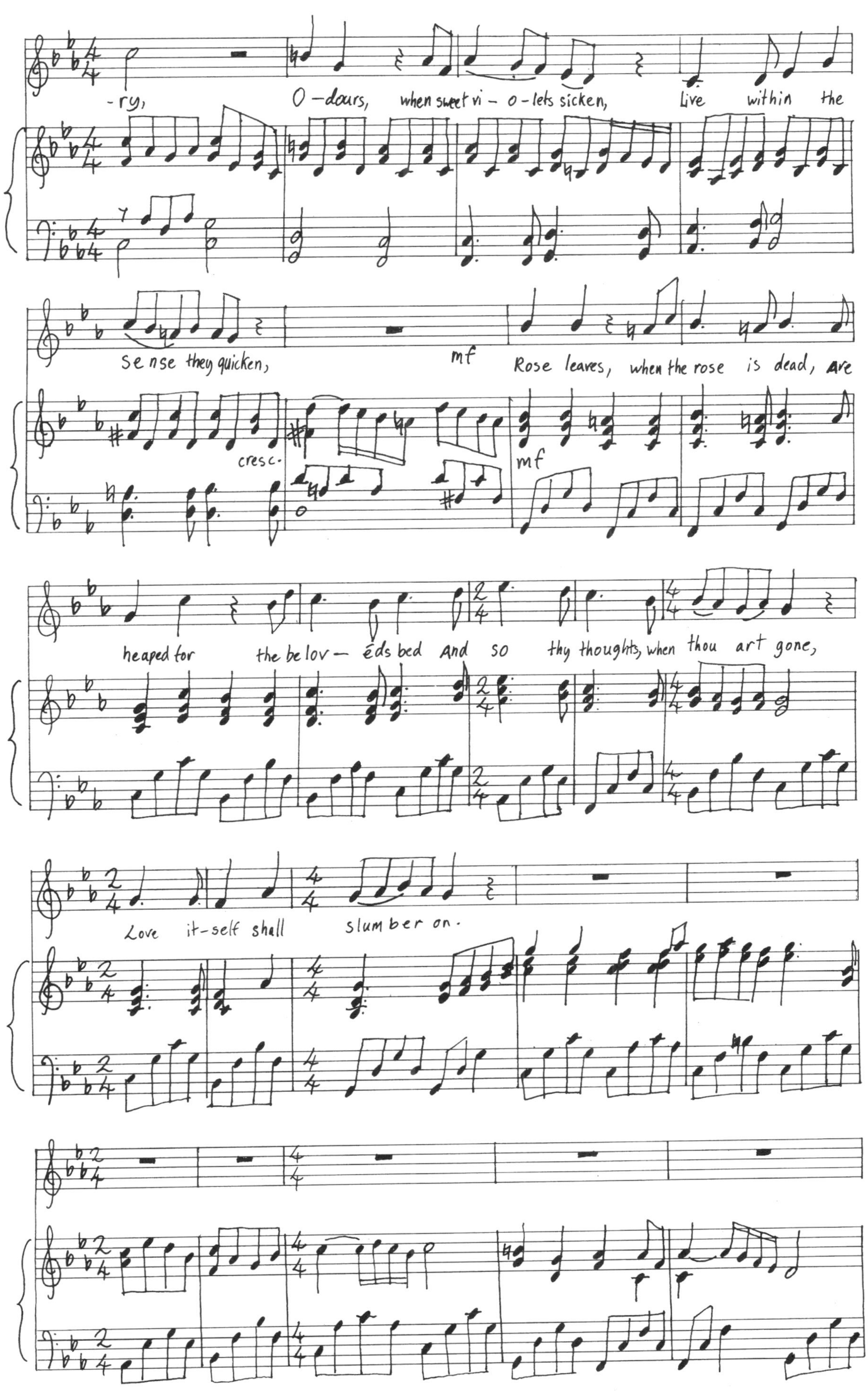

Fig. 11.20 continued

Fig. 11.20 continued

Practice questions and answers

Refer to the piece 'Music, When Soft Voices Die' and try to answer the following questions:

Question 1
What key is it in?

Question 2
How does the accompaniment avoid monotony?

Question 3
What key do we reach at verse 2 – 'Rose leaves' (bar 12)?

Question 4
What structure has the candidate used?

Question 5
What happens at bar 21?

Question 6
There are one or two slips in the piano writing (bars 8 and 33). What are they?

Answer 1
C minor (three flats and B naturals).

Answer 2
The accompaniment does rather look all the same on paper but this candidate has intelligently avoided monotony by breaking the harmonic pattern occasionally (e.g. bars 6 or 11), and by introducing semiquavers (bars 8 or 11) which not only avoids tedium but actually helps forward flow.

Answer 3
G minor (F#s and A naturals).

Answer 4
The form is A B C B, where A is verse 1, B is verse 2 (although it could be considered as A1), and C is the piano episode (but again, there are fragments of A within it). Unusually, the second verse is sung twice.

Answer 5
The piano provides an 11-bar episode between the two statements of verse two.

Answer 6
In the second beat of bar 8 the G in 'violets' will clash against the A♭ in the piano part. Similarly in bar 33, the B♭ on 'rose' will clash against the A natural beneath it. These are minor solecisms but worth mentioning – you need to proof read your compositions carefully to avoid these minor errors.

A FINAL STATEMENT

When assessing your compositions, your teacher will judge your work according to established criteria; your work will not be compared with the work of other candidates, but assessed on your own ability. Work is then moderated by external examiners to ensure uniformity of standards.

It is expected that your compositions may imitate other styles at this level; in no way will this penalise you, for traditional styles can be used creatively. Arrangements of other pieces are encouraged, although this seems not to be a popular option. Successful arranging requires as much imagination as a free composition; avoid any tendency to merely transcribe the chosen tune for other instruments or voices. If you think of your arrangement as if you were writing variations, then you might be more creative. Consider adding counter melodies or fresh harmonies; change the key perhaps, or modulate more freely.

Do not assume that 'difficult is best', or that your pieces must be lengthy. Marks awarded for composition are likely to be for quality rather than for length or the number of pieces submitted. The examiners are looking for evidence of **expressive ability**; twenty-four bars of **clearly written, sensitive music** with a **satisfying structure** is preferable to pages of incoherent note-spinning. Now over to you, and enjoy yourselves!

SUMMARY

▷ Be consistent in your chosen style.
▷ Quality not quantity – but don't be *too* short, or you may be penalised!
▷ Simplicity is often most effective.
▷ Be accurate with notation, especially when using a computer to record your piece.
▷ Aim for a well-presented folio with a good, clear recording.

12

Composing 2: Graphic notation and music technology

GETTING STARTED

In Western music, a thorough knowledge of *notation* has long been regarded as a pre-requisite for composers and performers alike. It is easy to forget, however, that a great deal of music around the world is not written down. Popular music, folk, jazz, and Indian music are among the styles which are either improvised or committed to memory. Staff notation is a well understood and useful tool, but it is by no means the only way of recording sounds on paper.

Even the most detailed and complex traditional score can indicate only a portion of the information required for a satisfactory performance – we still depend on the interpretation of the conductor, performer and the taught tradition for these signs and symbols to be fully realised, or brought alive, according to the composer's intentions.

During the last few decades there have been tremendous improvements in music education, including a movement away from an exclusive use of staff notation. Traditionalists might argue that the existence of alternative notation is necessary simply because staff notation has not been learnt properly. This may be partly true, but forms of graphic notation actually became necessary for some of the different styles that have evolved this century.

IGCSE	LONDON	MEG	NEAB	NICCEA	SEG	WJEC	TOPIC	STUDY	REVISION I	REVISION 2
✓	✓	✓	✓	✓	✓	✓	Graphic notation			
✓	✓	✓	✓	✓	✓	✓	Working with electronic instruments			
✓	✓	✓	✓	✓	✓	✓	Summary			

WHAT YOU NEED TO KNOW

▷ **Graphic notation**

A graphic score is one where the notation is invented by the composer for a particular piece; the signs and symbols (which may, of course, include traditional ones) are devised to represent ideas where approximation is appropriate. It can never be as accurate as staff notation, but is to be encouraged for GCSE if you take pains to record your intentions for performance.

A graphic score is certainly useful for those candidates who find staff notation difficult, and should not be thought of as inferior; contemporary composers such as Stockhausen and Berio have used graphic notation for their compositions where some degree of choice is desirable or necessary. This could be just the thing for you if you wish to explore textures of sound and spatial concepts, rather than melodies and rhythm in the traditional sense.

Once you have considered the sounds you wish to explore and the overall structure of your piece, you will need to select or devise suitable **signs** and **symbols** for the notation. The next important step is to work out a *key* so that you can clarify the interpretation of your symbols. You will need to consider the following criteria:

▶ How long or short do you wish the notes to be and how will you notate this?
▶ How will you notate pitch?
▶ How will you notate harmony? Are you keen to explore clusters of notes or do you prefer more conventional chords?
▶ Will you specify instruments or permit any combination that is available?
▶ Will you invent your own symbols for expression or retain the traditional ones?

There is an important maxim with all composition, that you should **hear the sound before you use the sign.** In other words, notation itself is not music, even though we use the same word, 'music', for the written sign as well as for the sound. **Notation** is merely an accepted way of **representing** sounds on paper. Only when these symbols are realised can we consider it to be music. Ask yourself these questions when composing a piece using graphic notation:

▶ Which instrument is playing the important part? Does it remain so, or does another instrument take over?
▶ How can I ensure that this instrument is heard to full advantage, and not swamped by the other parts?
▶ Should I choose a sound or instrument which contrasts with the other parts and therefore becomes conspicuous?
▶ Should I make it louder than the other instruments? Or is it easier to make the other parts quieter?

How would you interpret the signs in Fig. 12.1? In the notation in Fig. 12.1, no indication of duration (length) of notes has been indicated, so freedom is implied if not indicated on the score.

In (a) you need to relate the sizes of the boxes to each other – in terms of height (which can represent pitch) and width (which can represent duration). Could the boxes be used for blocks of chords? If so, the notes will be arbitrary because no pitch has been indicated.

In (b) we could think of the sounds as becoming quieter and each one higher than before, but are these sounds single notes, or chords? The key at the beginning of your piece would have to indicate this.

In (c) we have some traditional Italian dynamics, and it is good to use these. Why discard signs for the sake of it? The lines imply a glissando (or slide) up and down a scale. The length of the line gives an approximate duration of the glissando, and their position indicates fairly clearly when they should be played. Notice the overlap between all three. The notes used in the glissando would obviously depend on the particular instrument being used.

In (d) the series of dots would imply a cluster of single notes played at random, and in close proximity. The second cluster would be proportionately higher, depending again on the instruments being used. The final grouping of four dots is slightly bigger. Could this mean louder notes or longer notes? This needs to be made quite clear in the key to your piece.

The four groups of symbols carry a fair amount of information, some implied and some to be explained more fully in the key. Let us now consider ways of employing signs in a piece which explores textural and spatial effects.

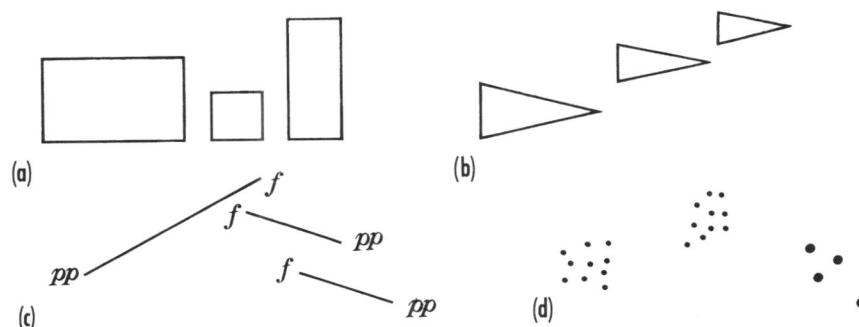

Fig. 12.1

Key to Fig. 12.2

The height of each square on the grid represents the total range of the instrument. The conductor is to indicate by means of a down-beat where each ten seconds has elapsed. This timing is to be regarded as approximate. The signs are more or less self-explanatory:

Rising or falling notes – random pitch, but observing the relative pitch position within the square.

A held note, then falling and rising slightly.

f   *mf*   *p*   As for conventional notation.

Cluster-blocks of chords, relative to its position in the square. The sustaining pedal may be used at the player's discretion.

Glissando (an upward slide).

Rapid 'shake' or trill; the two notes a semitone apart.

The graphic score in Fig 12.2 illustrates the first 40 seconds only of a piece.

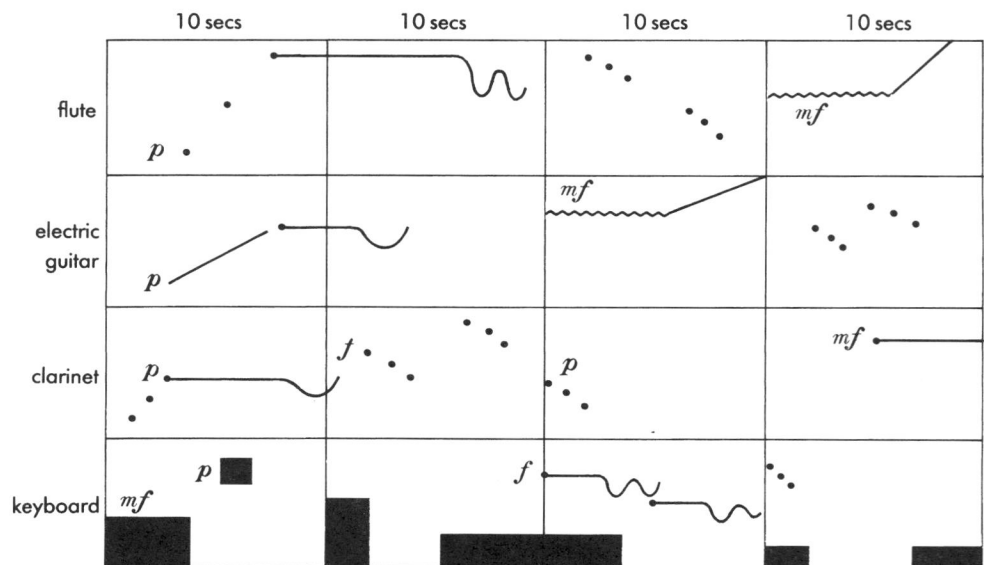

Fig. 12.2

You can see that by including the ten-second time-spans as 'bars' and also some traditional dynamic markings, it starts to take on some of the characteristics of staff notation. With careful thought, this sort of notation can convey a considerable amount of precision while retaining a certain element of freedom which provides a sense of spontaneity.

Given these suggestions, and the brief example above, could you experiment with this style of composition and notation to create an inventive piece? **Remember, the sound comes first, then the sign.** Don't fall into the unmusical trap of drawing meaningless lines and squiggles on paper and kidding yourself that it is music. Allow the instruments or parts to relate to each other, as if you were notating imitation or counterpoint more conventionally.

A final point: ensure that your performers give a first-class account of your piece, or it may sound a little pretentious. If a piece sacrifices a melodic content in the traditional sense, then more importance must be given to timbre and nuance (tone colours and subtle shading) to compensate.

▷ Working with electronic instruments

When GCSE Music was introduced, pupils had the opportunity to acquire a broad base of practical skills and the chance to explore a much wider range of musical styles than ever before. Pupils were able to use, for the first time, electronic keyboards, synthesisers and music computers as composing tools, in whatever genre they chose to explore; the keyboards and synthesisers could also be used for the performing elements of the course.

This short section will only be of benefit to those candidates who have not, as yet, worked with electronic instruments; it introduces them briefly, and then sets out to encourage you to use these new instruments. Most importantly, it suggests ways of using them more musically.

Differences between synthesiser and keyboard

First of all, the words 'synthesiser' and 'keyboard' are often used as if they are interchangeable. There are, however, important differences between them. In a nutshell, the many varieties of portable keyboard with their banks of automatic accompaniments are aimed at the home musician – and great fun they are too. The synthesiser, however, is much more versatile; it is essentially a professional musical instrument capable of multi-timbral sounds, which are altered or created yourself. It has a wide range of sounds, rhythms, pitches and durations. Developed well over thirty years ago, it is now a much-used instrument with rock musicians and modern composers. (This is not the place to go into electronic details – you can read elsewhere of oscillators, mixers, filters, envelope shapers and so on. It is a very complicated piece of machinery). It must be stressed that synthesisers too have many pre-set sounds, and also provide the user with the opportunity to plug in memory cards or floppy disks with even more built-in sounds. This has curtailed the desire for musicians to synthesise their own sounds; all music technology can encourage laziness, but in the hands of an enthusiastic and inventive musician can be used as creatively as traditional instruments.

MIDI

There is one technical detail that must be mentioned, as it is an important musical consideration. When choosing an electronic instrument for use in composition (or performance) try to obtain one that is equipped with MIDI (Musical Instrument Digital Interface) – you will find that most keyboards produced recently have this facility built in.

The digital system is widely used in electronics, and is used here so that everything you play on your keyboards or synthesiser is encoded as a series of numbers.

MIDI is a universal language which is utilised now on all makes of hi-tech equipment. If you connect a MIDI lead to your synthesiser's MIDI OUT socket and link it to the MIDI IN socket of another MIDI keyboard, information can be transmitted from your synthesiser to the other keyboard. For example, if you move the pitch bend wheel on your synthesiser, or play a note, this will then be duplicated on the keyboard. In this way several interconnected keyboards will produce a great variety of complex blends of timbres. This facility is used to good effect in the rock business where keyboard players use these layered sounds to good advantage by means of MIDI – listen to Jean-Michel Jarre's *Oxygène* album, for example.

If you choose to work with a portable keyboard with built-in rhythms, do make sure that you don't resort to simple 'button-pushing'. The pre-recorded sounds can be great fun to play with, but are so inflexible; you should be in full control of the instrument as a performer, and should select the different sounds inventively. An incessant rhythm on a keyboard is as relentless as a drum machine: vary it and think of a contrast in speed or dynamics if you can. Initially these factory pre-set sounds can be exciting, but the chances are that you will soon tire of them, especially those which imitate other instruments.

Both synthesiser and keyboard are invaluable as composing aids; you can experiment with chords and melodies until you are satisfied with the result. By processing your sounds they may be changed in pitch or repeated at different pitches at the same time (pitch shift), elongated (reverb), or repeated at specific intervals of time (echo/delay). Filtering will radically alter the sound quality. There are countless ways of working: music technology will offer you a direct and complete control over your sound – in volume, texture, pitch, timbre and articulation.

Recording

On completion of the piece, the point to consider is, how do you record your composition? Will you be content with the rather limited sounds of your keyboard for a recording? Could you bring your composition alive with more sophisticated equipment?

When submitting your scores or commentaries you may have to include a recording of your composition. If so, the examiner will want to assess your work alongside the recording. Although the quality of the recording is not assessed, it will make a more favourable impression if it is clear and well balanced. A tape recorder and microphone can be perfectly useful for a recording of your composition, but if you are working in a rock/pop style and wish to build up your piece in layers (i.e. multi-tracking), then a portastudio is what you need. These are essentially small mixing desks combined with a multi-track tape facility.

There is a whole range of these machines, and after instruction and experimentation you will soon master the basic elements of balancing your music, bouncing the tracks, mixing and equalisation. If you use the portastudio with a computer sequencer, you will obtain a sophisticated recording. Try to use a higher tape speed for best results, with Dolby C, DBX or Dolby S.

Use of computers

Do you have access to a computer with music software at school? Atari ST, PC, Apple Macintosh and Acorn are four good choices for music computer hardware. Although the sounds are created by machine, the selection process is made by you. All of your compositional work is stored on disk, and you can easily pick up where you left off.

There are many software packages now available – some rather complex to master initially, but very worthwhile as an aid to composing. Sibelius 6 or 7 with an Acorn is excellent, and the choice for the PC and Macintosh is enormous. If you want to invest in your own computer and music software, seek good advice from a reputable dealer.

Useful contacts: Apple UK (on freephone 0800 127753).
Acorn Education Sales Office (01223 254214).
System Solutions (01753 832212), or
The Upgrade Shop (01625 503448) for Atari advice.

Your school will probably have equipment like that mentioned so far. If so, do ask if you can have some hands-on experience; it may be just the thing for your compositions. Try out a drum machine, a wind controller or a guitar synthesiser; could it be used for your piece?

Many of you will be familiar with the above, and some of you may even own some of the equipment. But if this is new territory for you, and there is an opportunity to try it out, be adventurous – have a go! It may be just the thing that you are looking for.

SUMMARY

Graphic notation

▷   Devise signs and symbols that are clear and bold.

▷   Are you representing on paper what you really mean?

▷   Don't be frightened of using conventional music signs – they are universal.

▷   Emphasise timbre and nuance (tone colour and shading) in performance.

Electronic instruments

▷   Experiment! A dull piece on piano could sound brilliant if produced on a computer or portastudio with interesting instrumental sonorities.

Chapter

13

Useful theory

▷ **GETTING STARTED**

You may not find this section the most interesting, but music theory needs to be learnt thoroughly if you are to be sure of a top grade in GCSE. If you wish (a) to give a good account of yourself in the written papers; (b) to interpret your ensemble and performance pieces intelligently; and (c) to notate your compositions accurately – you should make sure that you are familiar with the theoretical knowledge contained in this chapter:

IGCSE	LONDON	MEG	NEAB	NICCEA	SEG	WJEC	TOPIC		STUDY	REVISION 1	REVISION 2
✓	✓	✓	✓	✓	✓	✓	Key signatures				
✓	✓	✓	✓	✓	✓	✓	Relative minor scales				
✓	✓	✓	✓	✓	✓	✓	Minor scales				
✓	✓	✓	✓	✓	✓	✓	Pentatonic scale				
✓	✓	✓	✓	✓	✓	✓	Whole-tone scale				
✓	✓	✓	✓	✓	✓	✓	Rests and note values				
✓	✓	✓	✓	✓	✓	✓	Intervals				
✓	✓	✓	✓	✓	✓	✓	Chords				
✓	✓	✓	✓	✓	✓	✓	Cadences				
✓	✓	✓	✓	✓	✓	✓	Ornaments				
✓	✓	✓	✓	✓	✓	✓	Form				
✓	✓	✓	✓	✓	✓	✓	General signs and symbols				
✓	✓	✓	✓	✓	✓	✓	Guitar chords				
✓	✓	✓	✓	✓	✓	✓	Transposing instruments				
✓	✓	✓	✓	✓	✓	✓	Practice questions				
✓	✓	✓	✓	✓	✓	✓	Summary				

▷ **WHAT YOU NEED TO KNOW**

▷ **Key signatures**   The seven sharps and seven flats are always used in a fixed order:

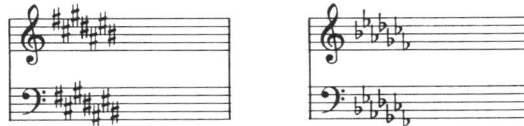

You may not actually use a key with all of the sharps or flats, but you should be aware of them just in case – it may turn up in a written paper, or in a performance piece. The order of the flats is quite easy to remember with a simple mnemonic.

British European Airways Do Good Charter Flights (or you can easily make up your own).

For the order of the sharps simply reverse this, into:

F C G D A E B – or make up a nonsense line to help you remember, as with the flats. (Farmer Charles Gets Drunk At Every Barndance...?)

You will need to know which scales contain these sharps or flats. The relative minor scales, which share the same key signatures are given in brackets:

C	major has no sharps or flats	(A minor)
G	major has 1 sharp	(E minor)
D	major has 2 sharps	(B minor)
A	major has 3 sharps	(F sharp minor)
E	major has 4 sharps	(C sharp minor)
B	major has 5 sharps	(G sharp minor)
F sharp	major has 6 sharps	(D sharp minor)
C sharp	major has 7 sharps	(A sharp minor)
F	major has 1 flat	(D minor)
B	flat major has 2 flats	(G minor)
E	flat major has 3 flats	(C minor)
A	flat major has 4 flats	(F minor)
D	flat major has 5 flats	(B flat minor)
G	flat major has 6 flats	(E flat minor)
C	flat major has 7 flats	(A flat minor)

Thus, if you are asked to enter the key signature for A major into the correct place – check first which clef you are in, then enter the necessary number of sharps (in this case 3 = F C and G sharps) after the clef and before the time signature:

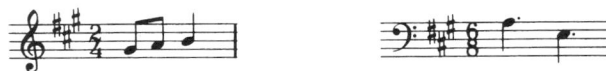

It is worthwhile practising some of these to help you remember. You should certainly know up to four sharps and flats very well indeed.

▷ **Relative minor scales**   Do not assume that every key signature you see is for a major key – there is a good chance you might be in a minor key. When you are working with minor scales you can work out the correct minor key signature from that of the major. (This may save you having to learn the minors by heart, but you will need to know all the major key signatures!) Take a minor scale and count up three semitones to find its relative major. They will share the same key signature. For example: A (minor) – count up through B flat and B natural to arrive at C (major) = no sharps or flats; or E (minor) – count up through F and F sharp to arrive at G (major) = one sharp (F sharp). Try some of these for yourself and check your answers with the above table of key signatures. Similarly, of course, you can count down (three semitones) from a major to a minor key.

▷ **Minor scales**   There are two types of minor scale, the *Harmonic minor* and the *Melodic minor*. Harmonic minors usually have the seventh note (leading note) raised a semitone by means of an accidental. So A minor, for instance, will have the same key signature as C major but the seventh note is G sharp and not G natural. Also, the scale is similar ascending and descending (see Fig. 13.1).

Fig. 13.1 A harmonic minor

The melodic minor scale (Fig. 13.2) has some of the difficult intervals ironed out, and is used more when writing smooth minor-key melodies. The 6th and 7th notes are raised on the way up, but flattened (that is, the key signature is applied) on the way down.

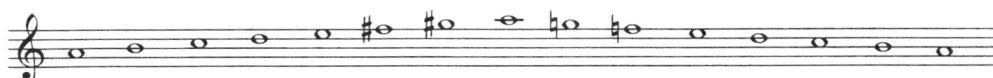

Fig. 13.2 A melodic minor

Again, you should practise some of the easier harmonic and melodic minor scales – up to four sharps or flats, perhaps.

▷ **Pentatonic scale**

This five-note scale (see Fig. 13.3), which omits the 4th and 7th degrees of our major scale, is used by many different cultures around the world. Chinese, Japanese, American Indian, American Negro and Scottish folk music have it. There is an illustration in Fig. 13.4

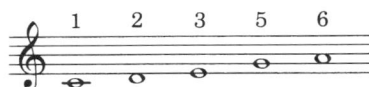

Fig. 13.3 Pentatonic scale

Fig. 13.4

(You could experiment with this scale, and perhaps use it as the basis for a composition or improvisation. The piano black keys form the pentatonic scale – use F sharp as your home note.)

▷ **Whole-tone scale**

Here there are no semitones at all, and the scale creates a nice feeling of vagueness (Fig. 13.5); so suitable for Impressionistic music!

Fig. 13.5 Whole-tone scale

Play the scale over several times until you are really sure of its sound, and then use it within a short composition of your own. Of course, you do not have to include whole-tones all of the time, just when you think it is appropriate!

▷ **Rests and note values**   Silence in music must be indicated as accurately as actual sounds. Many students get the semibreve and minim rests confused, and note groupings are often incorrectly written. The table in Fig 13.6 should help.

Name	Note	Rest	Value (when a beat = ♩)
semibreve	o	▬ *	4 beats
minim	♩(♩)	▬	2 beats
crotchet	♩(♩)	⸹(or ⌐)	1 beat
quaver	♪(♪)	⁊	½ (♩♩ = 1 beat)
semiquaver	♪(♪)	⁊	¼ (♩♩♩♩ = 1 beat)
demisemiquaver	♪(♪)	⁊	⅛ (♩♩♩♩♩♩♩♩ = 1 beat)

* This rest is also used to denote an empty bar (or complete bar's rest,) whatever the time signature.

Fig. 13.6 Silences in music

By adding a dot after a note, it can be made to last half as long again:

♩. = a dotted minim (1½ minims, or three crotchets)

♩. = a dotted crotchet (1½ crotchets)

♪. = a dotted quaver (1½ quavers, or ¾ of a crotchet)

Likewise with rests, we can lengthen by use of dots:

1½ crotchet beats rest = ⸹· or we can use two rests: ⸹ ⁊

Fig. 13.7 gives an example in 4/4 time:

Fig. 13.7

In 6/8 time (where the pulse is two dotted crotchets = 2 × 3 quavers) it will be written as in Fig. 13.8.

Fig. 13.8

It is worth stressing at this point that note stems must be correctly written. Below the middle line of the stave, stems must go up, and above the middle they come down. Only on the middle line itself do you have a choice. Fig. 13.9 illustrates this clearly.

Fig. 13.9

'A table to help with correct groupings'

The table (Fig. 13.10) should remind you of time signatures and their correct groupings. Be especially careful of 6/8 time which is often incorrectly grouped as 3 × 2 quavers, which is actually 3/4 time.

Fig. 13.10

Many modern composers use different time signatures from the above. 5/4 and 7/4 are very common now, but should not cause too much trouble for you. 5/4 is often thought of as 2 + 3, or 3 + 2, for example, and soon feels natural with practice. It gives a freer form of rhythm, and can be very effective when time signatures are changed within a single piece. Try composing a piece in an unusual time, or a mixture of time signatures.

Fig. 13.11 shows some rhythmic examples of less usual time signatures.

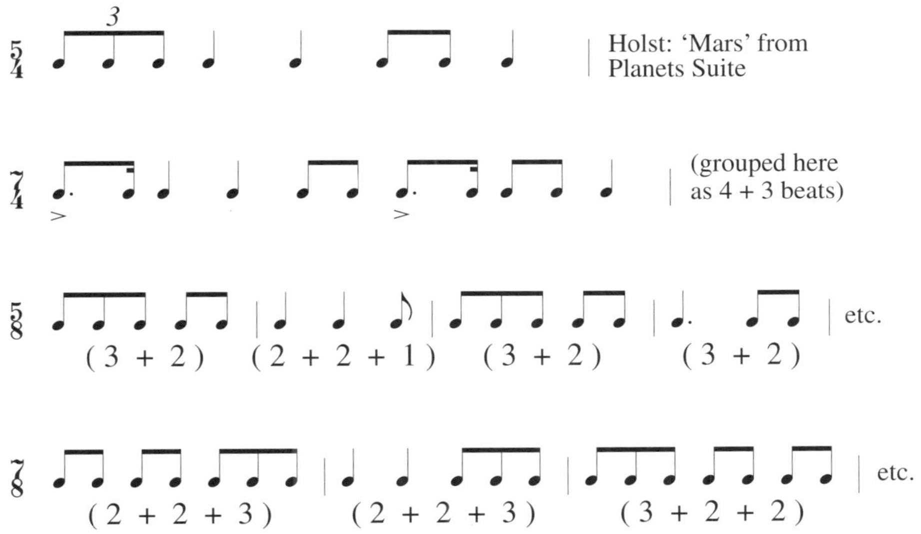

Fig. 13.11

These time signatures can be exciting rhythmically, producing jazzy effects.

▷ **Intervals**   An interval is the distance between any two notes. Think of the lower note as one, then count on up through the lines and spaces to the higher note, thus (a)  is an interval of a 5th, and (b)  is an interval of a 7th. If both notes are contained in the major scale of the lower note, it will be a **major** interval (for 2nds, 3rds, 6ths and 7ths) or a **perfect** interval (for 4ths, 5ths and octaves). So then, (a) will be a perfect 5th, and (b) is a major 7th.

If, however, the top note does not belong to the major scale of the lower note, another name has to be given, see Fig. 13.12.

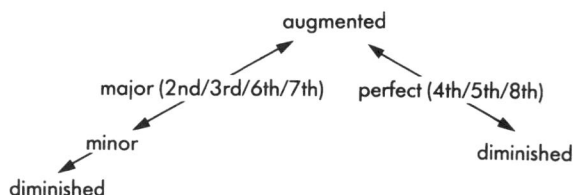

Fig. 13.12

The arrows in Fig. 13.12 represent a rise or fall of a semitone. Thus, an interval with the upper note a semitone higher than a major 6th, for example, is an augmented 6th, and a semitone less than a major will be a minor, etc.

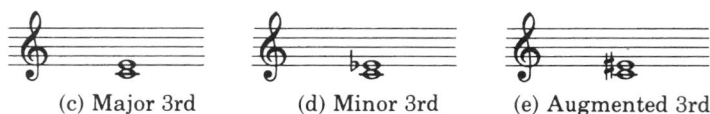

(c) Major 3rd   (d) Minor 3rd   (e) Augmented 3rd

Fig. 13.13

In the three examples in Fig. 13.13 we are using the scale of C major because the lower note of each interval is a C. In (c) both notes are present in C major, so the interval is a major 3rd; in (d) the upper note is a semitone lower than the 'true' note E, so the interval is a minor 3rd; and in (e) the upper note is a semitone higher than the correct note, so is an augmented 3rd.

Quick test

For practice, describe the intervals illustrated in Fig. 13.14. The answers are given at the end of this chapter on page 158.

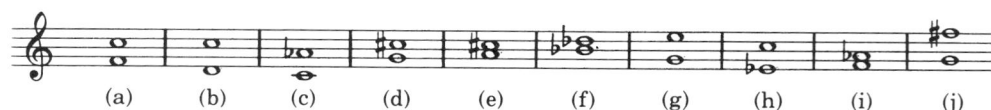

(a)   (b)   (c)   (d)   (e)   (f)   (g)   (h)   (i)   (j)

Fig. 13.14

For your compositions, and perhaps keyboard improvisations, you will probably be working with chords. You should become familiar with all the common chords of the scale. Fig. 13.15 gives you the chords of C major with the names we use for those chords.

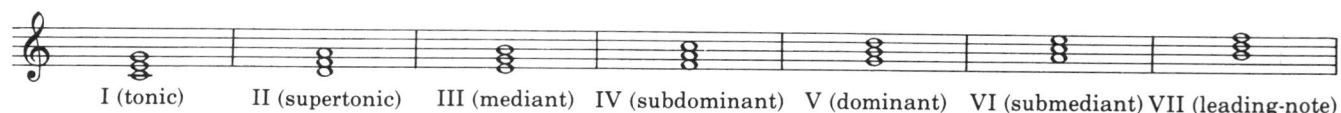

I (tonic)   II (supertonic)   III (mediant)   IV (subdominant)   V (dominant)   VI (submediant) VII (leading-note)

Fig. 13.15

▷ **Chords**   Harmony is the application of suitable chords to a melody, and the three most important chords in traditional Western music are the tonic (chord I), the subdominant (chord IV) and the dominant (chord V). With these three chords alone, it is possible to harmonise many pieces – from pop songs and twelve-bar blues, through to hymn tunes or a simple *lied*. The remaining chords, however, are frequently used in addition, to add flavour to the harmonisation, particularly chords II and VI.

▷ **Cadences**   A cadence is a full or half *close* in music, two chords at the end of a phrase or section to round things off. There are four types of cadence:

▷ **Perfect cadence**	chords V and I	Strong and final.
▷ **Plagal cadence**	chords IV and I	Final, but 'softer' like a church Amen.
▷ **Imperfect cadence**	chords I (or II or IV) and V	Incomplete because it goes away from the tonic.
▷ **Interrupted cadence**	chords V and VI	Unexpected as its name suggests; needs a continuing phrase to finalise.

The four cadences are shown in Fig. 13.16.

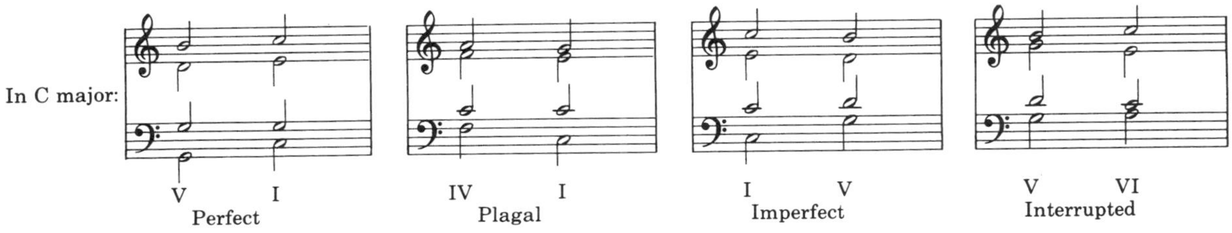

Fig. 13.16

▷ **Ornaments**   Ornaments are decorations in music. They have been used at all times to embellish a melody line, but in the Baroque and early classical times especially, spontaneous ornamentation was expected of a performer, even if it was not actually indicated in the music. Ornaments may be written as special signs, or as small notes against a larger one. You may find ornaments in your chosen performance pieces and set works, or you may wish to use some in your compositions. Fig. 13.17 gives some of the more common ones.

Fig. 13.17

A trill over a short note, played at speed, may be thought of as a mordent (see Fig. 13.18)

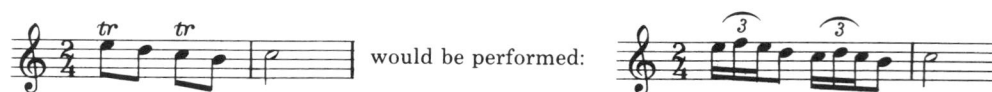

would be performed:

Fig. 13.18

Ornamentation is a detailed topic. If you require further information, consult a good text-book, or ask your teacher for advice. For GCSE, a working knowledge of the more common ornaments is perfectly satisfactory, but bear in mind that your interpretation of them, strictly speaking, should take into account the period in time of composition, and the overall speed of the piece – you cannot 'trill' as many notes in a fast piece as in a slow one.

▷ **Form**   Form is **structural shape** in music. Much of 'classical' music shows easily identifiable forms, but nothing is fixed in format, and many variants can be found. Composers write their music as they feel, not to suit descriptions in textbooks! We can only describe the average structures that composers have evolved, and must realise that there will always be diversity.

When young students start to think seriously about musical analysis, many think at first that a good composition is one where there is a wealth of good tunes, or ideas, one after the other. It is only through experience, good teaching and copious listening that they come to understand that repetition and contrast of a minimal amount of musical material is what helps to make a satisfactory composition. (Think of this when you work on your own compositions!) Themes are important, but so too is a contrast of key. Changes of key (especially in Classical times) mark out the significant landmarks in a work.

Before we consider whole movements and how they are structured, we must not forget that melodies and even phrases should be constructed in a careful way. A typical musical sentence (from a simple song, perhaps) might consist of 2 × 2-bar phrases, for example with a cadence in the middle and at the end. (See the section on Cadences earlier in this chapter). But composers try to avoid a feeling of 'squareness' (that is, predictable numbers of phrases and bars) by sometimes extending a bar. This will help to break up a monotonous pattern.

An example

Look at the 21-bar melody in Fig. 13.19 and play it through if you can. How has it been composed? Is it just a random collection of bars which 'happen to fit' together? Look in detail at the way each bar is part of the whole.

Fig. 13.19

The melody has been written in F major.

Bars 1–4   A four-bar sentence dividing into 2 × 2-bar phrases.

Bars 5–9   This time a five-bar sentence (immediately avoiding any predictable pattern). The extra bar (bar 8 really) is created by repeating bar 7 in sequence a third higher.

Bars 10–13 2 × two-bar phrases, both passing through new keys (G minor 10–11, by means of the F sharp leading note, and B flat major at 12–13 by adding the extra flat – E flat). This is a straightforward example of sequential modulation – the changing of keys by means of a simple repetition at a different pitch.

Bars 14–21 An eight-bar sentence. We are back in F major as we have lost the E flat. The interrupted cadence (chords V–VI in bars 16–17) demands an extension; notice how the last few bars make use of the very opening phrase. Bars 15 and 16 are a variant of bars 2–4; 18 = bar 1 (rearranged) and 19 = 2 and 3 in quicker notes (which is called diminution).

This may all sound rather complicated and rather pompous for a simple tune in F! However, it all serves to show how composers think and work – although many do all this automatically, of course. You should try to create melodies in a similar way. (See also Chapter 14 (2) Baroque Period – Things to Do no. 1.) Don't over-do the use of sequences, it can itself be very predictable. The great skill is in making a sculpted composition sound as if it has been conceived spontaneously.

Theme and variations

This is a common and popular form with composers of all periods and you may enjoy working with this yourself, in any style whatsoever. The simplest way of using this structure is for a theme (either original, or openly 'borrowed' from another composer) to be followed by several variations. There is never a set number of these, it is left to the discretion of the composer. Variations are different presentations of the rhythmic, harmonic and melodic structure of that theme.

A good example of early Variation form is so-called 'Harmonious Blacksmith' for harpsichord by Handel, or more properly, *Air and Variations* in E major. The theme is stated simply, in a singing style (cantabile) (Fig. 13.20).

Fig. 13.20 Theme

The first variation (Fig. 13.21) has more movement, but barely disguises the theme.

Fig. 13.21 Variation I

Whereas in the second variation (Fig. 13.22) the melody is (almost) absent but the chords remain unchanged:

Fig. 13.22 Variation II

The third variation (Fig. 13.23) retains the chordal framework and presents a flowing top line. Notice the very unusual time signature.

Fig. 13.23 Variation III

Variation four (Fig.13.24) uses the triplet figure (the running quavers) from the previous variation, but employs them here as a bass part.

Fig. 13.24 Variation IV

Finally, to make a flamboyant ending, Handel writes rapidly moving ascending and descending scales above the original chords for Variation Five (Fig. 13.25).

Fig. 13.25 Variation V

In later periods the theme was merely a starting point for varying mood pictures, albeit loosely linked to the theme in some way to give a feeling of unity. You may already know Andrew Lloyd Webber's *Variations*. This is based on a popular Paganini violin tune in A minor; several composers, including Rachmaninov (*Rhapsody on a Theme of Paganini*) have used the same theme for their variations. Try to get to know them, listening carefully all the time for references to the original melody. Note which variations you enjoyed the most. Were they the ones which contained the theme clearly, or the ones with clever changes of harmony or rhythm? You will find this sort of analysis automatic with practice, and you will probably enjoy your listening all the more for knowing what to listen out for.

Generally speaking, composers use the following devices to create their variations:

(a) Changing speed or time.
(b) Varying the rhythm.
(c) Transferring the theme (or fragments of it) to another line.
(d) Decorating the melody.
(e) Changing key.
(f) Using counterpoint, imitation or fugue.
(g) Isolating a fragment from the theme and developing it into something new.

These are only a few of the many ways that variations can grow from the original theme. You can probably think of several more. They can be combined, of course, so that for example, (a) +(b) + (d) + (f) + (g) might all be part of one variation – the possibilities are endless. The whole concept is one of **development**, that vital ingredient of all serious composition.

Rondo form

A rondo is a structure which alternates a recurring theme (which we shall call A) with contrasting episodes (B and C etc.). The number of episodes can vary, but a typical eighteenth century Rondo might run as follows:

A B A C A + coda *or* A B A C A D A + coda

You can see how the A section keeps on 'coming round' as its name implies. With Haydn and Mozart a Rondo was often found as the final movement of a Sonata or Concerto, and the theme was usually rather high-spirited and tuneful. You will probably know the rondo theme from the last movement (finale) of Mozart's *Eine Kleine Nachtmusik* (Fig. 13.26).

Fig. 13.26

Could you write a rondo? It need not be too complicated; make a strong A theme as it has to be heard several times, and give variety by putting you episodes into a different key.

Binary form

As its name suggests, this form is built in two sections, both of which are usually repeated:

Section A : :||:   Section B : :||:

Section B is sometimes longer than section A, and there is often a modulation to a new key towards the ending of section A. The original key will return before the end of the piece.

Ternary form

This is built up in three sections: A B A.

The middle section provides a contrast, and the composer may decide to vary the second A section, but it will be based on the same music.

Some melodies are constructed in a simple ternary form, such as the tune *All through the Night* (Fig. 13.27)

Fig. 13.27 *All through the Night* – trad. Welsh tune

Ground bass

Sometimes also called Passacaglia, this is where a musical figure (the *ground*) is repeated many times over in the bass part while *harmony* and *melody* are added above. Purcell was a notable exponent of this structural device; his most famous example is 'Dido's Lament' from his opera *Dido and Aeneas*. An extract is given in Fig. 13.28.

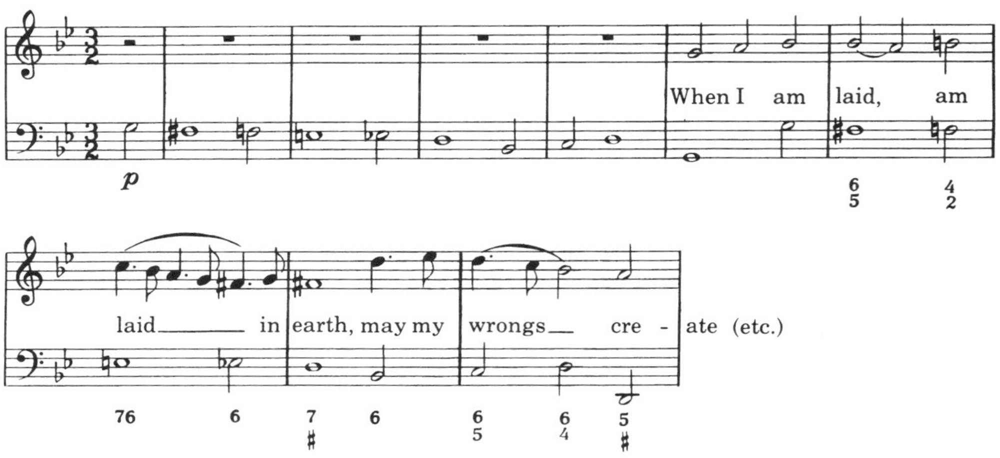

Fig. 13.28

In the extract, the bass part appears twice but the whole song contains nine consecutive statements of it. (Notice the figured bass – a musical shorthand for the harpsichordist).

The suite

A suite is a collection of dance movements. It was popular from the sixteenth to the eighteenth centuries, although the word is still used occasionally today by composers. Bach is regarded as one of the greatest composers of Suites. The most common movements with most early composers were the Allemande, Courante, Sarabande and Gigue. Between these last two movements were sometimes added a variety of other dances, such as a Gavotte or Polonaise, Bourrée etc. Most of these dance movements were in Binary form, and the same key was almost always used for each movement, with modulation within movements to provide variety.

You might consider writing a collection of short contrasted pieces, which you could group together as a suite. Any group of instruments will do, or it may be composed for just keyboard. Individual movements you might cast in Binary or Ternary Form, or you may like to try a set of short variations.

Sonata form

Sonata form is explained in Glossary 2 (Musical Words) and is illustrated in Chapter 14: (3) The Classical Period – Things to Do, no. 3. This is a most important musical form and you should try to understand it thoroughly, and apply this understanding by listening very carefully to symphonic movements that use Sonata Form. Try to note when musical subjects within the structure reappear – in the *Development* and *Recapitulation*.

▷ **General signs and symbols**

Most of the common Italian terms that you are likely to encounter are included in Glossary 2 at the end of this book. It still seems to be the custom to use Italian (although some composers prefer to use their native language). You should try to use appropriate markings in your compositions, so that you are communicating your intentions as clearly as possible in your notation. It is also important that you understand thoroughly the meanings of such words and terms when performing your solo and ensemble pieces.

Besides Italian, there are many signs that are useful in music. Some of the following you will probably know and use already, but it is a useful list for reference.

♩ = 120

A metronome marking, for measuring the speed of a piece. If ♩ = 60 represents one beat per second, then 120 must be two beats per second, and so on. Maelzel was the inventor of this clockwork device in the early nineteenth century. If you use a metronome for checking the suggested speed of your performance pieces, make sure that you read it correctly! Is it ♩ = 120 or ♩ = 120?

A crescendo marking; get louder.

A diminuendo marking; get softer.

Op.66

Optus 66 – the sixty-sixth work in a composer's catalogue of compositions.

Pause. (Written over a note:) Prolong the note at your discretion.

G.P.

General Pause. All performers must stop playing until indicated otherwise.

Repeat marks. Play the passage between the dots twice.

Ped. (or 𝔓𝔢𝔡.)

Use the right (sustaining) pedal on a piano.

Up bow for string players.

Down bow for string players.

Repeat this written note as eight semiquavers:

=  (More musical shorthand.)

𝄎 = repeat the previous bar.

Play an octave higher. The word 'loco' indicates a return to the ordinary pitch.

A double bar-line. Used to indicate the end of a piece or section. Also used when time signatures are changed e.g.: 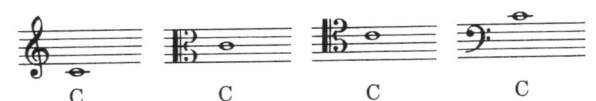 etc.

Staccato. Short, detached notes.

Staccatissimo. Very short notes.

Mezzo staccato. Half staccato, with a slight accent.

sf or fz

Sforzando. A short, forcefully accented note ( ).

gliss. or

Slide quickly from the lowest to the highest written notes. (For harp, trombone, piano etc.)

A slur. Play the notes smoothly and connected.

A tie. When two identical notes are joined, hold the second for its value without actually playing it.

Alto   Tenor
clef   clef

Alto and Tenor clefs – sometimes known as C clefs. The alto clef is used by the viola while the trombone, cello and bassoon occasionally use the tenor clef. The line indicated by the clef is middle C, so:

    C   C   C   C

are all the same pitch.

SATB

Choral music can be written out in two ways. The short score uses two staves, so that sopranos and altos share a stave, and the same with tenors and basses:

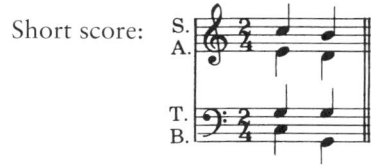

Short score:

(Notice how the usual way of drawing stems on notes has to be changed so that they fit clearly on the music.)

The more normal way is to use full score, that is, four staves:

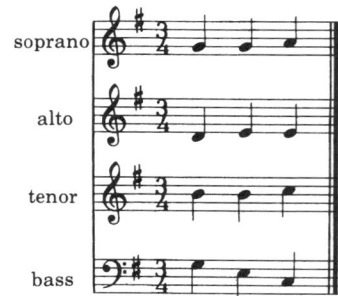

(Notice how the tenor voices use the treble clef. (They sound an octave lower.)

Guitar chords

Some of you may wish to teach yourself guitar so that you can join in the Ensembles. Fig. 13.29 gives you some of the common chords that you are likely to encounter. The small 'm' indicates that it is a minor chord; so that Em = E minor chord. The dots represent a finger position on the strings, and the cross indicates that you should not play on that string.

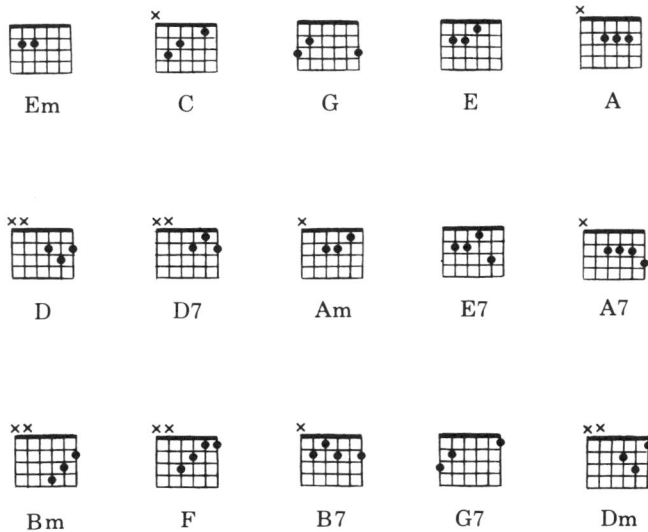

Em   C   G   E   A

D   D7   Am   E7   A7

Bm   F   B7   G7   Dm

Fig. 13.29

Chord sequences to practise

Beginners could try these as useful practice. More advanced players may find them helpful as chord progressions for a possible composition or improvisation:

(1) C   Am   Em   D   G7   C
(2) G   D   Am   Em   C   F   D7   G
(3) D   C   F   G   Am   Em   A7   D

▷ **Transposing instruments**

If you have used an orchestral score when studying your set work you may have wondered why some instrumental parts have different key signatures. Fig. 13.30 shows how Elgar sets out the instruments for the opening of his *Symphony No.1* in A♭ major (1908).

You will notice that the majority of instruments, whether treble or bass, use the 'correct' key signature of four flats for A♭ major. These instruments are said to be in Concert Pitch. The remainder are called transposing instruments; in other words, the notes seen and played sound at a different pitch. For example, a clarinet in B♭ reading [musical notation] will actually sound the note [musical notation]. The part is written one whole tone higher than it actually sounds.

Why is this the case? Surely it would be easier for all concerned if they were all the same? It stems from the early days of woodwind instruments when it was virtually impossible for clarinettists to play music with many sharps and flats. To make things easier for them, instrument makers produced clarinets in different sizes, which transposed into different keys. There are three types of clarinet in use today, the orchestral B♭ and A clarinets, and the smaller E♭ clarinet which is used mainly in military bands and occasionally in the orchestra.

You will read in Chapter 4, how brass players, in the days before valves had been invented, had to use the natural notes (harmonics) on their brass tubing. If they wished to change key, they had to insert 'crooks' of different lengths to raise or lower the overall pitch of their instrument. They always read in the key of C; if the music was in the key of D, they inserted a D crook. This is why brass parts of that time are based on a limited series of notes; players could not easily change crooks until the end of a movement. Today we have the fully-chromatic valved trumpet, but it is still a transposing instrument as it is usually built in B♭.

The golden rule with transposing instruments is that **written C sounds the letter name of the instrument** and you can then adjust all other notes accordingly.

So for the A clarinet, for example, written C sounds the A a minor third below: [musical notation] sounds [musical notation]

This is certainly confusing for the young musician confronted with this concept for the first time, but is something that experienced musicians get used to. Clarinet players in an orchestra usually take their A clarinets with them as well as their normal B♭s, so that they can swap over before a piece with awkward fingering. Trumpeters, however, are quite used to transposing at sight – so that they might well be using a B♭ instrument in a piece in E major and have to put the music up into F# major (a tone higher, and now into six sharps!). It is a skill which players of transposing instruments acquire with practice.

Here is a list of the main transposing instruments:

Piccolo:	sounds an octave higher than actually written
Clarinet in B♭:	written a tone higher than it sounds
Clarinet in A:	written a minor 3rd higher than it sounds
Bass Clarinet in B♭:	written a major 9th higher than it sounds
Cor Anglais in F:	written a perfect 5th higher than it sounds
Alto sax in E♭:	written a major 6th higher than it sounds
Tenor sax in B♭:	written a major 9th higher than it sounds
Horn in F:	written a perfect 5th higher than it sounds
Trumpet in B♭:	written a tone higher than it sounds
Double bass:	written an octave higher than it sounds

[Orchestral score layout showing instrument staves with key signatures:]
Flutes 1/2/3 & Piccolo
Oboes 1/2
Cor Anglais
Clarinets 1/2 in B♭
Bass Clarinet in B♭
Bassoon 1/2
Double Bassoon
Horns 1/2/3/4 in F *
Trumpets 1/2/3 in B♭
Trombones 1/2/3 & Tuba
3 Timpani *
Harp
1st Violins
2nd Violins
Violas
Cellos
Double Basses

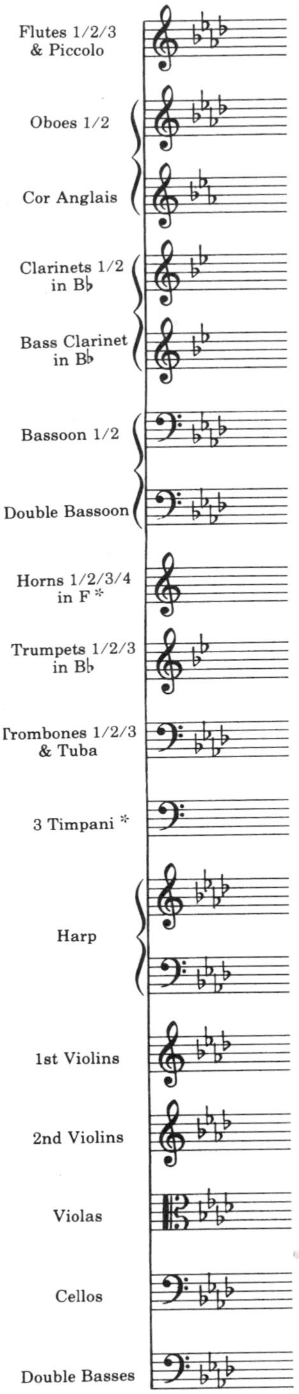

*It is the custom not to use key signature with horns and timpani.

Fig. 13.30

▶ PRACTICE QUESTIONS

These are not examination questions as such. They are given so that you can test yourself once you have studied this theory chapter. Remember that you will probably apply this knowledge with a real piece of music in any section of the exam. If you find any part of this difficult, be sure to ask your teacher to help you sort it out.

▷ **Question 1**

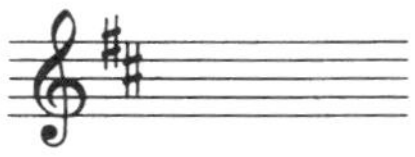

Fig. 13.31

(a) Name the major key that uses this key signature.
(b) Name the minor key that uses this key signature.
(c) Where would you write the same key signature into the bass clef?
(d) What major key has: (i) 4 flats; (ii) 3 sharps; (iii) 2 flats; (iv) 3 flats?
(e) What minor key has: (i) 3 flats; (ii) 2 flats; (iii) 3 sharps; (iv) 4 flats?
(f) What is the relative minor scale of: (i) E flat major; (ii) F major; (iii) D major?

▷ **Question 2**

Fig. 13.32

(a) How fast should this tune be played?
(b) How many beats in a bar?
(c) What type of rests are used in bars 3 and 4?
(d) What key is the piece in? (**Remember:** key signature first, then look for any accidentals).
(e) Explain how the ornaments in bars 1 and 4 are to be played.
(f) What intervals are used between the two notes marked at 1, 2, and 3?

▷ **Question 3**

Fig. 13.33

(a) Name two instruments capable of playing this music.
(b) What key is it in? How do you know?
(c) How fast would it go?
(d) How many beats in a bar here?

▷ **Question 4**

Fig. 13.34

(a) What instrument is likely to play this?
(b) How fast should it go?

(c) Explain 'con sord'.
(d) Describe the interval formed between the lowest and the highest notes of this short tune.
(e) What major key is it in? How do you know it is not a minor key?
(f) Using some manuscript paper, write it out in the treble clef at the same pitch.

▷ **Question 5**

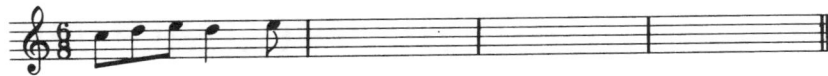

Fig. 13.35

Copy this out on to some manuscript paper four times.
Complete the melody using the notes from:

 (i) the pentatonic scale based on C;
 (ii) C major;
 (iii) A minor;
 (iv) the whole tone scale based on C.

Make sure that you use the given 6/8 time correctly, and that you end all four examples on the appropriate tonic.

▷ **Question 6**

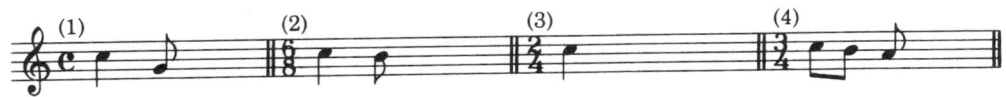

Fig. 13.36

Look at Fig. 13.36 and then complete it with the correct rests.

▷ **Question 7**

Fig. 13.37

Put in the correct time signatures in Fig. 13.37.

▷ **Question 8**

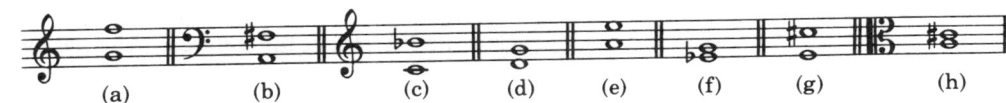

Fig. 13.38

Fig. 13.38 gives some further examples of intervals for you to describe. (Be careful to note changes of clef.)

▷ **Question 9**   Transpose the melody in Fig. 13.39 so that it would be suitable for: (i) B♭ clarinet; (ii) Horn in F; (iii) B♭ trumpet; (iv) Cor anglais; (v) Clarinet in A; (vi) Alto sax in E♭.

Fig. 13.39

ANSWERS TO PRACTICE QUESTIONS

▷ **Answer 1**   (a) D major
(b) B minor
(c)

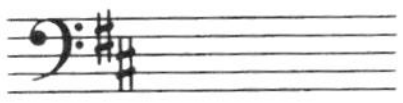

Fig. 13.40

(d) (i) A♭ (ii) A (iii) B♭ (iv) E♭
(e) (i) C minor (ii) G minor (iii) F# minor (iv) F minor
(f) (i) C minor (ii) D minor (iii) B major

▷ **Answer 2**   (a) ♩ = 96 crotchets per minute. Use a metronome to check different speeds.
(b) 𝄴 = 4 ♩ beats in a bar.
(c) ⌐ = a quaver (½ beat) rest.
        𝄽 = a crotchet (1 beat) rest.
(d) A minor (because of the G#).
(e) The turn ∾ would be played as four semiquavers:

The inverted mordent is played like this:

(f) (1) Perfect 5th (2) minor 6th (3) minor 3rd.

▷ **Answer 3**   (a) Piano or harp, because of the wide range of notes requiring bass and treble clef, and the long slide between the first two notes.
(b) E minor, because of the accidental D#.
(c) ♩. = 120. 2 dotted crotchet beats per second.
(d) 2 dotted crotchet beats in a bar.

▷ **Answer 4**   (a) The viola because it is the only instrument to use the alto clef.
(b) ♩ = 84. Use a metronome to check the speed.
(c) Use a mute (in full: con sordino).
(d) B♭ – F = a perfect 5th.
(e) B♭ major. There is no F# – the leading note for the relative key of G minor.
(f)

Fig. 13.41

▷ **Answer 5**   The bar given was designed to contain notes common to the four scales. Obviously, there are many ways of completing a melody, but remember the following:

(i) Pentatonic: use only C D E G A, ending on C;
(ii) C major: use C D E F G A B C, ending on C;
(iii) A minor: use A B C D E F G# A, ending on A;

(iv) Whole tone scale: use C D E F# G# A#, ending on C. This version will sound the most unusual with only four bars in the given exercise, but try experimenting with the scale. You may like to extend this one.

▷ **Answer 6**

Fig. 13.42

▷ **Answer 7**   (1) 6   (2) 2   (3) 4   (4) 9
              8   4   4   8

▷ **Answer 8**   (a) Minor 7th   (b) Major 6th   (c) Minor 7th
              (d) Perfect 4th (e) Perfect 5th (f) Major 3rd
              (g) Major 6th   (h) Major 3rd.

▷ **Answer 9**   To transpose a line of music higher or lower you must change the key signature as well. For example, if a melody in C major needs to be raised a tone into D major, you should first write in the appropriate key signature of two sharps and proceed to raise each note of the tune by one tone. Any accidentals will need to be altered so that the line remains parallel to the original. Don't assume that accidentals remain the same: e.g. B♭ raised a tone becomes C natural and C# lowered a tone becomes B natural.

(i) This needs to go up one whole tone, so our original key of G major now becomes A major with 3 sharps (Fig. 13.43).

Fig. 13.43

(ii) This needs to be written up a perfect fifth into the key of D major (see Fig. 13.44).

Fig. 13.44

(iii) The same as (i).
(iv) The same as (ii).
(v) This must be transposed up a minor third because that is the interval between A and C. B♭ major with 2 flats is a minor third above the original G major (see Fig. 13.45).

Fig. 13.45

(vi) Alto saxophones are written a major 6th higher than they sound, as that is the interval between E♭ and C. E major with 4 sharps is the key a major 6th above the original G major (Fig. 13.46).

Fig. 13.46

▷ **ANSWERS TO QUICK TEST**

Answers to the QUICK TEST intervals given on page 144, earlier in this chapter:

(a) Perfect 5th   (b) Minor 7th   (c) Minor 6th
(d) Augmented 4th   (e) Major 3rd   (f) Minor 3rd
(g) Major 6th   (h) Major 6th   (i) Minor 3rd
(j) Major 7th.

SUMMARY

▷ Learn key signatures (*thoroughly*, up to 4 sharps and flats).

▷ Know how to recognise a minor key: check the key signature first, then look along for extra accidentals in the music.

▷ Place the sharps/flats in the key signature correctly.

▷ Learn note and rest values.

▷ Make sure stems on notes are written correctly (♩ or ⌐?).

▷ Group notes correctly according to the time signature.

▷ Be able to recognise cadences by ear.

▷ Be familiar with the common musical ornaments.

▷ Know the familiar types of musical form.

▷ Have a working knowledge of transposing instruments (especially if you are composing for some of these, or are studying an orchestral set work).

History of music: 1550 to the present day

GETTING STARTED

This brief outline of the history of music starts in 1550. This is a date of convenience really, for by that time composers were writing music that is still widely heard today, and available in recorded form. Of course, there was a great deal of music before 1550 but notation was primitive, and not all musicians were able to write their compositions down. You may like to listen to some earlier music, for more and more is becoming recorded, but examination syllabuses rarely go much before our chosen date.

IGCSE	LONDON	MEG	NEAB	NICCEA	SEG	WJEC	TOPIC	STUDY	REVISION 1	REVISION 2
	✓	✓	✓	✓	✓	✓	1550–1600: The Late Renaissance Period			
✓	✓	✓	✓	✓	✓	✓	1600–1750: The Baroque Period			
✓	✓	✓	✓	✓	✓	✓	1750–1830: The Classical Period			
✓	✓	✓	✓	✓	✓	✓	1830–1900: The Romantic Period			
✓	✓	✓	✓	✓	✓	✓	1900 onwards: The Modern Period			
✓	✓	✓	✓	✓	✓	✓	Jazz			
✓	✓	✓	✓	✓	✓	✓	The world of Folk Music			
✓	✓	✓	✓	✓	✓	✓	The world of Popular Music			
✓	✓	✓	✓	✓	✓	✓	Summary			

> ## WHAT YOU NEED TO KNOW

> ### 1550–1600: The Late Renaissance Period

In the sixteenth century music was considered to be a highly important art. After the uncertainty of the so-called Dark Ages there was a rediscovery of culture and learning that had not been seen for many centuries. During this new period of Renaissance there was a burst of creativity in all the arts, and the music of this time attained a refined beauty and polish that make it a peak of artistic achievement of the last thousand years.

If you are only used to hearing music from later times, you may at first find sixteenth century music hard to understand. It tends to be *contrapuntal* and full of *imitation*; it was constructed with the old *modes*, for our more recent system of major and minor scales was yet undeveloped.

Listen to some sacred (religious) music by **Palestrina** or **Byrd**.

Palestrina was a master of contrapuntal composition, composing *masses*, *motets* and *magnificats*. He was chosen as a 'model' composer by the Council of Trent (1545–63), a committee convened by the Catholic Church to improve the state of church music. The Council considered that music was becoming too ornate and the words unintelligible as the voices were too interwoven; it was too worldly, as popular songs were often used as a 'theme' running through these interweaving parts. Only music of pure clarity was allowed; 'pure' implying that it was free of secular connections.

Byrd was a founder of the English school of *madrigal* writers, and also composed pieces for the *virginals*, but his church music perhaps represents his finest work. Try one of his three masses for unaccompanied voices, and notice how the vocal lines all merge beautifully with one another, and how the Latin words appear all mixed up together – but to glorious effect.

Besides church music, music in the home began to flourish. Madrigals by **Morley**, **Weelkes** and **Lassus** (to name but three) were sung in the wealthier homes, and *consorts* of instruments, such as recorders and viols had contrapuntal music written for them, as well as playing madrigals as instrumental pieces. Composers such as **Dowland** were beginning to write *art songs* with *lute* accompaniment. Keyboard instruments, such as the *virginals* and *spinet* became increasingly popular, and had attractive pieces by **Byrd**, **Gibbons**, and **Bull** composed for them.

Things to do

1. Listen to some sixteenth century religious music by Palestrina or Byrd – it doesn't really matter which piece you choose:
    (a) Is the tempo (speed) of the piece fast, moderately fast or slow? Does this tempo vary throughout the piece?
    (b) Can you understand the words? Are they sung in English, Italian or Latin? Find out what the words mean.
2. Listen to any madrigal from this period (preferably in English so that you can understand the words):
    (a) What is the mood of the madrigal? Is it bright and cheerful, relaxed or melancholy?
    (b) Is it about love? How does the composer express the words?
3. You may like to join a group of singers and try some madrigals. Some of the simpler ones can be performed with one singer to a line or part.

> 'Since singing is so good a thing,
> I wish all men would learn to sing.'
> (Byrd)

Try singing the madrigal *The Silver Swan* by Orlando Gibbons (set by WJEC for 1998) with a few friends. There is some evidence that it was originally a solo song with lute accompaniment, but as a madrigal it is set for SATBB, a five-part texture. Though less contrapuntal than many of its contemporary English and Italian madrigals, it provides a good, simple example of the madrigal idiom.

With its key signature of one flat it looks and feels much like the modern key of F major, but really it is in the Ionian mode (which corresponds to the white notes C–C on the piano) and transposed up a fourth. It modulates to the dominant at bars 10–11 ('against the reedy shore') and again at bars 17–18 ('death, come close mine eyes') which, unusually, gives this madrigal an almost Classical feel. It is also not usual practice for madrigalists to repeat music, as from bar 14 onwards (corresponding to bar 7 onwards); the overall structure is thus A (1–6) B (7–13) B (14–21).

4. These chords are extracted from the first line of the printed choral piece *Farewell, dear love*: Gm D B♭ F Dm Gm C D. Now use them as the harmonic basis for your own song in G minor. You need not change chords as quickly as Robert Jones, the original composer. For example, you could rearrange them like this:

$\frac{4}{4}$ Gm / / / | D / / / | B♭ / / / | F / / Dm | Gm / C / | D / / / :‖

Fig. 14.1

and then invent some new lyrics in a more modern style. You could soon have the basis of an attractive song – all grown from another, nearly four hundred years old!

5. Alternatively, use the Jones chord scheme as a recurring ostinato for an improvisation. Use spread arpeggios over the chords to maintain a sense of movement. You will need to finish with the tonic chord of G minor. Try an improvisation (i) exploring a feeling of sorrow, or (ii) entitled 'Farewell' – you may like to use these chords as the basis for a second section: F B♭ F Dm Gm D – G (major or minor).

6. Read up about the instruments of this period, and listen to further examples of consort music. Can you tell the difference between the sound of viols and the modern string family? Can you differentiate the various recorders? How does a lute differ from a Spanish guitar? Try to see inside a harpsichord and examine how the mechanism differs from a piano. When you listen to this early music, a live performance will be the most helpful as you can see everything that goes on, such as the frequent tuning of lutes and theorbos, for example. Failing this, choose the ensembles or choirs that specialise in the period. Here are some examples:

▶ **Vocal**
The Clerkes of Oxenford, director David Wulstan
The Hilliard Ensemble
Pro Cantione Antiqua
The Sixteen (choir and orchestra) director Harry Christophers
Monteverdi Choir (and orchestra) director John Eliot Gardiner

▶ **Instrumental**
Consort of Musicke, director Anthony Rooley
Jaye Consort of Viols
Musica Antiqua Koln (Cologne), director Reinhard Goebel
The New London Consort, director Philip Pickett
The Parley of Instruments, co-directors Peter Holman and Mark Caudle
Taverner Consort and Players (also with voices) director Andrew Parrott
Trevor Pinnock – solo harpsichord
The English Concert, director Trevor Pinnock.

7. For those who enjoy the music of this period and would like to find out more, try to find out about the following:
(a) Broken Consort; (b) the meaning of the word 'Renaissance'; (3) Fitzwilliam Virginal Book; (d) Viola da gamba; (e) Monteverdi (try the opening of his 'Vespers' 1610).

8. Obtain a copy of Thomas Morley's madrigal 'Now is the month of Maying' (set by WJEC for 1998) and try to hear a performance of it. Strictly speaking this is a Ballett – a type of madrigal which (as the name suggests) has a dance-like feel to it, and a fa-la refrain. This particular one is written for five parts: SATTB, and is mostly homophonic except for a few bars in the second half where the voices imitate each other contrapuntally. Notice the old-fashioned flavour to the words. Now try questions 1 and 2 in the practice questions section on p. 162.

9. Get to know *Though Amaryllis Dance* by William Byrd (also set by WJEC for 1998). This is written for SSATB (a five-part group of singers). Don't be put off (when listening) by the many repetitions of the words – it is great fun to sing when all the parts seem to chase each other. The words are typical of the period. Now try questions 3 and 4 in the practice questions section on p. 162.

Practice questions with answers

The following two questions refer to Thomas Morley's madrigal 'Now is the month of Maying' (see *Things to do*, no. 8 on p. 161).

Question 1
How does Morley produce variety in this piece?

Question 2
What structure does he use?

Questions 3 and 4 refer to 'Through Amaryllis Dance' by William Byrd (see *Things to Do*, no. 9 on p. 161).

Question 3
How is the dance-like mood produced in this madrigal?

Question 4
How does Byrd use his five-part choir?

Answer 1
By using a mixture of homophonic and contrapuntal textures, and by varying the dynamics for each repeated section.

Answer 2
Strophic form – each of the three verses uses the same music. Each verse is constructed as A A B B.

Answer 3
By strongly rhythmic contrapuntal melody lines which interlock with each other, producing a lively dance feel. To give just one example, the agile bass line in bars 4 and 5 'dances' along, fitting under the different rhythms above it.

Answer 4
The composer does not use his five voice parts all the time. Indeed, the first two bars are for the three lower parts alone. Using five parts (instead of a straightforward SATB) allows greater variety in the compositional texture. Notice how sophisticated the overall rhythmic effect is when the individual strands all fit together. Bar 14, for instance, has four different rhythms at the same time, with the soprano line producing a cross-rhythm against the two lower parts.

▷ 1600–1750 The Baroque Period

The word 'Baroque' is borrowed from architecture, where it suggests the elaborate twisting of the sometimes excessively decorated buildings of that time. Similarly, Baroque music is often full of ornaments and decorations.

This was a time of great change in music. By about the end of the seventeenth century the outdated modes had been replaced by our familiar major and minor scales, and harmony, as we know it, had started to develop. The viols became obsolete, and the more versatile violin family took their place. The great violin makers, **Stradivarius**, **Amati** and **Guarneri** flourished at this time.

Music was written to order in those days and composers all worked for a patron. This might be the church, where they were employed to provide all the music for church services; or a wealthy nobleman, where they were paid to entertain him and his guests at important social functions. King Louis XIV of France, for example, employed the composer **Lully** as his court composer.

There was a distinct move away from the sort of vocal music that Palestrina and Byrd had written in earlier times. Gradually, the melodic interest moved up to the top vocal line, and there was an effort to make the words become more distinct in themselves, and to write music which illustrated their meaning more dramatically.

The composer **Giovanni Gabrieli** and his uncle **Andrea Gabrieli** were, in their time, both organists at St Mark's in Venice. The splendid acoustics of this spacious building were exploited by these composers when they divided up their vocal and instrumental forces to form *antiphonal* effects. (This had a direct influence on the development of the later concerto principle, where forces were separated, instead of having one body of sound. This started with the concerto grosso and moved to the solo concerto in the late Baroque and Classical eras. This also had major implications for the concept of drama in music, in both vocal and instrumental spheres.)

A new invention, to be known as *opera*, started in Florence about the year 1600. The first operas were very different from the large-scale spectacles of modern times. They were largely recitative, with some arias and choruses. Although first produced in private homes, the first public opera house opened in Venice in 1637. The first audiences came to prefer the arias, for these were expressive and often showy pieces; people were drawn by a particular performer rather than the plot or even the music itself. A basso continuo was played throughout the opera by a harpsichord player, often supported by a cello. To save the composer from writing out every note, the harpsichordist would read from a figured bass.

Monteverdi is regarded as the first great composer of opera. He is accredited as the first composer to use *tremolando* on the violin as a dramatic effect, and he used a variety of instruments to accompany his operas – not yet the orchestra as we know it today, but certainly the foundation, a mixture of different tone colours, was being laid. Later in the century, **Alessandro Scarlatti** was the chief Italian composer of operas, but they are not often performed today, as they contain many arias in the lengthy *da capo* form and the plots are unacceptable to modern audiences.

The French composer **Couperin** wrote suites for the *harpsichord*, which gradually superseded the virginals and spinet. These suites contained stylised dances, often in binary or rondo form. Like **Corelli**, the English composer **Purcell** wrote trio-sonatas for two violins and the obligatory continuo (cello and harpsichord). Besides much church music, keyboard pieces and music for plays, he wrote only a single opera, *Dido and Aeneas*, as opera took longer to establish as a form of entertainment in England than on the continent.

The two great composers of the later Baroque period were undoubtedly **Bach** and **Handel**, both born in 1685 in Germany. You should familiarise yourself with as much of their music as you can – it is often strong and strident music, and if you are able to play or sing Bach or Handel you will realise how beautiful and enjoyable it all is. Notice how the Baroque principle of 'one movement, one mood' applies here, it is certainly expressive and full of feeling, but far less changeable than the music of, say, a hundred years later.

Bach

Coming from a large extended musical family, Bach lived and worked all his life as organist and kappelmeister within one area of Germany. A devoted family man (he was the father of twenty children!), he combined a strong and simple religious faith with a no-nonsense approach to life. After several organist posts he settled in Leipzig in 1723 as Cantor (head of music) at St Thomas' Church, where he taught and trained the choirboys, and provided music for the church services. His vast output includes the six Brandenburg concertos, four orchestral suites, the forty-eight Preludes and Fugues for keyboard, the Mass in B minor, the 'St Matthew' and the 'St John' Passions, the Christmas Oratorio, various concertos and sonatas, and over 200 church cantatas. His organ music continues to form the basis of the organist's repertoire.

Handel

Unlike Bach, Handel was a well-travelled, and worldly-wise man, but most of the pieces for which he is remembered today were composed in England. He studied in Italy, mastering the art of writing operas, before settling in England in 1712 as the foremost composer of Italian operas of that period. However, Handel was forced to turn his attention to the composition of oratorios when the public demand for Italian opera declined. His most famous example of this form is the ever-popular *Messiah*, composed in just three weeks, and first performed in 1742. Other examples of this genre include *Samson*, *Israel in Egypt*, *Saul* and *Judas Maccabaeus*. Everyone knows the *Water Music* and the *Royal Fireworks Music*, but you should try to hear some of Handel's *concerti grossi* and organ concertos. Although he was the composer of many fine fugues, Handel's music tends to be rather less contrapuntal than Bach's, perhaps reflecting his obvious interest in the art of writing operatic melody, where the attention is focused on the top melodic line.

Scarlatti

Yet another composer was born in the same year as Bach and Handel – Domenico Scarlatti, the son of Alessandro. A travelling keyboard virtuoso who furthered the development of keyboard music, he is considered to be the greatest of harpsichord composers, producing more than 500 one-movement sonatas in binary form, paving the way for the piano sonatas of the Classical period.

Things to do

1. The melody in Fig. 14.2 is the main theme to the first movement of Bach's third Brandenburg Concerto. Play it several times. How many times does this rhythmic figure appear in the extract: [rhythmic figure]? And this one [rhythmic figure]? Why does C sharp appear in the second and third bars? (It denotes a brief modulation (key-change) to D major, the dominant). Now listen to a recording of the whole movement, noting how often the two figures are used. Notice that the mood does not change ('one movement, one mood').

Fig. 14.2

You might like to compose your own melody (or fuller piece) using the minimum amount of musical material. Try to keep your piece flowing as Bach does, and maintain your opening mood. Fig. 14.3 gives you some short figures to get you started:

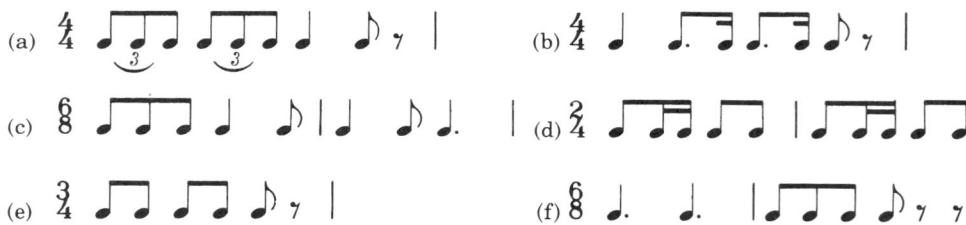

Fig. 14.3

Listen to other Baroque pieces and note how similar figures are developed.

Examples
(a) Bach 'Concerto for Two Violins' (third movement). See Fig. 14.4.

Fig. 14.4

(b) Handel 'Concerto Grosso' Op. 6 No. 1 (first movement). See Fig. 14.5

Fig. 14.5

Again, notice with these two pieces how the mood stays constant once established.

(c) Bach – Brandenburg Concerto No. 2 in F major. In the slow movement, the solo instruments (violin, oboe and flute) all take it in turns to develop this figure:

Fig. 14.6

and in the third movement, the high Baroque trumpet joins them in the rhythm:

Fig. 14.7

Try working out a theme of your own with similar rhythms.

2. You should be aware of the main types of Overture prevalent in the Baroque period: the *French Overture* and the *Italian Overture*.

(a) Listen to the Overture to Bach's Suite No. 2 in B minor (see No. 4 later in this section), or the Overture to Handel's oratorio *Messiah*. These two are examples of the so-called *French Overture*. There are usually two main sections. There is firstly a dignified slow section, characterised by dotted rhythms, often played as double dotted notes (see Fig. 14.8) although rarely written in this way. This is followed by a faster main section which is often in a fugal style (see No. 3 in this section for a better explanation of *Fugue*). Occasionally there is a brief restatement of the slow, dotted music to round off the Overture. The composer Lully, who was court composer to Louis XIV at Versailles, is associated with the early use of the French overture.

Fig. 14.8

(b) The *Italian Overture*, alternatively named 'Sinfonia', has three main sections:
  I a quick (*allegro*) section, which was often fugal;
  II a slow section (*adagio*);
  III another quick, dance-like section (*presto*).

The composer Alessandro Scarlatti is credited with the introduction of the Italian Overture, and used it in his many Italian operas. (With much development the Italian Overture led on to the Classical Symphony, as its 'quick – slow – quick' plan became enlarged into separate movements, and the Minuet was introduced as an additional movement. For a good example, try to listen to some of the short symphonies by **Thomas Arne**: No. 2 in F major recorded by Cantilena, conductor Adrian Shepherd, is an excellent one.

3. Make yourself familiar with the texture of fugue. Listen to any Bach Fugue for organ to see how it is composed. What exactly is fugue?

A fugue is a contrapuntal piece where the parts (always called voices, even in instrumental works) are highly imitative. It is a texture rather than a form, because no two fugues are alike after the opening (*exposition*).

A strand of melody (the *subject*) is played or sung unaccompanied in the tonic key. It is then imitated by a second voice, but in the dominant key this time (the *answer*). This answer can be 'real' if it imitates exactly, or a 'tonal' answer if it is an imitation with some slight changes. Likewise the third and fourth voices enter, tonic and then dominant. The entry of the voices may be in any order; the composer may choose. Fig. 14.9 is a plan of the start of a four-part fugue.

Once a voice has stated its subject or answer it continues immediately with another contrapuntal melody, known as the *counter-subject*, if each voice uses it. If not, it is generally known as a *free part*. Sometimes composers begin to state the subject, for example, when the fourth voice has reached its answer, and it then 'dries up'. This is called a *redundant entry*, and it gives the fourth voice the opportunity to state the counter-subject.

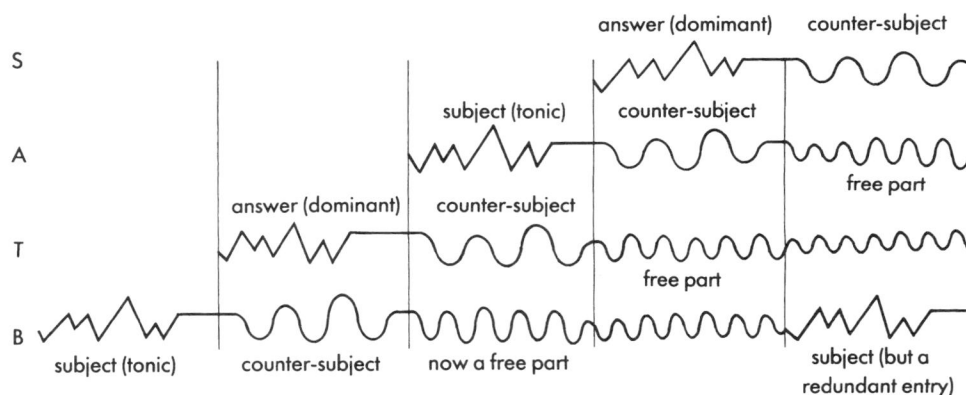

Fig. 14.9

Everything so far is part of the fugal exposition, as in sonata form where all the main themes are stated at the outset in the exposition. From this point on the composer is free to develop as he wishes. In the middle section of a fugue the composer may introduce the subject in related keys, usually avoiding the tonic; or he may introduce new ideas, which we call episodes, as a varied contrast to the subject. These episodes are often devised from a fragment of the original subject or counter-subject.

To round off the fugue satisfactorily, the subject will return again in the tonic key. The composer may decide to present it only once, or in several voices. After the last statement is made the coda brings the fugue to its conclusion.

4.   Obtain a good recording of Bach's Suite No. 2 in B minor for orchestra, and listen to the whole Suite carefully. It opens with a French Overture, which we used as an example in (2) above, and is followed by a set of shorter, stylised dances. The word *suite* today implies a set of short pieces, but Bach originally gave his four Suites for Orchestra the name *Ouverture*. He wrote No. 2 in Leipzig towards the end of the 1730s and scored it for flute, strings and harpsichord continuo. All seven items in this Suite are in the tonic key of B minor. Notice how the mood of each dance, once established, does not alter substantially. You may like to familiarise yourself with the whole Suite, but here we shall cover only the Overture, Rondeau, Sarabande, Menuet and Badinerie. (IGCSE for 1998 sets the Overture, Rondeau, Sarabande and Badinerie only.)

5.   You would enjoy listening to Bach's Suite No. 3 in D for orchestra. Whereas No. 2 is intimate in character, the third is more pompous and extrovert. Listen to Suite No.'s 2 and 3 and then try the following practice questions.

Practice questions with answers

The first four questions refer to Bach's Suite No. 2 in B Minor.

Question 1
How does Bach construct his Overture?   *(3)*

Question 2
Is the Rondeau (the second movement) a typical Rondo?   *(8)*

Question 3
What form does Bach use for both the Menuet and the Sarabande?   *(2)*

Question 4
Give a brief account of the Badinerie from Bach's Suite No. 2 in B minor.   *(5)*

The following questions refer to Suite No. 3 in D by Bach which is set by NICCEA for 1998. When you try these questions notice the mark weighting and make sure that the length and detail of your answer relates to this.

Question 5
Why is this piece called a Suite?   *(3)*

Question 6
Outline the movements and key scheme of Suite No. 3. *(4)*

Question 7
What is the instrumentation for this Suite? *(2)*

Question 8
Why did Bach choose the key of D major for this Suite? *(2)*

Answer 1
It is a French Overture, and has three sections: (a) slow with dotted rhythms in a solemn mood (b) a faster fugal secton in four parts and (c) a return to the slow section, again with dotted rhythms, which serves as a coda to the Overture.

(**N.B.** It is important to notice that this question is worth only three marks, and so demands a fairly brief answer and you should not spend too long on it. If there were more marks available you should go into more detail, using information from 2 and 3 above. For an excellent analysis of this Overture see *Musical Forms* I by Roy Bennett, published Longman 1987.)

Answer 2
We normally think of a Rondo structure as A + B + A + C + A, where the main theme A is in the tonic key, and the contrasting episodes B and C are thematically different as well as being in keys other than the tonic. In Bach's *Rondeau*, the episodes contain references to the main rondo theme, which is rather unusual (see Fig. l4.10).

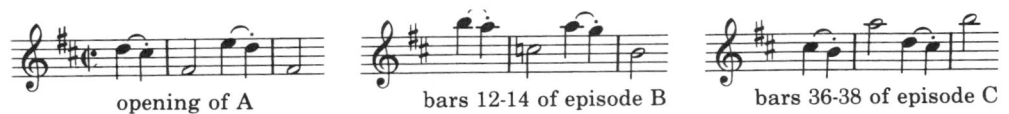

opening of A   bars 12-14 of episode B   bars 36-38 of episode C

Fig. 14.10

The contrast in this Rondeau is one of key more than one of melody. Episode B is in E minor, and episode C passes through the keys of A major, D major and F# minor. In answer to the question, therefore, this is a Rondo, but not a Rondo as in the later Classical style where the episodes would be thematically different.

Answer 3
They are both in binary form (A + B).

Answer 4
This lively piece in B minor acts as the finale to the seven movement Suite. The French title implies a frivolous and happy mood. The flute part is difficult – there are a lot of notes and the mood must remain light. The piece is constructed in binary form, where the basic dancing arpeggio figure is used in both sections (Fig. 14.11).

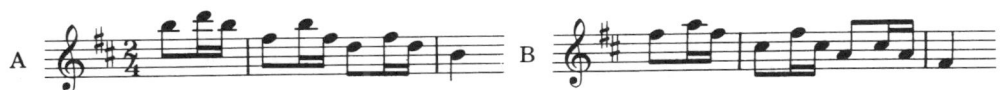

Fig. 14.11

The second half of the movement commences in F# minor (the dominant) and the tonic key returns finally in bar 32. There are only forty written bars, but each section is repeated, making a total of eighty bars in all. This fast-moving piece has something of the atmosphere which Mendelssohn perfected a hundred years later in his music to *A Midsummer Night's Dream*.

Answer 5
There are four Orchestral Suites by Bach, but the title is misleading, for in the Baroque days a collection of dance movements could have been entitled *Suite*, *Overture* or *Partita*. Bach's own title for his Orchestral Suites is actually *Ouverture*, but these works are best called suites (or partitas!) because they consist of an overture followed by a suite of dances.

Answer 6
1.   Ouverture: (Grave) D major – Vivace – Grave (repeat = Vivace – Grave)
2.   Air in D major
3.   Gavottes I and II in D major
4.   Bourree in D major
5.   Gigue in D major (6/8 time)

Answer 7
Two oboes, three trumpets, timpani and strings, with harpsichord continuo. The Air, however, is scored for first and second violins, violas and continuo only.

Answer 8
When Baroque composers wanted to include trumpets, which were in those days valveless and generally pitched in D, they wrote in that key.

▷ 1750–1830 The Classical Period

The word 'classical' is often loosely used when describing any music that is not pop or jazz but applied strictly, it refers to this short period of musical history which was dominated by Viennese composers. Indeed, Vienna was so important that we sometimes refer to this time as the Viennese period. **Haydn, Mozart, Beethoven** and **Schubert** were all concerned with Vienna, which was then undoubtedly the musical capital of Europe, and remained so for about a hundred years.

Composers were now using less counterpoint in their music; fugues were occasionally written, but far less than in Baroque times. *Sonata form* evolved in this period, and the *symphony* and *concerto* (not to be confused with the concerto grosso which phased out), *string quartet* and *piano sonata* were developed, and the modern *symphony orchestra* was born. Continuo parts were less used, and the *piano* eventually superseded the harpsichord. Schubert composed many art songs (*lieder*) and **Weber** created the first German operas.

This seems a lot to happen in a short time, but things evolved gradually, rather than appearing overnight. Haydn and Mozart perfected the new sonata form in their symphonies, climaxing the work of earlier, overshadowed composers. Classicism in music emphasises *order* and *form*, *gracefulness* and *beauty*, and it avoids the excessive emotion that was to be so apparent in music later, in the next century.

Haydn

Haydn and Mozart had great respect for each other's work, and were good friends, despite the age difference, but led very different lives. Haydn, from a humble background, sang as a choirboy at St Stephen's Cathedral in Vienna, and spent most of his working life in the service of the wealthy Esterhazy family. There he composed, and even dressed to order, and directed the orchestra and singers. In later life he travelled around Europe, thanks to his employer's generous pension, composing prolifically and enjoying his deserved success. Listen to some of the later symphonies (there is a grand total of 104 altogether), or part of his oratorio *The Creation*; his string quartets are rewarding to listen to, and everyone enjoys the Trumpet Concerto.

Mozart

In contrast, Mozart was much more of a free spirit. Having been taken all over Europe as a child prodigy by his father, Mozart found it hard to settle down as an adult. As a young man he had worked in the service of the Archbishop of Salzburg, but came to hate the system of patronage, which he equated with slavery. Once he was dismissed, in 1781, he became completely freelance and found it very difficult making ends meet. He wrote an enormous amount of music in his short life (he died at thirty-five), but was not really appreciated until after his death. You should listen to extracts of his operas: *The Marriage of Figaro* perhaps, or *Don Giovanni*, which are certainly operatic masterpieces. You are sure to enjoy his concertos – for piano, or violin or french horn, and you should get to know the last three symphonies (nos. 39–41), which were composed in less than six weeks in 1788. Remember when you listen to some of his late music, that it was composed at a time of great insecurity for him, and financial struggle, yet it shows tremendous calm and beauty.

Beethoven

Beethoven and Schubert were to link the Classical period of music to the *Romantic*. Their early music shows the strong influence of Haydn and Mozart, as you might expect, but they developed their own ideas and styles as they matured, their works increasingly showing their innermost feelings. Beethoven's so-called 'middle period', from about 1800, was a time of developing mastery. His works became more majestic (listen to the 'Eroica' Symphony, No. 3, or the famous fifth symphony (see Chapter 4, Analysis 4) and the beautiful E flat major 'Emperor' Piano Concerto). You will recognise his love of nature in the 'Pastoral' Symphony, No. 6. Beethoven had settled in Vienna by this time, leaving his native Bonn for good. Although he was never directly employed by the aristocracy or church, he had many wealthy acquaintances and survived by teaching, giving concerts and dedicating his music to his patrons.

Increasing deafness was a major problem for him, forcing him to give up his piano playing in public and eventually his conducting, but he continued to compose. His last period of composition, from about 1820, produced some incredibly personal works, demanding enormous concentration of the listener. It includes the last five string quartets, the magnificent Mass in D and his ninth and last symphony, the 'Choral', with its innovation of using voices in the last movement. This was a setting of Schiller's *Ode to Joy*, and expresses a striving for the heights of happiness.

It had been Haydn who added the Minuet as a regular third movement in sonatas and symphonies; Beethoven later substituted the faster, and often lighter Scherzo for the Minuet. He often expanded the coda compared to Haydn and Mozart, and made it an important feature of the composition. Beethoven would deviate from the usual four movements in his sonatas – there are examples in two, three, four and five movements. He would sometimes add a slow introduction, and at other times link movements together. Instruments in his lifetime were continually being improved, so he experimented with re-groupings within the orchestra, which has not radically changed to this day.

Schubert

Schubert was twenty-seven years younger than Beethoven, and lived in the great man's shadow in Vienna all of his short life. He was a very prolific composer – he wrote nine symphonies, keyboard pieces, and much fine chamber music, but he is best remembered for his development of the art song, or *lied*. Six hundred examples exist: many with fine melodies, but they are particularly satisfying because the piano accompaniment was by now regarded as an equal counterpart to the voice, often capturing the intimate atmosphere of the poem being set. Listen to *The Erl-King*, for example, where the piano represents the galloping of the horse, yet at the same time encapsulates the sinister mood of the poem.

Weber

Weber wrote piano and chamber music, and some orchestral music including three clarinet concertos, but is important for his German operas. *Der Freischutz*, first produced in Berlin, is considered to be the first romantic opera and contains chivalrous and supernatural elements based on an old German legend. *Euryanthe*, first heard in Vienna, had a weaker libretto and is less often heard. Finally, *Oberon* (set by WJEC for 1998 as a detailed study), composed for performance in London (where he died at the early age of forty in 1826) depicts fairyland, based on *A Midsummer Night's Dream* by Shakespeare.

Things to do

1.   Get hold of a collection of Mozart and Haydn Piano Sonatas – it doesn't matter which ones you choose. Examine the sort of accompaniments that are used by these Classical composers. They are rather fond of the so-called 'Alberti Bass', a recurring broken-chord (*arpeggio*) figure, such as in Fig. 14.12.

Fig. 14.12

Alberti bass does not always need to be in the bass clef, as you can see from the first two examples, it simply provides a flowing part to which a melody was added. Fig. 14.13 shows an example by Mozart.

Mozart: Piano Sonata in C (2nd movt.) K.279

Fig. 14.13 Mozart: Piano Sonata in C (2nd movt) K. 279

2. Perhaps you might compose a keyboard piece (in your own style) using broken chords as part of your accompaniment. Remember, it can become very tedious if you are not careful. Mozart was clever in the way that he subtly changed the shape of the figure, perhaps also passing it from one hand to the other, thus avoiding monotony and dullness. Make sure that you do the same!

3. Listen to the first movement of Mozart's *Eine Kleine Nachtmusik*. Meaning literally, 'A Little Night Music', this is his most well-known serenade – a set of four movements in relaxed mood for string orchestra.

     This first movement is in Sonata Form, and is a useful movement to help you understand the workings of this important Classical structure.

     Exposition: Fig. 14.14 is the first subject in G major, a vigorous theme made from arpeggios (broken chords), as was common with Mozart.

Fig. 14.14

The bridge passage, or transition (see Fig. 14.15) leads from the tonic key of G major into the dominant key (notice the C sharp, which confirms D major).

Fig. 14.15

Fig. 14.16 is the 2nd subject in D major.

Fig. 14.16

Notice the contrast in style and mood this makes with the first subject. A *codetta* (a short rounding-off section) completes this exposition. The repeat of the exposition may be ignored – it is left to the discretion of the conductor. *Development*: at first Mozart uses the strong opening of the first subject, but then develops the second part of the second subject (Fig. 14.17).

first subject now in D

f (based on Fig. 14.14)

p second subject
(based on Fig. 14.16b))

Fig. 14.17

As is quite common with Mozart this is a fairly short development section, and soon leads into the *Recapitulation*: first subject as in Fig. 14.14. The bridge passage starts the same as Fig. 14.15, but changes this time (Fig. 14.18) so that the second subject will start in the tonic key of G major, as was the custom.

Fig. 14.18 (compare this with Fig. 14.16a)

The *coda* is made to be rather longer than the codetta, and brings the movement to a very lively end. When you have read this carefully, listen several times to the movement to let it all sink in. **Remember**, *Sonata Form* is a structure used in symphonies, sonatas, concertos and chamber music. You should understand it thoroughly.

4. Listen to some String Quartets by Haydn, Mozart, Beethoven or Schubert, and familiarise yourself with the texture of this important Classical medium. Choose later works by Haydn and Mozart where all four stringed instruments are treated equally.

5. Listen to Schubert's Piano Quintet in A major (*The Trout*).

   If you have read through the preceding history sections and taken heed of the suggested things to do, you will be familiar by now with a wide range of music, from early madrigals and church music up to the standard classical structures. You will probably have heard some other chamber music before you listen to this work by Schubert, so it should not feel too 'new' for you.

   Instead of an analysis of this movement, here are some ideas for your own research which will help you to understand the piece and something of its background:

   (a) Why is this piano quintet called *The Trout* (or *Die Forelle* in German)?
   (b) Do you find the combination of piano, violin, viola, cello and double bass a satisfactory one for chamber music? It is actually an unusual grouping of instruments; which is the 'intruder' into chamber music? Is this unfounded? Should this instrument be used more often in this way?
   (c) Which is the most common ensemble of instruments for chamber music?
   (d) You are told the form of the 4th movement; how many variations does Schubert compose here?
   (e) How does Schubert treat each variation in this 4th movement? Consider each one separately. Is the theme present in each? Does he change key, or time, or speed? Which instruments are prominent?
   (f) Does Schubert use much counterpoint in these variations? If so, where?
   (g) Find out, briefly, about Schubert's life. Be aware of his life and times and the type of music writing and music making prevalent in that period.
   (h) Was Schubert an originator (devising new musical styles and ideas); or was he a per- fecter (summing-up or perfecting existing ways of composition)?
   (i) What sort of music did Schubert compose? Have some idea of his output and where *The Trout* quintet appears – early, middle or late in his career.
   (j) Can composers be more expressive when writing for only a few players? If so, why and how?

Practice questions

Having worked out your own ideas about chamber music, and listened carefully to these movements of *The Trout* quintet several times, answer the following GCSE-style questions:

Question 1
Name the instruments that are required for this quintet.   *(2)*

Question 2
How many variations are there in the 4th movement?   *(1)*

Question 3
Which variation is played in the minor key?   *(3)*

Question 4
Write a brief commentary on the last variation, explaining how Schubert makes
use of *The Trout* theme.   *(6)*

Question 5
Write a programme note for the 1st movement. In your answer refer to keys, textures
and anything that is of interest to a listener who may be hearing it for the first time.   *(12)*

1550–1830 – a final statement

This concludes only the third of the eight historical sections in this chapter, but before you proceed, it might be a good idea to reflect for a moment. Factual information of this sort has no value for its own sake. You are not a good musician just because you can remember intricate details of composers, pieces and dates. The main purpose in studying in this analytical and historical way is to gain a further insight into a piece so that we might understand it better and enjoy it more. Ideally, music should not have to be 'translated' into words; but once we have accepted that music is an examinable subject, we have to assess your responses to music by using words – we cannot measure your feelings.

Many people enjoy learning facts about music and there is nothing wrong with that. However, don't lose sight of the fact that music is all about sounds and expression and was never composed to give examination candidates something to study! It is a good thing that the GCSE boards recognise that an acquaintance with Italian terms, staff notation and so on, are only ways of increasing our awareness of how music works. The ability to express ourselves satisfactorily as a performer, or to respond sensitively as a listener must come from within ourselves.

1830–1900 The Romantic Period

In this period, composers showed less interest in the formal, or structural side of music, and began to emphasise the imaginative, and more emotional side. Art often reflects life; as Europe became more democratic, and power was removed from the aristocracy, so composers were influenced by this new belief in freedom. The Romantic composers were inspired by things outside music: landscape, literature, and the supernatural, for instance. Their music became more descriptive (see *Programme* music), often with unusual titles; the orchestra grew much bigger throughout the century as instruments were developed and improved.

Mendelssohn

We have seen how Beethoven and Schubert straddled two periods; some later composers wrote pieces that seemed Classical in outlook. Both **Mendelssohn** and **Schumann** certainly had Romantic attitudes, but composed in Classical forms. Mendelssohn helped to develop the concert overture – an overture that stands on its own. His *Hebrides* or 'Fingal's Cave' Overture is a good example for you to listen to. This sea-picture is cleverly suggestive of swell, storm and calm – yet is composed in traditional sonata form, where the rippling calm is the exposition and the storm is the development section. His oratorio *Elijah* (still very popular with choral societies today) was written at a time when composers wishing to write religious music were concentrating on large works for the concert hall rather than small-scale vocal pieces for use in church services.

Rossini

Rossini was the most outstanding opera composer of the earlier Romantic period. You might listen to parts of *William Tell* or *The Barber of Seville*: the overtures to these are particularly exciting.

The later Romantics

As the century progressed, Romantic music became more complex and abundant, and different styles emerged. The more conservative 'Classical' Romantics, such as **Brahms, Dvorak, Tchaikovsky** and **Bruckner** continued to write symphonies; the forward-looking Romantics – **Berlioz, Smetana, Liszt, Rimsky-Korsakov, Mussorgsky,** for example, turned to the *symphonic poem* (or *tone poem*), where they were unconstrained by the normal sonata form expected of a symphonist. Although there was not a great deal of religious music written, much fine chamber and piano music appeared. Nearly all of **Chopin**'s works were for piano, and Liszt wrote extremely difficult piano music to show off his prodigious technique.

There was a development of musical nationalism at this time. **Glinka, Borodin,** Mussorgsky, **Balakirev** and Rimsky-Korsakov in Russia, the Norwegian **Grieg,** and Smetana and Dvorak in Czechoslovakia – all tried to express the spirit and character of their own country by using its folk tunes and dances, and rhythmic idioms in their music.

Wagner was a sort of nationalist, using the old German legends of gods, heroes, giants and dwarfs as the background to his music dramas (as he preferred to call his operas). For Wagner, the ideal work of art had an equal unity between music, words, costume and set; he even wrote his own libretti. His vast 'Ring' cycle of four operas (*Der Ring des Nibelungen*) took a period of nearly twenty-five years to complete, and with the generous patronage of King Ludwig II of Bavaria, Wagner was able to build his own opera house in Bayreuth, Germany. Wagner used the *leitmotiv* – a continually recurring theme which is associated with a character, object or event. He also increased the size of the orchestra and was to be very influential as an orchestrator for a long time to come.

Another highly successful opera composer was the Italian **Verdi,** who was born in the same year as Wagner, 1813. Whereas Wagner was an operatic innovator, Verdi continued, at first, on the same Italian-style lines as his successful predecessors – Rossini, **Bellini** and **Donizetti** – approaching opera through the voice, with a more subservient orchestra; this was the converse to Wagner, who conceived opera as being, in musical terms, a union of voice and orchestra.

You should try to hear an opera by Verdi or Wagner – preferably in the opera house! It will be a very memorable experience.

Practice questions, notes and answers

Here are some specimen London questions on Berlioz's *Le Carnival Romain* Overture, which is a set work for study by London for 1998. Read through the questions and the notes which follow before you start your answers.

Question 1

Turn, in your score, to bar 37 where the violas repeat the cor anglais theme. Listen from this bar up to bar 53. After listening to the extract, answer these questions:
(a) What is the key at bar 37?   *(1)*
(b) Name the instruments which play the counter-melody at:
    (i) bars 41–43;
    (ii) bars 45–48.   *(3)*
(c) Write notes on the texture and instrumentation of the accompaniment.   *(6)*

Question 2

Write a description of the section from the beginning of the Allegro Vivace section (bar 78) to bar 127. Refer to themes, keys, instrumentation and any other important musical elements.   *(20)*

Notes

▷   By now it should be apparent that you need to know your chosen work very well indeed; you must be prepared to answer a wide range of short questions on it. This overture is 440 bars long; it is unlikely that you will be asked in detail about a very long extract, but you will need to know it all.

▷   Read the questions several times, noting the exact wording. What are they asking you? In question 2 you are specifically asked to mention themes, keys and instrumentation, but there is scope within the question ('and any other important musical elements') for you to elaborate further.

▷   For a larger question (i.e. question 2, worth 20 marks), list the points that you want to include in rough before you begin your answer. This will help you to decide on the content and how you can best arrange it into paragraphs. Then read the question once more.

Now, attempt the questions, then compare your answers with the model answers that follow.

Tutor's answers

Answer 1

(a)   E major (A new key signature of four sharps, and the chord of E G# B = E major.

(b)   (i)   1st flute and 1st clarinet play a counter-melody; the 1st bassoon is playing another counter-melody to the viola theme.

(ii)   Cor anglais (corno inglese).

(c)   From bar 37 to bar 53 the texture is quite thin or it would cover the undoubled solo viola melody. The accompaniment up to bar 44 is a simple effect of semi-quaver pairs (on the beat) in the strings answered back on the off-beat by the second clarinet and three of the horns. The counter-melody (see (b) above) adds richness to this soft accompaniment. Bar 44 has more wind semiquavers to lead to the cor anglais counter-melody at bar 45. The upper wind play soft repeated semiquavers behind the viola and cor anglais melodies, while the first violins play an off-beat descending single-quaver pizzicato figure. Bar 50 has a sudden crescendo up to bar 51 (*sf*) and comes back down to a soft level in bar 52, leading to the new section at bar 53. The *sf* (sforzando) chord in bar 51 has extra instrumentation: four horns and the pair of wide-ranging bassoons.

Answer 2

This overture (1844) is based on a saltarello from an earlier opera, *Benvenuto Cellini* (1838). A saltarello is a lively type of Italian dance and the opening of *Roman Carnival* uses this 6/8 A major melody to create an immediate lively impression to the lengthy introduction.

Bars 78–127, marked 'Allegro Vivace', is an exciting section – scampering music with typically-Berlioz colourful, imaginative orchestration. We can think of this as the first subject in the tonic key of A major, but it is a different saltarello theme to that heard in bar 1. The staccato violins are muted (con sordini) and Berlioz has indulgently asked at the beginning of the score for a minimum number of strings (at least 15 each of first and second violins, 10 violas, 12 cellos and 9 double basses). He has cleverly treated the lower strings in bars 78–101 with a soft drum roll effect.

The strings and wind alternate in a dialogue of echo effects for some time (bars 82–86, 90–94, 109–111 and 118–120). At bar 85 the theme seems to start up again in the violins, but Berlioz changes it so that it hints at the key of the relative minor (F# minor). There is a third version of the melody starting at bar 94 (back in A major) and the rhythm here is of continuous quavers. There is an effective *ppp* section starting at bar 102 in the violas and cellos, which leads to a brief development of the main melody. There is an unexpected change to C major at bar 112. Berlioz keeps it all soft (until 126) in rhythmical anticipation of the very loud tutti second subject which is to come at bar 128 in the dominant key (E major). Two crescendo bars (126–7) of repeated brass quavers herald this loud tutti.

Things to do

Listen to the Symphonic Poem *Vltava* by Smetana (set by WJEC for 1998). Use the advice given in Chapter 1 in the section on Coursework and Examination Techniques, and listen constructively to it several times. Are you able to analyse it for yourself yet? Some people can feel the structure of a piece by just listening with concentration; if you can obtain a score of the piece so much the better. If you are still finding set work analysis rather difficult, here is a brief description of *Vltava*:

Smetana composed a set of six symphonic poems between 1874 and 1879, and they were published as a cycle entitled *Ma Vlast (My Country)*. The six pieces each describe a different element of Bohemian history: (1) *Vysehrad* is the castle of mythological kings of Bohemia (now Czechoslovakia) which overlooks the River Vltava. (2) *Vltava* depicts the river. (3) *Sarka* portrays a Bohemian Amazon leader. (4) From *Bohemia's Fields and Groves*. (5) *Tabor* is an epic of Hussite warriors and (6) *Blanik* is a legendary resting-place of dead Hussite heroes – the piece is a description of Czech knighthood.

You may, of course, like to hear some of the others in the cycle, but in this country *Vltava* is by far the most popular. We are not too familiar with Bohemian history, and this may well be the reason; 'Vltava' is a highly effective description of the course of a river.

The opening represents the source of the river, and characteristic 'water music' is shared by the two flutes (Fig. 14.19).

Fig. 14.19

The clarinets enter at bar 16 (representing a second stream). (Might the intermittent violin pizzicato chords be representing light reflecting off the stream – or is it a splashing effect? You must decide). The river is growing – with added instruments and a general crescendo – and the main Vltava river theme arrives at bar 40 (see Fig. 14.20).

Fig. 14.20

This is an appropriately majestic theme in E minor for the river, and its accompaniment has plenty of flowing semiquavers to give it movement. At bar 80 the river passes a hunt in the woods, which is suitably depicted by the use of horns and trumpets playing typical hunting calls (Fig. 14.21).

Fig. 14.21

This section is written in the key of C major, a necessary change after seventy-nine bars centred on the tonality of E. It all continues until Smetana calms it down in both volume and speed, returning to E major in bar 102.

The river now enters a populated district, and we hear a polka (a traditional Czech dance; this one is Smetana's own composition) which represents the music for the dancing of peasants at a village wedding. Clarinets and bassoons double the violins in the G major melody (Fig. 14.22).

Fig. 14.22

This dance section of *Vltava* lasts for sixty-three bars. As with the 'Hunting' section, Smetana allows the music to wind right down as if the river has flowed on past the event.

He writes a bass (tonic) pedal on G from bar 161–186, and effects a marvellous modulation from the key of G major into A flat major, a semitone shift which is a good example of Romantic writing; this would have been considered too 'daring' in earlier periods. He uses the long-held G as part of the new chordal link into A flat (Fig. 14.23)

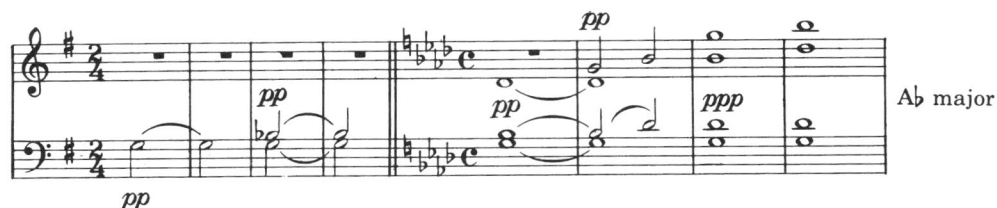

Fig. 14.23

This new section is perhaps the most Romantic of the piece. It depicts water nymphs bathing and playing in the moonlight. Flutes, clarinets and harp are prominent as the flowing river accompaniment, and high muted divided strings play an ethereal melody in slow-moving minims representing the water nymphs (Fig. 14.24).

Fig. 14.24

Gradually more instruments are added as the river becomes more turbulent. A dominant pedal of the original key (i.e. the note B) arrives at bar 229 and after ten bars of orchestral crescendo – again with flutes and clarinets prominent as at the very beginning – we have a restatement of the main *Vltava* river theme in the home key. It leads on this time to the climax of the whole work, the St John Rapids, where the composer brilliantly depicts the foaming cascades and rushing torrents. Listen out for the shrieking piccolo at the height of the musical furore. (With all the richness of this music, it is an amazing fact that Smetana was totally deaf when he wrote it.)

Finally, at bar 321, again over a dominant pedal (on B) a fortissimo (*fff*) climax suddenly drops right down to *pp*, and then scurries up the scale to the last statement of the main theme of the piece, this time in a triumphant E major, portraying the broad flow of the Vltava as it reaches Prague, the capital (Fig. 14.25).

Fig. 14.25

At bar 359, we hear the brass and woodwind play the *Vysehrad* (castle) theme which is also used in the first symphonic poem of the set. (Fig. 14.26).

Fig. 14.26

Smetana remains in E major until the end of the piece. For the last time, he allows the volume to decrease to *ppp* and rests with just the violins on a pause. The work ends with a *fortissimo perfect cadence*.

Practice question and student answer

Here is a pupil's answer to a set work question with examiner's comments.

Question
Write a paragraph on the musical ways in which Smetana describes the river in *Vltava*.

Student answer

'Good. Concise use of relevant detail'

'Good. You start to answer the question straight away.'

'Good. Clear, short answers.'

'Don't waste time on irrelevancies.'

'Correct, but in the wrong place. Avoid after-thoughts with good planning'

Smetana establishes his water effect immediately by using flutes and clarinets in a persistent semiquaver movement. This is to represent trickling mountain streams which later form the river itself. He cleverly orchestrates this section with pizzicato and punctuated chords to give the effect of light reflecting off the water, or of splashing water against rocks. The main theme for the river is suitably majestic and has a flowing movement as an accompaniment; this theme returns later. The climax to the work is where the orchestra plays fortissimo for the St John rapids. All the instruments here have turbulent rhythms, and the combined effect would be good for a film where people shoot the rapids in a canoe. The work has a long coda all based on one chord before it finishes with a loud perfect cadence. Some imaginative harp writing is used as a reminder of water during the water nymphs section.

'Personal responses and imaginative uses for music have their place – but not here. This question requires only a paragraph so don't waste it.'

▷ 1900 onwards: The Modern Period

The compositions that have appeared this century reflect rapidly-changing times. Two horrific World Wars, and enhanced awareness of the world around us through television and radio have raised our social conscience; artists aim to reflect life, and comment on it far more than ever before.

In 1900 there were two main groups of composers: those who continued the Romantic tradition (the *Neo-Romantics*); and those who were inspired by *Impressionism*.

Neo-Romantics

Elgar, Vaughan Williams, Holst, Bax, Mahler, Richard Strauss and **Sibelius** all developed Romantic writing further from the styles of Brahms and Wagner. They all had their different characteristics of course – some continuing the nationalist movement with the collection and use of folk-music – but did not radically change the nineteenth century symphonic tradition.

Impressionists

Debussy, however, was greatly influenced by the developments of the Impressionist painters, such as Cézanne and Monet. By using unconventional harmony, *overtones* and *whole-tone scales* he produced many pieces with atmospheric, shimmering effects. (Notice the dreaminess in his piano prelude *The Submerged Cathedral* or the orchestral *Prélude à l'Après-midi d'un Faune*, for example). His music felt very different and new at the time, yet was still basically tonal (see *tonality*). **Ravel, Falla** and **Delius** were others to be inspired by Impressionism.

Anti-Romantics

Some composers became decidedly anti-Romantic, however.

Prokofiev composed lively and often discordant music, until commanded by the Russian authorities to revert to 'easier', more lyrical music. **Stravinsky** used contrasting styles in his long composing life. Having assimilated the colourful nineteenth-century symphonic style from his teacher Rimsky-Korsakov, he produced several successful ballet scores, including *The Rite of Spring* and *The Firebird*, which broke new ground with their driving, complex rhythmic structures and general move away from anything approaching conventional 'sweetness' of melody and orchestral sound. Continuing to reject all things romantic, he experimented with *polytonality* and with rhythm and melody, none of which was very popular with audiences at the time. In fact, *The Rite of Spring* caused the biggest riot from an audience ever known when it was first performed in Paris in 1913. In contrast to this forward-looking work, Stravinsky also looked back to the eighteenth century: he would combine the simpler forms of that time with the flavour of modern music. This we now call *neo-classicism*. (Listen to his *Pulcinella* ballet suite: he is avoiding emotional intensity, re-producing the calm and clear textures of pre-Romantic times).

Bartók in Hungary had been influenced by Wagner and Strauss, but he also gradually changed his style, choosing to absorb the rich resource of Hungarian folk-tunes into his work.

Schoenberg had also started his career as a neo-Romantic. His *Verklärte Nacht* (*Transfigured Night*) sounds as if it might be a late work by Brahms. In time, however, he came to feel that the use of tonality was no longer valid as a vehicle for expression, and after much soul-searching, devised the strict twelve-note method known as *serial composition*. Key sense was now abandoned, and all chromatic notes became equal to one another. His followers were **Berg** and **Webern** who treated this new *atonal* method in their own individual ways.

Jazz

Jazz was a strong ingredient in American music, especially with **George Gershwin**. Listen to excerpts of his opera *Porgy and Bess*, or the well-known *Rhapsody in Blue*. **Charles Ives** used *polytonality* in some of his pieces, as he remembered from childhood the clashing sounds of rival marching bands. **Copland**, in his ballet scores especially, managed to capture the Wild West flavour. Try *Billy the Kid* or *Rodeo*.

Music since 1945

Since the end of the Second World War there has been an incredible development in *electronic technology*. We can all now listen to and enjoy high-quality music at the touch of a switch, and come to know music that we may not otherwise encounter. In all ages there have been both innovatory composers and reactionary composers. The reactionary ones prefer to work within an existing and accepted style, perfecting as best they can the current musical language. Others, however, are rather more revolutionary. The so-called avant-garde composers are continually seeking new ways of expression, new instruments and new structures.

Since 1945, **Britten**, **Tippett**, Stravinsky, **Shostakovich**, Vaughan Williams and **Walton** are among the most important names in the traditional methods of composition. They are all individuals, of course, but nonetheless, they can be grouped within the mainstream of twentieth century music. The avant-garde composers are also diverse in style, and space permits only the mention of a few. The Italian **Berio** sometimes gives the performer a choice of actual notes to play. Originally a serialist, he has written electronic as well as orchestral music. The Polish composer **Penderecki** has written notable religious music with voices used in strange new ways – whispering, chanting, murmuring, whistling and so on – besides normal singing. **Stockhausen** has written many electronic works and sometimes allows choice to the performer as to where and when he should play. **John Cage** has written for the prepared piano, and *aleatoric* pieces based on random sounds. He is notorious for his *4'33"* piece, which consists of absolute silence from the performer! **Messiaen**, from France, has used birdsong and complicated Indian rhythms in much of his work, which is strongly religious.

Opera

Opera is much the same today as ever – a mixture of art, stagecraft and business wrangling. Financial problems are always dominating opera houses, and those in charge of them are often unwilling to try new works that may not sell tickets! Opera-goers tend to be very conservative anyway, not always giving a chance to something new. Despite all this, there have been some operatic masterpieces this century. Berg's *Wozzeck* (produced 1925) and Britten's *Peter Grimes* of 1945 are notable examples. The latter was an instant success in an artistically-deprived post-war Britain, but Berg's opera, with its dissonance and *sprechgesang*, met with initial hostility. *Wozzeck* is now well established in the repertoire; new music always takes time to become accepted!

Television, with all its modern technology, allows great opportunity for dramatic effect, and composers have been composing operas specifically for this medium. **Menotti's** *Amahl and the Night Visitors* was the first example in 1951, and more recently Britten composed *Owen Wingrave* for television in 1971.

This century has seen an extremely wide range of techniques and styles in its 'classical' music, and it is often very hard for the listener to feel any sense of unity or continuity between the countless schools of thought. It is impossible to speculate on the future of serious music; there will always be experimentation – and much will fall by the wayside – but it will be interesting to see in years to come whether or not composers eventually 'lighten' their music by introducing elements that will be more immediately appealing for the ordinary listener. You must try all styles. Some will probably be not to your taste, but give it a chance! Listen intelligently, and think what feelings the composer might be trying to express, even though the language may be strange to your ears.

Things to do

1. Make up a composition in Impressionist style, using chords that have a feeling of timelessness about them. Aim for a relaxed atmosphere if you can by avoiding chords that are too 'definite'. Try chords like the ones in Fig. 14.27.

Fig. 14.27

It may be helpful to have a picture in your mind as you are working, even if you don't acknowledge this in the eventual title. 'Fog' or 'mist' perhaps might get you thinking of the right atmosphere. If you are using the piano, you can obtain some marvellous foggy effects with the sustaining pedal; with a synthesiser you can experiment until you find the right sound.

2. **Stravinsky:** *Symphony of Psalms* and *Petrushka – The Shrove-Tide Fair*
    Stravinsky is a most important composer of this century, and you should become familiar with some of his work. He was born in 1882 near St Petersburg (once called Leningrad), where his father was a bass singer at the Opera House. Although his parents persuaded him to study law, he was a keen musician. In 1902 he showed some of his compositions to Rimsky-Korsakov and was taken on as a pupil by him. At about this time he met Diaghilev, the director of the Ballet Russe, and went on to compose ballets for the company, *Firebird* in 1909, *Petrushka* in 1910–11, and *The Rite of Spring* in 1911–13.

    The 1917 Revolution forced Stravinsky to leave Russia and he settled first in Switzerland, then France and finally America at the beginning of the Second World War. He became a nationalised American and made Hollywood his home until his death in 1971.

    His music seemed to change as often as his life. His early ballet scores had Romantic influences, notably from his teacher Rimsky-Korsakov. Then followed his radical works of the First World War, his lengthy neo-Classical period, and finally in his last years, he turned to serialism, where he was working in note rows, thirty years after Schoenberg and Berg had first created the process.

    Listen to his *Symphony of Psalms* (1930) which bears the dedication: 'composed to the glory of God and dedicated to the Boston Symphony Orchestra on its 50th anniversary'. All his life Stravinsky was a sincere member of the Russian Orthodox Church. Now try questions 1–3 in the practice question section which begins on p. 180.

When you have become familiar with this first Psalm, try to analyse the other two yourself. Do you find the work expressive? Does it have the power to move us in the same way as more openly emotional works, and if so why do you think this is?

Now turn to some of Stravinsky's Ballet music. Listen to *Petrushka* and try to answer question 4 in the pratice question section on p. 181.

3. Get to know *Les Miserables* by Alain Boublil and Claude-Michel Schönberg. The following numbers are set by WJEC for 1998:

    ▶ I Dreamed a Dream
    ▶ On My Own
    ▶ Do You Hear the People Sing?

    Les Miserables, first heard in Paris in 1980, reached the Barbican Theatre in London in 1985. Since 4 December 1985, it has been staged at the Palace Theatre, London. It is an adaptation of the lengthy classic novel by Victor Hugo, and should not be judged by the standards of nineteenth-century opera, nor by the standards of twentieth-century pop music – it is in a genre of its own. No attempt will be made here to put these three songs into a dramatic context. Reference to keys and bar numbers are based on the Piano/Vocal Selection (Wise Publications, London 1986).

4. To conclude our look at 'serious' works written between 1550 and the present day, we shall take just one more piece and present you with a series of points to ponder over. These are not the sort of questions that you will encounter for your exam, but they aim to encourage you to develop opinions and ideas of your own. The danger of reading analytical information in the form of study notes, questions and answers, is that it can all become over-technical and can gloss over the most important element of any work of art – that of feeling. Here we can only be subjective; in other words, there is no real right or wrong, only personal opinion.

    Ask yourself:

    ▶ Do I like this piece? If not, why not? Is it because I shouldn't like it – or my friends won't like it?
    ▶ Is it because I've never heard it before?
    ▶ Have I really understood the 'message' or emotion behind the music?

    Listen to Penderecki's *Threnody to the Victims of Hiroshima*. Here you must find out your own background information; we shall say nothing technical about this piece whatsoever, except that Hiroshima was the Japanese city where the first atomic bomb was dropped in 1945. Assuming that you know that anyway, and are familiar with the historical consequences of that horrific event, the very title conveys its emotive content before you even hear a note. This is not intended to be armchair listening – you will realise that immediately! Ask yourself what the composer is trying to do, and decide whether the experiment is a success. Above all, keep an open mind when you are listening, then consider the following. (Answers will not be provided.)

    1. Has Penderecki managed to create a mood, or range of moods, appropriate to that suggested by his title? Do you find the piece moving?
    2. Listen to the instrumental effects the composer has used. Are the musical ideas appropriate? If so why? Do you think the sounds are effective or just gimmicks? Indeed, is there a future for this type of serious orchestral composition in our age of new sound technology?
    3. Should the piece have more melodic content?
    4. Can you see this style of music 'surviving' in the sense that other composers could use it for less emotive pieces?
    5. Is the sole purpose of music to entertain or please? Do you consider it a good thing that composers should disturb the listener, by rousing a social conscience? In your opinion is music a suitable vehicle for making serious comment?

Practice questions and answers

Listen to Stravinsky's *Symphony of Psalms* and try to answer questions 1–3 (see *Things to do*, no. 2 on p. 179).

Question 1

What words does Stravinsky use for the *Symphony of Psalms*?   *(2)*

Question 2

How does Stravinsky's orchestra for the *Symphony of Psalms* differ from a normal symphony orchestra?   *(8)*

Question 3

Write a commentary on the first Psalm in *Symphony of Psalms*. Consider the use of vocal and instrumental textures in your answer, rather than keys.   *(10)*

Listen to Stravinsky's *Petrushka* before trying to answer the following question (see *Things to do*, no. 2 on pp. 179–80).

Question 4

How does Stravinsky capture the mood of *The Shrove-Tide Fair*?   *(4)*

Questions 5–7 refer to three numbers from *Les Miserables* by Alain Boublil and Claude-Michel Schönberg. Read through *Things to do*, no. 3 on p. 180 before you attempt to answer.

Question 5

What is the structure of the song 'I Dreamed a Dream'?

Question 6

Discuss the unusual harmony of verse 3 in 'On My Own'.

Question 7

(i)   In what form is the song 'Do You Hear the People Sing?'?
(ii) Describe the tonality of the song.

Answer 1

He uses verses from the three Psalms and they are set in Latin. (1) Psalm 38: 13–14; (2) Psalm 39: 2–4; and (3) Psalm 150 (complete). The three movements are performed without a break.

Answer 2

The most obvious difference is that upper strings (violins and violas) are not required at all. Other sections are large. In the wind there are four flutes and a piccolo doubling on fifth flute, four oboes and a cor anglais, three bassoons and a double bassoon, but clarinets are not required. In the brass there are four horns, four trumpets in C and a D trumpet, three trombones and a tuba.

In the percussion section he writes for timpani and bass drum. There is also a harp and two pianos. The average symphony orchestra would not use as many flutes, oboes or bassoons, and would require clarinets. The trumpet section would be smaller (probably three), and the piano, if used, is not normally doubled. Stravinsky has selected a different series of timbres in composing this work.

Answer 3

Stravinsky writes quite a long introduction for orchestra – twenty-five bars of irregular time signatures with flowing semiquavers punctuated unpredictably by chords. The French horn and solo cello hint at the first choral melody which is then stated by the contraltos. Stravinsky requests that children's voices be used where possible in preference to adult sopranos and contraltos. This first melody has seven bars written on only two different notes! The full choir answers with a single homophonic phrase, then a four-bar link of semiquavers leads to another seven-bar phrase for altos using the same two-note melody. Stravinsky is aiming for understatement here, avoiding the emotional impassioned sound that characterised much choral music prior to his time.

A single punctuated chord leads to a tenor line, joined later by sopranos (or trebles), who sing a four bar phrase on only one note. The accompaniment all through consists of the semiquaver figure, and spiky woodwind writing, often in fairly low registers, especially for oboes. The build-up commences at figure 10 when the altos and basses begin a more conventional choral statement, joined three bars later by the other voice parts. The climax is reached at figure 12 with bare, homophonic chords marked *ff*. The Psalm ends in a stark, unemotional way. The work finds its power from understatement; its austerity seems to underline the importance of the text: 'Hear my prayer O Lord and consider my calling with thine ears'.

Answer 4

The very opening suggests the hustle and bustle of a fairground with its sideshows and crowds of spectators. Stravinsky composes with several things going on at once, and uses a perpetual motion within the orchestra to convey an excited atmosphere. Apparently Stravinsky had heard a barrel-organ while working on this score and orchestrated the very tune, cleverly suggesting a creaky old barrel-organ by his skilful writing for woodwind instruments. Similarly, he borrowed another tune, a French dance melody this time, and used it to suggest a wandering musician with a music box playing for his dancer. This is interrupted immediately by the syncopated theme of the opening, again implying many things all going on at once.

Answer 5

Introduction – F major, bars 1–3
        A A – verses 1 and 2, F major, 8 + 8 bars.
          B – verse 3 is a bridge section, 10 bars long:

$$\text{D} \mid \text{Gm} \mid \text{D} \mid \text{G} \mid \text{C} \mid \text{Fm} \mid \text{C} \mid \text{F Gm} \mid \text{F Gm} \mid \text{C}$$

Fig. 14.28

        A1 – verse 4, F major, 8 bars and a one-bar link modulating up to G major.
        A2 – verse 5, G major, 8 bars long.
        A3 – verse 6 + coda, 8 bars + overlapping coda, G major.

Answer 6

The key for the first two verses is D major, although both end on a chord of A major. Verse 3 plunges straight into the following chord scheme:

$$\text{B}\flat \text{ Cm}\flat 5 \mid \text{B}\flat \mid \text{Gm B}\flat \mid \text{E}\flat \mid \text{Em} \mid \text{B B7} \mid \text{Am7} \mid \text{C7} \parallel \text{F (v. 4)}$$

Fig. 14.29

The most unusual element in this progression is the abrupt (but most effective) change from E♭ to an E minor chord.

Answer 7

(i) Ternary form: A (verse 1) – B – A (chorus 2) – B – A (verse 3) – coda.
(ii) Verse 1 is in F major. The B section starts in A minor but works its way to G for a strong dominant preparation of C major for the chorus. Sections B and A (verse 3) are then repeated, and the five-bar coda ends softly in C minor.

▷ Jazz

At the time when modernist composers in Europe and America were evolving a different musical language, another very different type of sound-world was born. This was to be known later as jazz. This is not the place to give a detailed history of jazz. It is such a diversified area of music that space permits only a concise introduction to the background, its styles and musicians.

With so many different styles to listen to, it is actually rather difficult to define what jazz actually is. Improvisation is a major ingredient, and strong feeling and high energy are nearly always present. For a long time jazz was categorised as just another section of popular music, not to be taken too seriously. But this is no longer the case, for although a novelty in 1900, it was firmly established as an important musical genre by around 1930, and given serious attention by major composers such as Stravinsky and **Kurt Weill**.

You will probably know that during the eighteenth and nineteenth centuries the slave trade transported thousands of Africans to America. It takes little imagination to picture the incredible hardship that those people endured – the claustrophobic journey, the humiliation of slavery auctions and the cruelty of perpetual work.

Music to the African is a natural part of life. Small wonder that it was used to express sorrow and grief. Work songs were, as the name implies, sung in time with work; the regular beat of these songs was timed to fit to hammer blows, or whatever. When they were not working, simple instruments were fashioned from everyday objects to beat in time with the songs.

There were differences, obviously, between African music and American (which was basically white European anyway). The African music tended to use pentatonic (five-note) scales (see Chapter 13), whereas the American used the seven-note major and minor scales. Strong rhythm and drumming was a vital ingredient of African music, and everyone would want to join in the performance – with clapping, singing or dancing. This was very different from the European way of doing things, where a composer would write for certain players, and the audience would only 'join in' by applauding at the very end. During the course of time, black and white music was to mix. The slaves heard around them European tunes, and military band pieces. When slavery ceased in 1865, with the ending of the American Civil War, many white bands split up and there were cheap instruments around for the blacks to play: trombones, cornets and clarinets. Before long, there were black bands in most southern American towns. Their music 'jazzed up' the spirituals (religious hymn-like songs – the slave-owners had tried to convert their slaves to Christianity) and the 'white' marches in an exciting way – by adding 'blue' notes (see *Blues*) and bending notes slightly out of true pitch. Many of the freed slaves found work on the railways and made up more worksongs, often in a 'call and response' style. They were free from slavery, but still faced enormous hardship and racial persecution. Their sadness still found expression in their songs – 'singing the blues' was a way of releasing their feelings, and it was often primitive and emotional. The so-called 'blues scale' includes the flattened or 'bent' 3rd and 7th (see Fig. 14.30).

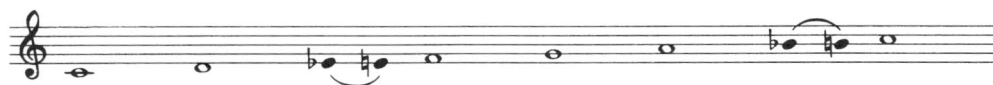

Fig. 14.30

The twelve-bar blues was later to be a standard jazz chord progression, see Fig. 14.31.

Fig. 14.31

This familiar chord scheme is a framework upon which a song or improvisation can be built.

Birth of jazz

New Orleans was the city associated with the birth of jazz. Bands would play in the dance-halls, bars and on the Mississippi river boats. There were usually six players: clarinet, cornet, trombone, piano or banjo, string bass and drums and these bands are generally referred to as 'Dixieland' or 'trad' jazz bands. When there was no room for a band, a pianist would play, and a favourite style at the turn of the century was *ragtime*. Much of this music, by **Scott Joplin** and others, was written down and published. It was the first black music to really be accepted by the whites, who went on to write rags themselves. (This, of course, has a similarity to 'classical' music, where music is written down accurately.)

In 1918 the American navy closed down most of the bars in New Orleans and many of the jazz players were forced to travel north to find work. In this way, the popularity of jazz was to spread, and with the help of gramophone recordings and the development of radio, jazz was soon to be heard all over the world.

In the 1920s, *boogie-woogie* was a popular piano style. This was a fast-moving bass part in a twelve-bar blues framework (see Things To Do no. 2 at the end of this section).

Swing

An economic slump put many jazz musicians out of work and it was some time before jobs could be found. When things did improve (by about 1933), a new style of jazz appeared, known as swing. It used 'blue' notes (see *Blues*) as before, and the old 'call and response' from the worksongs, and sometimes a boogie bass, but somehow it sounded new because it was played by larger bands – as many as thirteen players, instead of the usual half-dozen. Now things had to be written down. Band leaders such as Benny Goodman and Paul Whiteman made careful arrangements for big bands and the players now had to be able to read their parts or learn everything by heart. The arranger usually scored for four instruments in the saxophone section, five in the brass section, and four in the rhythm section. A feature of swing was the use of short, repeated figures, called *riffs*. They were passed around the band in a 'call and response' way. Sometimes a soloist would change the riff, to avoid monotony, by adding an idea of his own, but Goodman always kept a tight control on his players – the parts had to be played as written!

Be-bop

Swing was superseded by a new style in the 1940s – be-bop (or bop for short). Some musicians (such as Dizzy Gillespie and Charlie Parker) were tired of using riffs and working from arrangements. The be-bop bands were smaller, so that the soloists became more prominent. The rhythms used were far more sophisticated than in swing, often using Cuban-style rhythms (such as the *cha-cha*, *conga* or *rumba*), and the drummer played in a 'cooler' way, mainly on cymbals. The bass line was a perpetually-moving pizzicato string bass part. Be-bop music was often based on popular songs, but the melody was replaced by a highly chromatic decorative line, with complicated chords – to such an extent that the original song could easily become unrecognisable!

Modern jazz

Modern jazz dates from about 1950. Musicians like Gerry Mulligan, Miles Davis and Gil Evans came to prefer simpler harmonies and rhythms to those of be-bop. The West Coast of America became the focal point for modern jazz. Some players began to use instruments not formerly associated with jazz: flute, horn and cello, for example. The Modern Jazz Quintet (MJQ) used classical pieces arranged in a jazz style in their concerts, and included vibraphone. This style of marrying classical to jazz was called *Third Stream* music.

Jazz today is very much a mixture, because some players prefer to revive earlier styles – Kenny Ball and Acker Bilk in this country have worked in the traditional (trad) jazz style based on the New Orleans 1920s bands – while others pursue modern jazz or swing. The National Youth Jazz Orchestra is a good example of a band which plays swing. Jazz trios are fairly common – the pianist Oscar Peterson is probably the most well-known musician to work mainly with string bass and percussion. Free-form jazz is where the music contains no common chords or obvious melodies, it all being based on free improvisation. Finally, bands such as Chicago and Blood, Sweat and Tears use a mixture of jazz and rock.

Jazz to listen to

The following alphabetical list of names is but a selection of great jazz musicians for you to get to know and enjoy. You may like to find out about some of these colourful characters. They certainly make interesting reading, as well as listening!

Louis Armstrong	trumpet and vocals
Count Basie	band leader/piano
Bix Beiderbecke	cornet and piano
Big Bill Broonzy	blues singer and guitar
Dave Brubeck	piano/composer
Kenny Clarke	drums
John Coltrane	multi-instrumentalist
Miles Davis	trumpet

Duke Ellington	composer/band leader
Ella Fitzgerald	singer
Stan Getz	tenor sax
Dizzy Gillespie	trumpet (notice his 'vertical' trumpet)
Benny Goodman	clarinet/band leader
Herbie Hancock	keyboards
Woody Herman	clarinet/alto sax/band leader
Earl Hines	piano
Billie Holiday	singer
Scott Joplin	ragtime piano and composer
Glen Miller	trombone/bandleader
Charles Mingus	bass/composer
Thelonious Monk	piano
Jelly Roll Morton	piano
Gerry Mulligan	baritonesax, composer and arranger
Charlie Parker	alto sax/composer
Oscar Peterson	piano
Django Reinhardt	guitar
Bessie Smith	blues singer
Art Tatum	piano
Fats Waller	piano
Muddy Waters	guitar/singer

Things to do

1. Listen to some Scott Joplin piano rags, and see if you can write one of your own. A rag usually has four main themes (each sixteen bars long) = A B C and D.

   The plan then should be: A A B B A C C D D which makes it quite a lengthy piece. Yours can be much shorter, of course, the structure is entirely up to you. You will probably need to improvise at the keyboard first. Work out an 'oom-pah' bass part for the left hand first, using simple chords, then add a catchy melody above it, with syncopation.

2. If you are a keyboard player practise a boogie style. You will need to master the left hand part first, and there are all sorts of variations to it. Try the simplified version in Fig. 14.32 first.

Fig. 14.32

When you feel happy with this rather tricky bass part add on the suggested chords with the right hand. It is really a twelve-bar blues with a decorative bass.

3. Listen to some Swing music by Benny Goodman or Count Basie. Can you hear the riffs? Now listen to some 'trad' jazz played by Kenny Ball or Acker Bilk. Which do you prefer – swing or trad? Why?

4. Try to compare Be-bop with Swing by listening to some appropriate Dizzy Gillespie and Count Basie.

5. Try using simple chords and then adding some 'foreign-sounding' notes to them. For example in Fig. 14.33.

C chord + F♯   D minor chord add C♯

Fig. 14.33

How do you like the sound of these? Experiment at the keyboard as often as you can, noting which chords you particularly like, and why.

6.   Can you think of ways in which worksongs could be used today? Make up one for a particular job, making sure that it has a very strong rhythm. Perhaps you could use the pentatonic scale (C D E G A only) as the African slaves did. You may like to include some harmony, and a 'call and response' pattern. Fig. 14.34 shows two well known spirituals which are good examples of 'Call and response' – you may find them useful as starting points for your worksong.

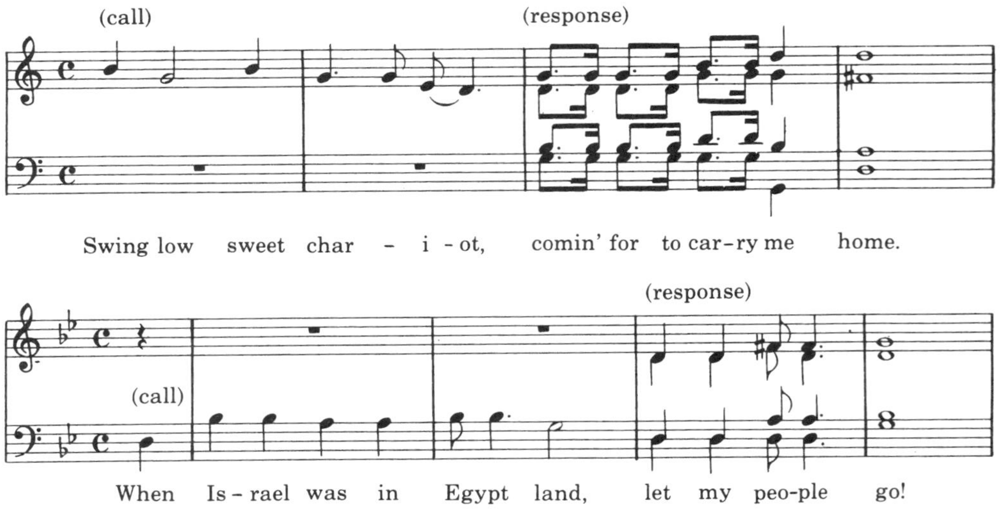

Fig. 14.34

7.   The marching band was very popular in nineteenth century America (and indeed, still, is). Try writing a march tune, using either 2/4 or 4/4 time. Write it for keyboard first, and if you are satisfied, you may like to arrange it for instruments.

▷ The world of Folk Music

Every year throughout Britain, Ireland and America, millions of people are entertained by folk and traditional musicians in folk clubs, pubs, on concert stages and at folk festivals without the vast publicity that has surrounded all other styles of popular music since recording was invented. To a casual listener, the folk genre is perhaps the most misunderstood of all twentieth century popular music. This is not the place for a detailed history, but you might enjoy listening to the following folk styles.

Cajun
This music comes from the south-east of the USA, developed by French settlers who trekked from eastern Canada (Acadia, now Nova Scotia; from 'Acadian' comes the abbreviation 'cajun') at the end of the eighteenth century. The standard line-up for cajun bands today is an accordion, fiddle and guitar, and perhaps some percussion (a triangle or rubboard) an acoustic or electric bass, drums, extra fiddles and guitars. The music is a mix of dance tunes, songs and cajun blues reflecting their oppression over the years.

Bluegrass
A name adopted in the mid-1940s to mark its origins in the Bluegrass state of Kentucky, where this style of string band music flourished. It is a sort of country music jazz with instruments such as banjo, guitar, dobro (a modified guitar with raised strings and an inbuilt metal resonator to produce an acoustically amplified sound), mandolin and fiddle. Exciting effects are produced when the lead is taken by the mandolin, and an essential flavour of bluegrass is the melodic, three figure style of banjo picking.

Country music
Country music (in Britain we tend to call it 'country and western') is centred, as it has been since the mid-1950s, around Nashville USA. It is hard to define, as there are so many artists who have mimicked country music. It can encompass the hillbilly ballads of Hank Williams, the sad tones of Jim Reeves or Johnny Cash, the mountain music of Bill Monroe,

the traditional Irish style of Daniel O'Donnell, and even the parodying of The Rolling Stones. It is too simplistic to call country the white man's blues – the cry of people doomed on the land or in the large city ghettos.

One vital strand of country came from the traditional folk carried by British emigrants, but the increasing commercialisation within Nashville created a country music industry where increasingly the acoustic roots of the style were forgotten. '*Western swing*', another brand of country, is a lively blend of dixieland jazz, polkas and Texan country music.

Folk music to listen to

Try to hear recordings by some of the following folk singers:

Joan Baez	American folk singer, politically conscious. Associated at one time with Bob Dylan. Try her *Where Are You Now My Son* album (1973).
Harry Belafonte	American folk singer and actor. His *Calypso* album (1956) became the first ever album to sell a million copies. Belafonte was one of the few black artists who broke down race and class barriers through popular music.
Ian Campbell Folk Group	British folk group 1956–78. In 1962, *Ceilidh at the Crown* was the first ever live folk club recording to be released. For a while, Dave Swarbrick (best remembered as fiddle player with Fairport Convention) was a member. Try *The Sun is Burning* (1970).
The Chieftains	An Irish folk band with various personnel changes since the late 1950s. The first album *Chieftains 1* (1964) introduced their skilled interpretations of traditional Celtic tunes. In recent years they have worked with rock musicians Mike Oldfield and Van Morrison, classical musicians such as James Galway (try *The Celtic Connection – James Galway and The Chieftains* 1990), and have contributed to film soundtracks.
John Denver	American singer most popular in the 1970s; try *The Best of John Denver* (1974). His simplistic approach has been attacked by the music critics, but nevertheless Denver achieved a mass popularity which is the envy of most artists.
The Dubliners	A Dublin, Eire folk band founded in 1962. Try *The Dubliners: 25 Years Celebration* (1987).
Fairport Convention	The inventors of British folk-rock created an atmosphere that allowed traditional music to be played in a rock context. The band has had an incredible number of members since its formation in 1967. Try the compilation albums *History of Fairport Convention* (1972) or *The Best of Fairport Convention* (1988).
Julie Felix	American singer and an early champion of the folk-styled singer/songwriter movement. Try *This is Julie Felix* (1970).
Gordon Giltrap	Renowned and innovative English guitarist. Try *The Best of Gordon Giltrap – All the Hits Plus More* (1991)
Woody Guthrie	American folk singer (1912–67) and prolific song-writer. A pioneer and leading source of inspiration for the 1960s folk revival in Europe and the USA.
The Incredible String Band	UK folk group founded in 1965. Various personnel and styles: try *The Incredible String Band* (1966) and the compilation album *Relics of the Incredible String Band* (1970).
Burl Ives	Celebrated American folk ballad singer. He was also an actor, and an editor of folk music. Many songs are associated with him, for example *Big Rock Candy Mountain* and *I Know an Old Lady who Swallowed a Fly*.
Bert Jansch	Scottish guitar player and one-time member of Pentangle. Try *Bert and John* (1966, with John Renbourn).
Leadbelly	Hudson 'Huddie' Leadbetter (1889–1949) played several instruments, and sang folk and blues, but was best known for his mastery of 12-string guitar. He performed in a primitive, powerful style.

Ralph McTell	One of Britain's leading folk singers in the 1960s. His best known song is *The Streets of London* (1974). Try *The Ralph McTell Collection* (1978).
Joni Mitchell	Canadian singer/songwriter and guitarist with a love of open tuning (retuning to exploit the richness of the open strings). Try any album: *Clouds* (1969), *The Hissing of Summer Lawns* (1975), or *Night Ride Home* (1991).
Tom Paxton	American folk singer and composer. A central figure of the folk revival, he wrote several songs that became standard folk club material, such as *The Last Thing on my Mind*. Try *The Very Best of Tom Paxton* (1988).
Pentangle	Active from 1967 until 1972, this folk band featured two remarkable guitarists, Bert Jansch and John Renbourn. Pentangle's style used both original and folk material. The band later reconvened with new personnel. Try *The Pentangle* (1968), *Anthology* (1978) or *One More Road* (1993).
Pete Seeger	American folk singer and songwriter, best known for popularising songs such as *Little Boxes*, *Where Have All The Flowers Gone* and *We Shall Overcome*, but an important figure in the development of free speech through folk music.
James Taylor	American singer and songwriter. Try *The Best of James Taylor – The Classic Years* (1990).

▷ The world of Popular Music

We started our brief guide to the history of music with the year 1550. With a similar convenience, this outline of the main developments in pop music will start in 1950. There has always been 'popular' music, of course, that is, music for ordinary people to sing and dance to, but pop music, as we know it, is an industry based on the selling of records, and more recently, pop videos. This quick-moving world goes hand in hand with fashion and dance crazes; some lasting for only a matter of weeks, others for rather longer periods. This is a very different tradition to the world of 'classical' music, although sometimes the two cultures come very close to each other. Some pop composers use styles that invoke serious composers (e.g. the 1967 No. 1 hit *A Whiter Shade of Pale* by Procol Harum has an organ counter-melody lifted from Bach). Similarly, there was a vogue at one time for taking well-known Classical pieces and dressing them up with appropriate drum backing and increased speeds into a pseudo-pop style (e.g. Mozart's 40th Symphony).

Pop music has rarely been original in real musical terms. Since bursting out in the 1950s, it has absorbed a rich variety of styles from the classical, jazz and folk traditions, as well as from within itself. It has always been associated with young people, often making a powerful and pervasive social impact.

In 1954 a song called *Rock around the Clock* was released on the Decca label. It was number one in the British and American charts the next year and used as the title song in a rock 'n' roll film in 1956. The singer was **Bill Haley**, with his backing group **The Comets**, and the song was to make him the first real pop star. Although we think of him (and perhaps his music) as rather old hat now, it came at a time when teenagers on both sides of the Atlantic were ready for something 'modern', and they could afford to buy records after the deprivations of the Second World War. New pop magazines and periodicals (*Melody Maker* and *New Musical Express*) were appearing and began to 'hype' up these new idols, and popularise them further, as did the rapid expansion of television at this time.

Rock 'n' roll

Rock 'n' roll was derived from skiffle, which was a simple type of rhythmic song as sung by **Lonnie Donegan**, **Tommy Steele** and others. Skiffle was a British, not American, style and tended to use home-made instruments instead of normal ones – the washboard (used then for scrubbing clothes and played by scraping thimbles on it!) and tea-chest + broomhandle basses, for example. The lyrics were black-American blues style. Rock 'n' roll used the twelve-bar blues chord progression (borrowed from jazz), but it was used in a quicker and livelier fashion. It was at this time that the guitar gained enormous popularity, often using an electric pick-up to amplify the sound. **T-Bone Walker** was one of the first non-jazz musicians to use an electric guitar on record.

Elvis Presley (1935–1977) was younger, and far livelier than Bill Haley, and soon overtook him in popularity. Presley was the first white singer to sing in a 'black' style, and the effect of all this energetic and overtly sexual music and movement must not be underestimated. There were campaigns against the evils of rock 'n' roll! To some extent, there have been expressions of outrage over each new rock style ever since. Other important names then were **Buddy Holly** (1936–1959), **Jerry Lee Lewis**, **Little Richard** and **Gene Vincent**. **Chuck Berry**, a black rock and roller, tailor-made many of his lyrics to appeal to teenagers (*Roll Over Beethoven*).

A 1950s TV programme called *Oh Boy!* featured British pop music and encouraged many of our own singers and groups. **Cliff Richard** and his backing group **The Shadows** became well known in 1958 and are still performing and recording nearly forty years later. The Shadows were also an instrumental group in their own right, releasing many singles and albums of memorable numbers, some of which were vocal. The basic line-up for most groups at that time was lead guitar, rhythm guitar, bass guitar and drums, and this rarely changed – sometimes an electronic organ would be added.

In the early 1960s a Liverpool group came to the forefront of the pop business, capturing worldwide media attention as never before – **The Beatles**. The song-writing team of **John Lennon** and **Paul McCartney** produced many million-selling hits that have become pop 'classics', re-arranged for all combinations of voices and instruments, and which are still often heard in their original versions. Countless other 'Mersey-sound' groups were formed in the 1960s to emulate the success of the Beatles: **Freddie and the Dreamers**, **Gerry and the Pacemakers**, **The Swingin' Blue Jeans** to name but three, but none of these were to overtake the amazing 'Beatlemania' that took hold in the middle of that decade.

By 1966 the Beatles style was becoming less stereotyped. The words became more important than in the earlier songs; listen to *Eleanor Rigby* for instance. Their 1967 LP *Sergeant Pepper's Lonely Hearts Club Band* is a milestone in the history of pop music, for besides a colourful and attractive cover to the album, there was a common theme of loneliness in several of the songs and several tracks merged into the next – a new departure in pop recording. The Beatles' visit to India had led to an interest in the sitar, which they used occasionally on their records.

The Rolling Stones were perhaps the main rivals to the Beatles, but were less 'polished' musically and in appearance generally. They were able to relate to rebellious teenagers (and consequently upset the parents) with the gyrating antics of the lead singer Mick Jagger and the suggestive lyrics of the songs. This aggressive style of performing had the same sort of effect on the older generation as Elvis Presley had had several years before.

At this time in pop history we can start to see a separation between the commercial 'Top Ten' songs and the more serious, known generally as 'underground', which obviously appealed to smaller numbers of people. **Frank Zappa** was an inventive 'acid rock' musician who showed little interest in the three minute single, concentrating instead on making 'progressive' LP records. **The Grateful Dead** and **Jefferson Airplane** were two other notable bands who experimented with form, occasionally incorporating elements of jazz and Eastern sounds, often with long solos.

Attention switched from Britain in 1968 to the West Coast of America when the 'psychedelic' Flower Power movement briefly bloomed. The basic motivation behind this trend was a non-political pacifist resistance to the Vietnam War, with a flower as a symbol of love and peace (Beatles: *All You Need is Love* and John Lennon's *Give Peace a Chance*). Unfortunately it gave further publicity to the widespread use of drugs, associated for so long with the jazz and pop scene. This was the heyday of huge rock festivals, where thousands would gather to hear a dozen groups or more. The most famous festival of all was Woodstock.

While rock and beat music was at its height, folk music was enjoying a revival, although with never quite the same frenzy that Beatlemania was able to produce. Various styles of folk music developed – 'protest' music from **Bob Dylan**, and later 'electric folk' from **Steeleye Span** who re-arranged traditional folk material into a contemporary idiom. Listen to Dylan's song *Blowin' in the Wind* as an example of his protest against war and his interest in civil rights. Dylan is still performing and recording today; he has changed styles several times, in keeping with changing tastes, which may account for his continuing popularity. He became a Christian in 1979 and has written some religious rock songs. In Britain, Cliff Richard, who first became popular in the late 1950s, celebrated Christianity in his own style.

Another folk-rock musician who emulated the Dylan style was the British singer **Donovan** who also played a straightforward folk-guitar style in the mid-60s. (Listen to his song *Colours*). In America, **The Byrds** recorded a Bob Dylan song *Mr Tambourine Man* in folk-rock style, and two other groups worked in a similar way – **The Lovin' Spoonful** and **The Mamas and the Papas**. **Simon and Garfunkel** were an immensely successful American duo in the mid-60s. Listen to *Sound of Silence* (1966) and *Bridge Over Troubled Water* (1970). Paul Simon and Art Garfunkel eventually went their separate ways as solo artists. Most people know *Bright Eyes* which Garfunkel recorded in 1979 as a theme from the cartoon film *Watership Down*. It was number one in the pop charts for six weeks.

The 1960s was the decade for super-groups, where the best musicians from several bands would play together. **Cream**, in the late 60s, included drummer Ginger Baker and the revered guitarist Eric Clapton. Although they made albums using all the latest technology, it was in stage performances that they really came alive; extended solo improvisations would be framed by references to their album songs. The Beatles eventually folded as a group, but each went his own way as a musician. Paul McCartney went on to form **Wings** with Linda, his wife, and John Lennon made a very successful solo career until his tragic assassination in New York in 1980. The Rolling Stones are still recording and performing after thirty-five years or more, and **The Who** reformed for a tour in 1989, even though their first hits date from 1965. Their early concerts featured amplifier and guitar smashing, and extensive use of screeching feedback – the noise made when a microphone or guitar pick-up is too near a loudspeaker. Their theatrical rock-operas *Tommy* and later *Quadrophenia* were a style to be developed later by **Alice Cooper** and **David Bowie**. *Tommy*, more of a song cycle than an opera, was another attempt to make an album with a coherent theme; it was later turned into a film by Ken Russell, the controversial film director. *Jesus Christ Superstar* and *Hair* are other popular rock musicals from this time.

Another performer was the late **Jimi Hendrix**, regarded by many as one of the finest rock guitarists of all time. He made distorted sounds with a 'wah-wah' foot-pedal to help create his unique blues-based style.

Led Zeppelin were formed in 1968 by **Jimmy Page**, another excellent guitarist of the period. This group tended to shun publicity, preferring to release albums rather than single records. New dramatic laser stage effects combined with brilliant high-volume musical skill led to a new name for this style – 'heavy metal'. **Deep Purple** is another band you should listen to.

Black music

Everything mentioned so far has been British or American White Music, but nearly all pop stems in some way from the music of Black America. The Blues developed at the end of the nineteenth century, and came from the songs and chants of the negro slaves working in the cotton fields. This turned into Rhythm and Blues (R 'n' B), a very influential force on pop music. Soul Music (popular in the 1970s) came from Rhythm and Blues and Gospel Music. **Aretha Franklin** and **Otis Redding** are two early Soul singers of the 1970s. Tamla Motown is well-known in the world of Black Music. It is a very large record company in Detroit which produced records by **Diana Ross and the Supremes**, **Stevie Wonder** and many others. The production of all these singers became so distinctive that 'Motown' is now a word that implies a style of black pop music. One feature is the constant repetition of the 'hook-lines' (the chorus title lines) so that they really stick in the memory.

Ska, Blue Beat, Rock Steady and Reggae are all styles of Jamaican music from the 1960s onward. You can easily recognise Reggae by its emphatic off-beat rhythm and the singer's West Indian accent. **Bob Marley** (who died in 1981) is regarded as the greatest Reggae artist; he was Rastafarian and politically-minded. (Rastas believe in peace and brother-hood, and that they will eventually return to Ethiopia, their spiritual home.)

The 1970s

The commercial pop music of the 1970s is not so memorable as that of the previous decade. It was a time of light-show spectacles and loud volume, demanding very large concert halls to stage the required effects. Ticket prices naturally reflected the cost of these extravaganzas. As before, many singers and groups were famous briefly, but soon forgotten. Some of the more successful include: **T-Rex, Slade, Rod Stewart, Wizzard, 10 CC, Abba, Status Quo,**

Queen, Elton John, Chicago, Leo Sayer, Kate Bush, The Bee Gees, Blondie and Police. Emerson, Lake and Palmer used themes from serious composers, such as Sibelius and Copland, and re-arranged them in a heavier style, performing with real showmanship. Keith Emerson, the keyboard player, was one of the first to use a Moog synthesiser. Pink Floyd has created very successful stage shows (e.g. *Dark Side of the Moon*) using sophisticated electronics and a superb control of sound and textures. Genesis started with an inventive concept album approach, but were later to move away to a more mainstream rock sound.

You should try to hear Mike Oldfield's album *Tubular Bells* of 1973–4 which is a blend of rock and light classical styles. Oldfield recorded nearly everything himself on this LP by multi-tracking and overdubbing. In 1992 he made a new version of this pop classic. Which of the two do you prefer, and why?

The 70s saw the arrival of Disco music. The vital ingredient here was the dance rhythm, not so much the tunes or instruments used. Donna Summer was the first real disco star in the mid-70s, and the film *Saturday Night Fever* with the Bee Gees' music encouraged many companies to produce Disco records. All sorts of unlikely people cashed in by making disco music – even old singles and classical tunes were re-arranged for people to dance to.

Funk was first played by James Brown way back in the mid-60s and it developed in the 70s. It has blues, jazz and rock ingredients and tends to use distorted sounds, syncopated rhythms and a percussive bass-line (slap-bass). It is black dance music with a strong jazz feel. Try songs by Kool and the Gang (e.g. *Funky Stuff*).

Punk, the 1980s and 1990s

One new style to arrive in the late 1970s was Punk Rock – an aggressive and shocking style, often with depressing lyrics. For its followers, it was more than just music; it was a whole lifestyle. Safety pins were used as jewellery (in the most unlikely places), and hair was dyed and shaped in outrageous ways. The infamous Sex Pistols and later The Clash were the epitome of this raw and extremely unsophisticated pseudo-style. The guitar sound is often distorted and simple to the point of banality, usually without solos. It had virtually disappeared in 1979, although some bands tried to keep the Punk tradition alive. Later punk music was often so fast and incoherent, that it is referred to as 'Oi music'!

Hip-hop, with its derivative rap, was the new black music of the 1980s. Disc-jockeys developed the style by rapping (speaking rhythmically) over records whose sound they modified by 'scratching'.

'New Age', in complete contrast, was soothing instrumental music, based on the softer kinds of classical, folk and jazz music. It was more of a mood than a style.

Names from the 1980s include: The Pretenders, The Jam, Roxy Music, Michael Jackson, Kraftwerk, Madness, Culture Club (with Boy George), Phil Collins, Spandau Ballet, UB40, Frankie Goes to Hollywood, Lionel Richie, Duran Duran, Wham! Eurythmics, Madonna and Pet Shop Boys. Names in the 1990s include: Sinead O'Connor, MC Hammer, Bryan Adams, Nirvana, Simply Red, Def Leppard, New Kids On the Block, AC/DC, George Michael, Sting, Whitney Houston, Bon Jovi, U2, REM, Guns 'n' Roses, Paul Weller, Blur and Oasis. This lengthy list is probably more familiar to you than the earlier names, and you will know much of the music. No-one can predict which way pop will turn next. Rock music has inspired countless cults and fashions in four decades, and the fragmented nature of the nineties pop music scene – goth-rock, rap, rave, heavy metal, house, dance, techno and grunge (to name but a few) – suggests that there is plenty more to come. Perhaps the wheel will turn full circle and we will revert to the simplicity of the 50s and 60s. Maybe there will be a folk revival, or something completely new. Black and white music will almost certainly continue to blend together, enhanced by new technology and changing social conditions. This is the way pop music has always evolved. Listen carefully to as much as you can, thinking as you do so about the origins of a particular style. Enjoy it!

Songs to listen to

Below is a list of the groups and singers that have been mentioned in the above section on pop music. With so many performers in all areas of popular music, space does not allow mention of everyone. Try to get hold of albums by performers that you have not heard before, and listen to them carefully.

Are the words political? Is the song trying to make a social comment, or is it simply a fun song for dancing to? How is the song put together? Is it too repetitive, do you think? Is there a solo for any particular instrument – if so, does it fit in well with the rest of the song? Perhaps you will hear two versions of the same number, by different performers. Which do you prefer and why?

Bill Haley and the Comets
Lonnie Donegan
Tommy Steele
T Bone Walker
Elvis Presley
Buddy Holly
Jerry Lee Lewis
Little Richard
Gene Vincent
Chuck Berry
Cliff Richard
The Shadows
The Beatles
Freddie and the Dreamers
Gerry and the Pacemakers
The Swingin' Blue Jeans
The Rolling Stones
Frank Zappa
The Grateful Dead
Jefferson Airplane
Bob Dylan
Steeleye Span
Donovan
The Byrds
Lovin' Spoonful
The Mamas and the Papas
Simon and Garfunkel
Cream
Eric Clapton
Wings
John Lennon
The Who
Alice Cooper
David Bowie
Jimi Hendrix
Led Zeppelin
Deep Purple
Aretha Franklin
Otis Redding
Diana Ross and the Supremes
Stevie Wonder
Bob Marley and the Wailers
T-Rex
Slade
Rod Stewart
Wizzard
10 CC
Abba
Status Quo
Queen
Elton John

Chicago
Leo Sayer
Kate Bush
Bee Gees
Blondie
Police (with Sting)
Emerson, Lake and Palmer
Pink Floyd
Genesis
Mike Oldfield
Donna Summer
James Brown
Kool and the Gang
Sex Pistols
The Clash
The Pretenders
The Jam
Roxy Music
Michael Jackson
Kraftwerk
Madness
Culture Club (with Boy George)
Phil Collins
Spandau Ballet
UB40
Frankie Goes to Hollywood
Lionel Richie
Duran Duran
Wham!
Eurythmics
Madonna
Pet Shop Boys
Sinead O'Connor
MC Hammer
Bryan Adams
Nirvana
Simply Red
Def Leppard
New Kids On The Block
AC/DC
George Michael
Sting
Whitney Houston
Bon Jovi
U2
REM
Guns 'n' Roses
Paul Weller
Blur
Oasis

Things to do

You may like to follow up some of the groups or singers that have been mentioned by considering some further songs in more detail. London (for 1998 and 1999) has included five Sting songs as set works (from his second solo album *Nothing Like the Sun*, released in October 1989), and here we shall consider three of them:

▶ *An Englishman in New York*
▶ *Fragile*
▶ *They Dance Alone*

If you have worked your way through the various set works in Chapter 4, you will have a good idea how to go about studying new songs. In addition, this present section of rock and pop will have given you some awareness of where Sting would fit into the plethora of styles and influences which has developed over the last sixty years or so.

When you have listened to these three songs and have become familiar with both the tunes and the words, try to work out any influences on them. You should form your personal responses to each song:

(a) Is it the lyrics or the tune you most like?
(b) Is the song different from the ordinary? If so, is it the use of voice/voices or instrumental solos that are played which make it sound fresh?

Practice questions and answers

Question 1
Compare the middle solo in *An Englishman in New York* (just after 'brighter than the sun') to the song's introduction.

Question 2
Describe the eight-bar episode in *An Englishman in New York* which begins 'Modesty propriety'.

The following are questions from the London 1998 Specimen Paper.

Question 3
Turn in your music score to the beginning of the song *Fragile*. Listen to bars 1–17 (end of verse l). After you have listened to the extract answer the following questions.

(a) What is the key in 5–8?   *(1)*
(b) Describe the sound of bars 1–4. Mention both the *texture* and the *rhythm* of
     the music.   *(3)*

Question 4
Write a description of the song *They Dance Alone*. Refer to **three** different themes,
keys, instrumentation, rhythm and any other important musical elements.   *(20)*

Answer 1
The solo is twelve bars long, whereas the introduction, which is based on the same chord scheme, has only eight bars. The gentle saxophone, first heard at the opening with mainly long-held notes is more lively, the piano adds a jazzy mood, and the bass has a busier part. Just before the voice returns, there is a strange four-bar 'solo' from a drum machine which does not really relate to the rest of the song.

Answer 2
This episode uplifts the song, because the section is made up mainly of major chords, and this contrasts well with the E minor feel to the rest of the song. The chords are:

D | A | Bm | F# | G | A | F# | Bm

Fig. 14.35

The melody is treated sequentially, falling at first, then rising in the second half.

Answer 3

(a) E minor.

(b) This introduction is gentle in volume and mood, the texture is thin and the tempo is quite free (rubato). Static chords underpin a Spanish guitar melody of four one-bar phrases. It all has an improvisatory feel to it. Synthesizer wind chimes and a distant maracas effect add atmosphere to this opening. The chords are indefinite: Em11 A/B D/E A/B. (A/B = A major, with a bass note B).

Answer 4

Before analysing this song it might be helpful to mention something of its background. Sting interrupted his 1987 *Nothing Like the Sun* tour to appeal for Amnesty International in Mendoza, Chile. For political reasons Amnesty was not permitted to hold the concert in Chile, but by holding it right on the border, Chileans could obtain a mountain pass to get there. In the event, fifteen thousand Chileans attended and Sting heard the plight of around 2000 people who had gone missing. He saw many women carrying pictures of their missing menfolk, each with the words 'Donde Estar?' (Where are they?). His song *They Dance Alone* is about these women.

There are three verses arranged as follows:

Introduction: 4 bars, A major
A – Verse 1: introduction 4 bars + 8 bars vocal
B – Refrain: 10 bars
A – Verse 2: 4 + 8 bars
C – 8-bar episode + 8-bar Spanish voice-over
A – Verse 3: 4 + 8 bars
B – Refrain: 10 bars
C – 8-bar episode
D – Coda: 16 bars (fade)

There are three main themes in this song: (i) the introduction, after a static bare fifth chord, has a rising semiquaver figure, played gently on saxophone; (ii) the pan-pipe theme starting at bar 5 which gives a South American flavour; (iii) the refrain B starting at bar 17 (F#m–A).

Most of the chords and keys are nearly related to the home key of A major, but the hook of the song title is given a sense of climax by effectively brightening the harmony in the refrain. Four bars of F#m–A suddenly changes to:

$$ \text{G–D} \mid \text{G–D} \mid \text{E–Dm6} \mid \text{E–Dm6} \mid \text{Dm6} \mid \text{E–F\#m} $$

Fig. 14.36

before returning to its more restrained mood. The harmony and rhythm of the coda is different to the rest of the song. It has an indefinite key – more C#m than the tonic A major, and the rhythm is busier with a more energised saxophone input before a fade-out.

The instrumentation is effective at the opening. The background side drum has military overtones, which is contradicted by the gentle pan-pipe theme. The saxophone obbligato is a favourite hallmark (he uses it in a similar way in *An Englishman in New York*, and there are subtle guitar in-fills, again reinforcing the South American atmosphere. The regular rock instruments – synthesiser, bass guitar and drums are used as one would expect in a mainstream rock song.

They Dance Alone was actually banned in Chile, because General Pinochet (the brutal dictator from 1973–1990) considered the lyrics subversive!

▷ A FINAL COMMENT

The world of pop and rock is immense; songs that were 'outrageous' in the 1960s are classics today. Groups that were regarded as rather unwholesome by parents are now accepted, through the fullness of time, and often enjoyed. Familiarity does not always breed contempt!

Enjoy your pop music, and try to widen your listening. Young people are often wary of admitting that they like or dislike a particular sound for fear of alienating themselves from their friends. Stand your ground – and convert the others!

SUMMARY

▷ Listen widely – try unfamiliar styles that you have not heard before.

▷ Make short notes from tape or CD covers – this is how you build up your knowledge.

▷ As you listen think of the structure of the piece/song, its instrumentation, mood changes, solos, words etc. Get used to thinking analytically.

Glossary I
Composers mentioned in this book

The following table contains brief details of composers whom you will have encountered in the book. The GCSE exam no longer places much emphasis on dates and similar factual detail, but this table is included to reinforce the information given in Chapter 14 and elsewhere. You may find some helpful notes here towards your chosen set work, but regard the Recommended Listening as the most useful column – try to hear some of these pieces, thinking as you do so about the advice given in Chapters 3 and 4 about **how** to listen to best advantage.

Composer	Dates	Country	Types of music	Recommended listening
J.S. Bach	1685–1750	Germany	Concertos, organ music, cantatas etc.	Brandenburg Concertos
Balakirev	1837–1910	Russia	2 symphonies, piano music	Tone poem: Tamara
Bartok	1881–1945	Hungary	Piano music concertos, operas	Concerto for Orchestra
Bax	1883–1953	England	7 symphonies, tone poems	Tone poem: Tintagel
Beethoven	1770–1827	Germany	Symphonies, opera, concertos, chamber music etc.	Pastoral Symphony
Bellini	1801–1835	Italy	Operas	Extracts: Norma
Berg	1885–1935	Austria	Operas, string quartet	Violin Concerto
Berio	1925–	Italy	Electronic and avant-garde music	Sequenza III
Berlioz	1803–1869	France	Operas, overtures, symphonies, Requiem	Roman Carnival
Bizet	1838–1875	France	Operas, symphony in C major	Jeux d'enfants
Borodin	1833–1887	Russia	Symphonies, opera, 2 string quartets	Polovtsian Dances
Brahms	1833–1897	Germany	Symphonies, songs, chamber music	Academic Festival Overture
Britten	1913–1976	England	Choral music, operas etc.	Serenade, Op. 31
Bruckner	1824–1896	Austria	9 symphonies, masses	Symphony No. 5
Bull	1562–1628	England	Music for viols, organ, virginals	Any piece
Byrd	1543–1623	England	Masses, madrigals, motets	5-part Mass
Cage	1912–1992	America	Avant-garde music; 'prepared piano'	Imaginary Landscape
Chopin	1810–1849	Poland	Piano music	Any piece
Copland	1900–1991	America	Ballet scores, orchestral, chamber	Rodeo/Billy the Kid
Corelli	1653–1713	Italy	Concerti grossi	Christmas Concerto
Debussy	1862–1918	France	Piano, orchestral, chamber	La Mer

Composer	Dates	Country	Types of music	Recommended listening
Delius	1862–1934	England	Operas, orchestral, chamber	On Hearing the First Cuckoo in Spring
Donizetti	1797–1848	Italy	Operas	Excerpts: Lucia di Lammermoor
Dowland	1563–1626	England	Lute songs, lute solos	Any piece
Dvorak	1841–1904	Czechoslovakia	Orchestral, opera, chamber, choral	New World Symphony
Elgar	1857–1934	England	Orchestral, choral, chamber	Cockaigne Overture
Falla	1876–1946	Spain	Ballet scores, orchestral	The Three-Cornered Hat
Gershwin	1898–1937	America	Songs, opera, orchestral	Rhapsody in Blue
Gibbons	1583–1625	England	Church music, madrigals	Madrigal: The Silver Swan
Glinka	1804–1857	Russia	Operas, orchestral, chamber music	Overture: Russlan and Ludmilla
Grieg	1843–1907	Norway	Piano music, orchestral, songs	Piano Concerto
Handel	1685–1759	Germany (nat. Eng.)	Concerti grossi, choral, operas, oratorios	Excerpts: Messiah
Haydn	1732–1809	Austria	Symphonies, string quartets, oratorios, masses	Symphony No. 104
Holst	1874–1934	England	Operas, orchestral, choral music	Suite: The Planets
Ives	1874–1954	America	Symphonies, sonatas	Three Places in New England
Joplin	1868–1917	America	Piano rags	The Entertainer
Kodaly	1882–1967	Hungary	Orchestral music, educational music	Hary Janos Suite
Lassus	1532 –1594	Netherlands	Madrigals, masses, motets	Madrigals (any)
Liszt	1811–1886	Hungary	Piano, orchestral transcriptions	B minor Sonata
Lully	1632–1687	Italy	Operas, church music	Any opera excerpt
Lloyd Webber	1948–	England	Musicals	Requiem
Mahler	1860–1911	Bohemia	Symphonies, songs	Symphony No. 4
Mendelssohn	1809–1847	Germany	Symphonies, piano, songs, chamber music	Violin Concerto
Menotti	1911–	Italy	Operas, orchestral	Amahl and the Night Visitors
Messaien	1908–1992	France	Orchestral, organ, choral music, songs	Oiseaux Exotiques
Monteverdi	1567–1643	Italy	Operas, madrigals, church music	Beatus vir
Morley	1557–1603	England	Madrigals, church music, lute songs	It was a lover and his lass
Mozart	1756–1791	Austria	Orchestral, chamber, church music, etc.	Symphony No. 40
Mussorgsky	1839–1881	Russia	Operas, orchestral, piano	Night on a Bare Mountain
Paganini	1782–1840	Italy	Violin music	La Campanella

Composer	Dates	Country	Types of music	Recommended listening
Palestrina	1525–1594	Italy	Masses and other church music	Missa Brevis
Penderecki	1933 –	Poland	Orchestral, choral	Threnody for the victims of Hiroshima
Prokofiev	1891 –1953	Russia	Symphonies, operas,	Romeo and Juliet chamber, piano, etc.
Purcell	1659 –1695	England	Church music, opera, harpsichord music	Excerpts: Dido and Aeneas
Rachmaninov	1873 –1943	Russia	Symphonies, operas, piano music	Piano Concerto No. 2
Ravel	1875 –1937	France	Orchestral, chamber,	Bolero piano, operas, ballets
Rimsky-Korsakov	1844 –1908	Russia	Orchestral, operas, choral, etc.	Scheherazade
Rossini	1792 –1868	Italy	36 operas	Any opera overture
A. Scarlatti	1660 –1725	Italy	115 operas, 500 cantatas	Any operatic extract
D. Scarlatti	1685 –1757	Italy	500 harpsichord sonatas	Any sonata
Schoenberg	1874 –1951	Austria	Orchestral, choral, chamber music	Verklarte Nacht
Schubert	1797 –1828	Austria	Symphonies, piano, chamber and church music, songs	Unfinished Symphony
Schumann	1810 –1856	Germany	Symphonies, piano, chamber music, songs	Carnaval for piano
Shostakovich	1906 –1975	Russia	Symphonies, piano, chamber music	Symphony No. 5
Sibelius	1865 –1957	Finland	Symphonies, songs, chamber music, tone poems	Finlandia
Smetana	1824 – 1884	Bohemia	Tone poems, operas, chamber music, etc.	Vltava
Sousa	1854 –1932	America	Marches for band	El Capitan
Stockhausen	1928 –	Germany	Electronic and avant-garde music	Mixtur
J. Strauss I	1804 –1849	Austria	Waltzes, polkas	Radetzky March
J. Strauss II	1825 –1899	Austria	Waltzes, polkas, operettas	Thunder and Lightning Polka
R. Strauss	1864 –1949	Germany	Tone poems, operas, songs, orchestral	Don Juan
Stravinsky	1882 –1971	Russia	Orchestral, choral, operas, ballets etc.	Rite of Spring
Tchaikovsky	1840 –1893	Russia	Symphonies, ballets, chamber music, songs	Violin Concerto
Tippett	1905 –	England	Symphonies, operas, piano and vocal works	Concerto for Double String Orchestra
Vaughan Williams	1872 –1958	England	Symphonies, chamber, vocal works etc.	Wasps Overture
Verdi	1813 –1901	Italy	Operas, Requiem	Excerpts: Requiem
Vivaldi	c. 1678 –1741	Italy	Concertos, church music, operas	Four Seasons
Wagner	1813 –1883	Germany`	Operas (music dramas)	Excerpts: any opera
Walton	1902–1983	England	Symphonies, chamber, orchestral, choral	Facade

Composer	Dates	Country	Types of music	Recommended listening
Weber	1786 –1826	Germany	Operas, orchestral, piano music	Oberon Overture
Webern	1883 –1945	Austria	Orchestral, chamber, vocal, serial music	Five Pieces for Orchestra
Weelkes	c. 1575 –1623	England	Madrigals, church music, lute muslc	Hark all ye lovely Saints
Weill	1900 –1950	Germany	Operas, symphonies	The Threepenny Opera
Williamson	1931–	Australia	Symphonies, vocal, orchestral, songs	Any work

Glossary 2
Musical words

Music is one of those subjects that contains many technical terms and foreign words. You will not need to learn all of them by any means, but this glossary contains a brief explanation of words that you may come across in your GCSE course. For fuller explanations you should consult a good music dictionary, such as the *Oxford Companion to Music*. Look up the words *in italic* in the Glossaries in this book.

A cappella	Unaccompanied choral music.
Absolute music	Abstract instrumental music – i. e. not *programme music*.
Accelerando	(accel.) – quicken the pace.
Accent	Extra force given to a particular note, and indicated like this:
Accidental	A sharp, flat or natural which does not form part of the *key signature*.
Adagio	Slow, but faster than *largo*. A slow movement is often called an adagio.
Air	A simple tune for instrument or voice.
Alberti bass	Using broken chords to create a flowing accompaniment part.
Aleatoric music	Music where the performer is allowed to play parts of a piece based on chance – the composer allows some degree of choice.
Allegretto	Fairly quick, but not as much as *allegro*.
Allegro	Quick and lively, but not as fast as *presto*.
Allemande	A dance movement in moderate 4/4 time; part of the Baroque *Suite*.
Alto	(1) The lowest female voice. (2) A clef which the *viola* uses.
Amati	Family of sixteenth and seventeenth century Italian *violin* makers, based in Cremona.
Andante	A walking speed, but not too slow.
Anthem	Protestant church equivalent of the Latin *motet*; now a term used for short religious choral pieces.
Antiphony	Groups of performers answering each other across a space (hence antiphonal music).
Arco	An instruction for string players to use the bow, after a passage marked *pizzicato*.
Aria	A solo vocal piece in *opera* or *oratorio*, often composed in *ternary form*.
Arietta	A short or light *aria*. Sometimes applied to an instrumental piece.
Arioso	*Aria*-like. Applied to a melodic type of *recitative*.
Art song	An artistic setting of a poem for voice and accompaniment, normally piano. This usually refers to nineteenth century *Romantic* songs (see *Lieder*).
Atonal	Music without a sense of key (*tonality*), by *Schoenberg* and others in early 1900s, which led on to *serial composition*.
Augmentation	Treating a melody so as to lengthen its note-values.
Avant-garde	Very modern music – often experimental.
Bagatelle	A short instrumental composition, often for piano.
Ballad	(1) From the sixteenth century, a term applied to a simple and popular song for solo voice, often describing an event of the day. (2) In the nineteenth century, either a narrative-type song, or a sentimental English drawing-room song.

Ballade	An instrumental composition (with no one particular form) by *Chopin, Brahms, Liszt* and others. They are supposed to have narrative associations.
Ballett	A type of *madrigal* with a 'fa la' refrain.
Barcarolle	A song or instrumental piece, usually in 6/8 time, suggesting Venetian gondolas.
Baroque	A word borrowed from architecture suggesting an ornamented, detailed construction. The name is used musically for the period 1600–1750.
Bass	(1) The lowest male voice. (2) The lowest note of a chord or composition. (3) The lowest member of a family of instruments, e.g. bass clarinet. (4) The lowest *clef*.
Basso continuo	Sometimes just 'continuo'. A type of *bass* line used in the *Baroque* period, with figures underneath it from which a *harpsichord* player would work out the correct harmonies. The bass line would often be doubled by a *cello*.
Be-bop	A jazz innovation of the early 1940s using *chromatic harmony* and complicated, fast-moving melodies.
Bel canto	Literally 'beautiful song'. An operatic term for a brilliance of vocal execution and beauty of tone as heard in eighteen/nineteenth century *operas* by *Bellini* and *Donizetti* etc.
Binary form	A common musical structure, especially in the *Baroque* period. In two parts, the first changing key, the second returning to the home key before the end. Both parts are often repeated.
Bluegrass	A brand of American *country*, descended from 'hillbilly' music.
Blues	A style of music, associated originally with American Negro *spirituals*. It generally has a mood of intense sadness and loneliness. Twelve-bar blues is a very common simple chord progression used in popular music. A 'blue' note is a note of the scale flattened (often the 3rd and 7th) which gives a characteristic *jazz* effect.
Bourree	A dance movement from the *Baroque* suite, in quick 2/4 time, beginning with an upbeat.
Cadence	See page 144
Cadenza	A solo vocal or instrumental passage, usually inserted into a *concerto* for display purposes.
Cajun	A distinctive style of French-American folk music with *concertina* or *accordion* prominent in the accompaniment.
Calypso	A type of West Indian music; strong rhythmically and often with topical words.
Canon	A *contrapuntal* composition, or section of music where a melody given by one part is imitated exactly by one or more others, usually with overlapping.
Cantabile	In a 'singing' style; flowing and clear.
Cantata	A choral work, with or without solo voices, and usually with orchestral accompaniment. It may be sacred or secular (non-religious) .
Canzona	A sixteen/seventeenth century short instrumental work, somewhat resembling choral music, and often in several movements.
Cassation	An eighteenth century type of lighter orchestral music in several movements, often played outdoors. Sometimes called *Serenade* or *Divertimento*. This century Malcolm *Williamson* has written several Cassations for children.
Catch	A type of amusing vocal *round*, often bawdy, by *Purcell* and others up to the nineteenth century.
Chamber music	This is not a precisely defined term, but it refers to music for a small group of players who are regarded as soloists on equal terms. (See *Duet, Trio, String Quartet, Quintet, Sextet, Septet, Octet* and *Nonet*.)
Chorale	A hymn tune of the German Protestant Church. *J.S. Bach* harmonised hundreds of these tunes.
Chorale prelude	An instrumental piece (usually for organ) based on a *chorale*.
Chord	Any combination of notes played together – whether pleasant or not! (See *Triad*.)
Chorus	(1) Refrain to a song, frequently recurring. (2) A group of singers singing in harmony. (See *SATB*.)
Chromatic scale	A scale which goes up or down in *semitones*.
Classical	(1) A style of music from 1750–1830. (2) A style of work that is standardised and 'accepted', not modern. (3) Opposite to light or popular music.
Clavier	(German = Klavier.) Term meaning 'keyboard'.
Clef	Sign which fixes the location of notes onto the stave and placed at the beginning of each line of music. Treble, *alto, tenor* and *bass* clefs are used today.
Coda	A section of music to round off a *movement*.
Coloratura	A very agile style of vocal music; the very high register of the soprano voice.
Concerto	Generally a work for one or more soloists with accompanying orchestra. (See *Concerto Grosso* and *Cadenza*.)

Concerto grosso	Seventeenth/eighteenth century type of orchestral music with interplay between a larger group of players (the ripieno) and a smaller group (the concertino). Try some of *Bach's* six Brandenburg Concertos.
Concord	A chord which seems to be at rest harmonically (hence consonance: opposite to discord or *dissonance*).
Conservatoire	Special college for higher musical training.
Consort	Old English for a group of instruments.
Contrapuntal	A combination of two or more melodies which make musical sense – they are then said to be in 'counterpoint' to each other.
Counterpoint	See *Contrapuntal.*
Country (and Western)	White American folk music, a forerunner of rock 'n' roll.
Courante	Dance movement in three time in the *Baroque* Suite. Usually in a running, rapid tempo.
Crescendo	(Cresc.) Getting gradually louder.
Cyclic form	(1) Work (e.g. *song cycle*) in several sections which has a unifying mood or theme. (2) Work which uses a recurring musical subject in each movement.
DC (Da Capo)	Go back to the beginning. A Da Capo *aria* (as used by *Handel*) returns to the opening section.
DS (Dal Segno)	Go back and play from the sign (𝄋) – not the beginning.
Development	A section of music (usually in *sonata form*) where themes are 'developed' – modified or expanded in some way according to the inventiveness of the composer.
Diatonic	Music that concerns itself with major/minor scales. The opposite to *chromatic.*
Diminuendo	(dim.) Becoming gradually softer.
Diminution	Treating a melody so as to shorten its note-values.
Disco	A strongly rhythmic dance from the 1970s.
Dissonance	A sense of 'clashing' or jarring *chords.*
Divertimento	A light-hearted work in several movements for a small instrumental group. (See *Cassation.*)
Dixieland	An early jazz style for a small band, with *choruses* and improvised verses.
Dodecaphonic	*Twelve-note music.* A style of composition as devised by *Schoenberg* in the 1920s. See also *serial music.*
Dominant	The fifth note of a scale, (in C major = G); or the chord formed above this note.
Drone	A constantly repeated or long held note.
Duet (duo)	A combination of two performers (sometimes with an accompaniment), or a piece for two.
Dynamics	Loud and soft expression marks.
Electronic music	Music that involves the use of synthesisers or pre-recorded tapes.
Embouchure	A term used for the application of a mouth-piece to a brass or wind player's lips.
En dehors	Play prominently.
Episode	A section of music within a *rondo* or a *fugue* intended to form a contrast.
Equal temperament	See *Temperament.*
Exposition	The opening section of *sonata form* which presents the main musical themes.
Falsetto	A high register of singing for male altos.
Fanfare	An introductory flourish for *trumpets* (or other instruments imitating them).
Fantasia	(Or fantasy/phantasie/fancy.) A vague title given by some composers, when they require a 'free' rather than a set form.
Figured bass	A musical shorthand from the *Baroque* period, whereby figures were added to a bass line for the harpsichord player to embellish with appropriate *chords.* (See *Basso Continuo.*)
Fine	Literally 'finish'. Written at the end of a repeated section of music to indicate the end.
Folk song	A song made up long ago and handed down aurally, the words often differing from region to region. Some composers this century (e.g. *Vaughan Williams, Holst, Bartók*) have collected folk songs and used them in arrangements of their own.
Form	Structure in music (e.g. A B A = *Ternary Form*).
Formalism	A supposed fault in Russian composition; the Soviet authorities denounced *Shostakovich* and *Prokofiev* in the 1930s and 40s for excessive emphasis on 'form' rather than 'content'.
Forte (*f*)	Loud.
Fortissimo (*ff*)	Very loud.

Frets	Marked divisions on the neck of a lute, viol or guitar to indicate fingering positions.
Fugue	A *contrapuntal* composition with strict rules of construction especially in the *Baroque/Classical* times. A set number of 'parts' or 'voices' are used, with the main 'subject' being heard in each part initially. *J.S. Bach* was a great writer of fugues.
Funk	A 1970s pop derivative of *soul* music.
Fusion	Attempts to merge jazz music with other musical styles, notably *Classical* and Asian.
Galliard	A three-beat dance from the fifteen/sixteenth centuries.
Gavotte	An old dance in 4/4 time which usually began on the third beat of the bar; it was used sometimes in the *Baroque suite*.
Gigue (jig)	A lively dance in 6/8 or 12/8 time; often the last movement of the eighteenth century *suite*.
Glee	A short choral piece for men's voices, very popular in England about 1750–1830.
Glissando	(Or gliss.) A slide from note to note, especially used on harp, trombone, piano and stringed instruments.
Gospel	The dominant church music of black America since the 1930s, and a major influence on all styles of black music.
Grave	Italian word for 'slow and solemn'.
Ground bass	(See also *Passacaglia*.) A piece of music built over a short recurring bass phrase. *Purcell* was a master of this form.
Harmonic progression	A series of chords.
Harmony	The art of adding appropriate chords to a melody.
Heavy metal	A style of rock which emphasises volume and intensity, which was most popular in the 1980s and early 1990s.
Hip-hop	1980s style of *rap*, which added 'scratching' onto records.
Homophonic	Music where the parts or voices move together instead of showing rhythmic independence (as in counterpoint or polyphony).
Honky-tonk	A form of *country* music (named after the taverns of the American south-west), featuring amplified steel and lead guitars in songs which often dealt with worldly things.
Hook	In pop music, a word or short phrase that is repeated. The 'catchy' part of the song.
Idée fixe	(See also *Leitmotiv*.) A recurring motto theme or figure associated with a person or action. *Berlioz* uses this idea in his *Symphonie Fantastique*.
Imitation	A *contrapuntal* action, where one voice or part 'copies' another – strictly or freely.
Impressionism	(From painting.) A term for music (by *Debussy* and others) where the expression seems to hint at something rather than state it dramatically. Tone-colour and harmony are used to give an 'impression' – with soft, vague outlines.
Impromptu	Title for a short piece, usually for piano, giving an impression of spontaneity.
Improvisation	Music made up on the spot.
Incidental music	Music for a play; songs, dances and perhaps an overture to enhance the drama.
Intermezzo	(1) Title for a short piano piece (e.g. by *Brahms*); (2) An instrumental item during an opera played while the stage is empty.
Interval	The distance measured between any two notes.
Jazz	A type of music with strong *syncopations* that came originally from Negro music in New Orleans. Although now branched out into many different styles, an important element is that of *improvisation*.
Jingle	A catchy tune – e.g. music for a television advertisement.
Kappelmeister	German for 'Musical Director'; and later for 'resident conductor' of an orchestra.
Key signature	Sharps and flats at the start of a piece to indicate the key; this is then repeated at the beginning of every line.
Larghetto	Slow and dignified, but less so than *largo*.
Largo	Slowly and broadly.
Latin-American music	A general name for dance rhythms which originated in South and Central America, which have influenced Anglo-American pop since about the 1920s.
Leading note	The seventh note of a scale.
Legato	Play smoothly. Connect the notes.

Leitmotiv	'Leading-motive'. A recurring theme associated with a character or object in operas – especially those by *Wagner*. (See also *Idée Fixe*.)
Lento	Slowly and broadly
LH	Left hand.
Libretto	(Plural libretti.) The text of an opera or oratorio.
Lied	(Plural Lieder.) A German *art song* with piano accompaniment. *Schubert, Brahms* and *Schumann* wrote many fine Lieder.
mf	Mezzo forte = rather loud.
mp	Mezzo piano = rather soft.
Madrigal	A type of *contrapuntal* vocal composition, which flourished in the sixteenth and seventeenth centuries. *Morley, Weelkes* and *Byrd* wrote madrigals, which were often about love in some way.
Magnificat	The hymn of the Virgin Mary ('My soul doth magnify the Lord') which is commonly set to music.
Mass	A service of the Roman Catholic Church. A musical mass usually has five sections (Kyrie, Gloria, Credo, Sanctus with Benedictus, and Agnus Dei). Try *Haydn's* 'Nelson' Mass.
Mazurka	Originally a Polish dance in three time. *Chopin* wrote over fifty piano mazurkas for concert use.
Mediant	The third degree of a scale.
Melodic	(1) Music that emphasises the melody, rather than harmony; (2) A type of minor scale.
Minuet and trio	Often the third movement of a *Symphony* or a *Sonata*, favoured by *Haydn* and *Mozart* and other *Classical* composers. Both Minuet and Trio are in two sections – and each is repeated before the Minuet is played once more, thus producing an overall *ternary form*.
Moderato	Use a moderate speed.
Modes (modal)	A scale system in use for hundreds of years before our present major/minor system evolved. Play the white notes on a piano for an octave from any note to produce a mode (e.g. A–A = Aeolian mode, useful for a folksong-like effect).
Modulation	Changing from one key to another.
Molto	Very (e.g. Allegro molto = very fast).
Motet	A church composition for voices, usually in Latin. (See *Anthem*.)
Movement	A self-contained section of a larger work, e.g. a *symphony* normally has four movements.
Music drama	Title given by *Wagner* to his later *operas*, which were intended by him to be a balance between music and drama.
Music hall	*Ballads* and comic songs performed by artists appearing in these British theatres in the half century before 1930.
Musical	A stage show of light entertainment (largely American influenced). Examples include *Oklahoma* (1943) by *Rogers* and *Hammerstein*, and more recently, *Evita, Cats*, and *Phantom of the Opera* by *Andrew Lloyd Webber*.
Musique concrète	A term coined by a group of Paris musicians experimenting in the 1940s with the rearrangement and reproduction of existing sounds by electronic means.
Mute	A device to clip on to a stringed instrument or insert into a brass instrument to deaden the tone slightly. (See *Sordino*.)
Nashville sound	A 1950s trend where vocal backing groups and strings were added to the recordings of *country* songs.
Neo-classical	Term given to a style of music by *Stravinsky* and others which deliberately avoids the expression of strong emotion. It was a reaction against the *Romantic* style of the late nineteenth century. Smaller orchestras were used (as in *Classical* days). Listen to 'Pulcinella' by *Stravinsky*.
Nocturne	Originally music alluding to the calmness of night-time, but now occasionally used as a title without 'nocturnal' connotations. Try *Debussy's* set of Nocturnes for orchestra.
Nonet	A group of nine players, or music for them.
Obbligato	E.g. aria with obbligato flute – a term used where an instrument has a solo role, often in conjunction with a solo singer.
Octave	Eight notes, e.g. C – C or G – G; an *interval* of a perfect 8th.
Octet	Eight players or a piece for eight players.
Ode	A piece of music written in celebration of something, e.g. *Ode for St Cecilia's Day* by *Purcell* or *Handel*.
Opera	A play set to music – e.g. *Carmen* by *Bizet*. Sometimes the word is used to mean a company which performs opera, or the building where it is performed (e.g. the Paris Opera).

Operetta	A form of light *opera* with spoken dialogue replacing *recitative*.
Opus	Literally a 'work'. Composers often give their compositions opus numbers, e.g. Op. 1, as a way of cataloguing them.
Oratorio	A large-scale religious work for choir, solo singers and orchestra. One of the best loved is *Messiah* by *Handel*.
Orchestration	The art of scoring out a composition for an orchestra.
Ornaments	A general term for the decorations that are used in music (use a music dictionary to look up trill, mordent, and turn, or see Chapter 13).
Ostinato	An 'obstinately' repeated figure or phrase.
Overture	An opening piece of music to an *opera* or *oratorio* (often said to be in 'French' or 'Italian' style depending on its structure). A Concert Overture (e.g. *Fingal's Cave* by *Mendelssohn*) stands in its own right.
p	Piano = softly.
pp	Pianissimo = very softly.
Partita	An alternative word for *Suite*.
Partsongs	Short unaccompanied choral pieces written in several parts, often *SATB*.
Passacaglia	Another word for *ground bass*.
Passing note	A note which passes between two others
Passion	A choral work which sets the Easter story. *Bach* composed a 'St Matthew' Passion and a 'St John' Passion.
Pastorale	A term to indicate a countryside atmosphere.
Pedal	(1) Ped. is an instruction to use the sustaining pedal on the piano. (2) In harmony, a long held (or repeated) note in any part.
Pedal Board	The set of foot pedals on a church *organ*.
Piu mosso	More movement; quicker.
Pizzicato	(Pizz.) An indication to pluck the strings.
Plainsong	An ancient form of church music – a single line of singing for unaccompanied voices in a free rhythm. Gregorian chant survives today.
Plectrum	A plastic 'plucker' guitarists use for strumming.
Polka	Dance in 2/4 time, originally from Bohemia.
Polonaise	Dance in 3/4 time, originally from Poland.
Polyphonic	*Contrapuntal* music – the so-called polyphonic age was the time of *Palestrina*, *Byrd* and *Lassus*.
Polytonality	Music composed in two or more keys at the same time. *Bartók* and *Holst* sometimes used this method of composing.
Prelude	Originally an 'opening' piece – perhaps to a *Suite*; it became a favourite pairing to a *Fugue* (e.g. *Bach*'s 48 Preludes and Fugues for *clavier*). Some composers use the word instead of *overture* to open their *operas*; others use the word for any self-contained piece (e.g. *Chopin*'s Preludes for piano).
Prepared piano	A way of producing new effects: the American composer John *Cage* instructs the pianist to insert screws in between certain strings!
Presto	Very fast.
Prestissimo	As fast as possible.
Programme music	Music that attempts to describe something – landscape, or the supernatural perhaps (e.g. the river *Vltava* by *Smetana*).
Proms	The annual Henry Wood Promenade Concerts held mainly at the Royal Albert Hall in London, July–September. First held in 1895, some seats are removed from the arena for young people to stand with cheaper tickets. You are not allowed to walk around however!
Quarter-tone	The *semitone* is the smallest interval in Western music, but some composers have experimented with intervals half this size, making use of quarter-tone pianos, and other new finely-tuned instruments.
Quartet	A group of four players, or music for four people.
Quintet	A group of five players, or music for five people.
Raga	In Indian music (which is improvised rather than written down) a cross between a melody and a scale. There are many ragas, each made for a certain time of day or night.

Ragtime	An early piano *jazz* style with a syncopated melody played against a regularly accented beat in the left hand. Scott *Joplin* is the important composer of piano rags.
Rallentando	(Rall.) Slow down.
Rap	A style of black music with rhythmically spoken vocals (which are often unintelligible).
Recapitulation	(Recap.) In *sonata form*, the section which reprises the main themes after the *development* section.
Recitative	(Recit.) Speech-like singing in an *opera* or an *oratorio*, often used to give information or fill in the story. The words tend not to be repeated (unlike the *aria* which it usually precedes).
Reggae	A pop style of West Indian origin, much played in the 1970s. The basic unit is a two-bar phrase, with the third beat of bar two accented.
Requiem	A *Mass* for the dead; notable examples are by *Mozart, Berlioz* and *Verdi*.
RH	Use the right hand.
Rhapsody	A title for a piece of music, suggesting a free form or *fantasia*. Try *Rachmaninov*'s Rhapsody on a theme of *Paganini*.
Riff	A short repeated musical pattern in *jazz* and pop; similar to *ostinato* in *Classical* music.
Ritardando (Rit)	Gradually slower.
Ritenuto (Riten)	Hold back, slower – immediately.
Ritornello	A passage for full orchestra which keeps 'returning' after a solo section in a *Concerto Grosso* or similar work.
Romantic	A period of musical history (c. 1830–1900) when composers were keen to depict emotional feelings and their response to things outside music, such as literature or landscape. (See Chapter 14, page 172).
Rondo	A form popular in the *Classical* and later periods where the sections appear as A-B-A-C-A. Sections B and C are contrasting *episodes* to the recurring Rondo theme.
Round	A short vocal *canon* for unaccompanied singing e.g. *London's Burning*.
Rhythm 'n' blues	A strongly rhythmic type of popular music which combines *blues* and *jazz*. The singer and guitarist *Chuck Berry* is a good example to listen to.
Rubato	A freedom of *tempo* for expressive purposes.
Salsa	A form of Latin-American music developed in New York in the 1950s and 1960s by Cuban and Puerto Rican musicians.
Saltarello	A lively Italian dance, often in 6/8 time.
Sarabande	A slow dance in 3/2 time, originally from Spain. A regular part of the old *suite*.
SATB	Short for: *Soprano, Alto, Tenor* and *Bass*; the regular voice parts of a choir.
Scherzo	Literally 'a joke'. From *Haydn* and *Beethoven* onwards a faster version of the *Minuet and Trio*, and usually (when used) the third movement of a *symphony* or sonata. It tends to be very lively – not particularly funny.
Semitone	Half a tone – the smallest distance between any two notes in Western music.
Septet	A group of seven players, or a work for seven.
Sequence	A repeated pattern at a higher or lower pitch (see page 93).
Serenade	Originally a work for outdoor use (to sing outside a lover's window); in *Classical* days it was a lighter instrumental piece for a few players – often wind players. *Mozart*'s *Eine Kleine Nachtmusik* is a popular string serenade.
Serial music	Music by *Schoenberg* and others which treats all notes of the *chromatic scale* equally. It is therefore *atonal*.
Sextet	A group of six players, or a work for six.
Sforzando	(*Sf*) or (*Sfz*) – an indication to give a 'forced' emphasis to a particular note.
Sinfonia	Literally 'sounding together'. The old name for what was to become the *symphony*; it is also used for the name of an orchestra – e.g. London Sinfonia.
Singspiel	A type of *opera* with extensive chunks of spoken dialogue, popular in the eighteenth century. German is used instead of Italian.
Ska	A forerunner of *Reggae* which flourished in the 1960s, adding elements of Jamaican music to *Rhythm 'n' blues*.
Skiffle	Originally 1920s black American music, adopted in Britain in the 1950s when using improvised instruments to perform American folk and *blues* songs.

Sonata	A four movement work for one or two instruments, depending on whether a piano accompaniment is required. Early sonatas by *Domenico Scarlatti* had just one movement.
Sonata Form	A Classically-developed structure which was frequently used for first movements in *sonatas, symphonies, concertos* and *string quartets*. It tended to follow this plan: *Exposition:* first subject in the *tonic* key. Bridge passage, or transition. Second subject in the *dominant* key. Codetta finishing off the exposition. *Development:* some of the main themes (from the above) are developed. *Recapitulation:* nearly the same as the exposition, but all in the same key this time. *Coda:* an ending.
Song cycle	A set of songs linked by a common theme. Try Vaughan *William's Songs of Travel.*
Soprano	The highest female voice.
Sordino	(Con sord.) Use a mute on the instrument.
Soul	An important form of black music in the 1970s, originating as a secularised version of *Gospel* music.
Spiccato	A method of playing rapid detached notes on stringed instruments, the bow bouncing off the strings.
Spirituals	American Negro religious folk-songs.
Sprechgesang	A sort of 'speech-song', originated by *Schoenberg*, where the voice just touches the note without actually sustaining it.
Staccato	Short, crisp notes – indicated thus ♩ ♩ ♩ ♫
Stradivarius	A name for the excellent violins made by Antonio Stradivarius in the seventeenth/eighteenth century (see Chapter 14, page 162).
String quartet	Two *violins,* a *viola* and a *cello;* or a work for this combination of instruments.
Strophic form	Term used when a song uses much the same music for each verse.
Study	(French = étude) – a piece which originally set out to provide practice for a certain technical difficulty; now it often has artistic merit as well (e.g. *Chopin*'s Studies)
Subdominant	The fourth degree of a scale; or the chord above that note.
Submediant	The sixth degree of a scale; or the chord above it.
Suite	A collection of short movements – in the *Baroque* suite they were mainly dances: e.g. *Allemande, Courante, Sarabande* and *Gigue.* Later on, it came to be the name for the instrumental extracts from an *opera* or ballet.
Supertonic	The second degree of a scale; or the chord above it.
Swing	The 'Swing' Band era was during the 1920s and 30s; Benny Goodman was one of the first band leaders to produce a swinging *jazz* style.
Symphony	(1) A four-movement work (rather like a *sonata*) for orchestra which developed around the time of *Haydn.* At least one of the movements will be in *sonata form.* (2) A short way of referring to a symphony orchestra – an orchestra large enough to play symphonies.
Symphonic poem	Or Tone Poem. A one-movement work for orchestra based on a story or sequence of events, e.g. *Vltava* by *Smetana* which describes the course of a river.
Syncopation	A rhythmic effect made when a weak beat is accented.
Tango	A favourite ballroom dance in the early part of this century. Originally from Argentina, its characteristic rhythm is ♩. ♪ ♩ ♩
Temperament	A word used in connection with tuning of instruments. Modern keyboard instruments use equal temperament where each semitone is made to be an equal interval. Thus G flat and F sharp are made to be the same sound. With this system it is possible to change key without any 'sour' notes sounding.
Tempo	'Time', i.e. speed. (Tempo primo – an indication to return to the original pace.)
Tenor	A high male voice; a clef sometimes used by cello and bassoon.
Ternary form	A three-part structure (designed as A B A), where the second A section is a repeat of the first.
Theme and variations	A popular form. A melody (either borrowed or original) is chosen by the composer, and any number of variations are created around it. Sometimes the theme may be simply decorated, or missing in a variation altogether. Listen to *Brahms' Variations on the St Anthony Chorale.*
Timbre	The 'colour' or sound quality of a particular instrument.
Toccata	A keyboard piece with difficult finger-work.
Tonality	A sense of key – where a piece is composed around a certain scale. (See also *Polytonality* and *Atonality*.)
Tone poem	See *Symphonic poem.*
Tonic	The 1st degree of a scale; or the chord above it.

Traditional jazz	A name for both the earliest, New Orleans style of *jazz,* and for the Anglo-American revival of the music ('trad') in the 1940s and 1950s.
Transcription	A work rearranged for another instrument; *Liszt* transcribed hundreds of orchestral pieces into piano pieces.
Transposition	Moving a piece higher or lower to another key.
Transposing instrument	One that produces notes either higher or lower than actually written. A horn in F will be written a perfect fifth higher than it sounds. Other examples: trumpet in B flat, clarinet in B flat – here written C sounds B flat.
Tremolando	(Tremolo.) A rapid bowing on a stringed instrument – for dramatic effect.
Triad	A three-note chord, e.g. C–E–G.
Trio	A group of three players or a work written for three.
Tutti	Literally: 'everyone' – an indication in a piece that all should play.
Twelve-note music	See *Serial music.*
Unison	All parts sounding the same note.
Valves	The mechanism on a brass instrument for producing different notes.
Variations	See *Theme and variations*
Vibrato	The slight 'wobble' that a singer or player produces to improve tone quality.
Virtuoso	A top-class performer.
Vivace	Lively.
Voluntary	A composition for church organ.
Walking bass	Term for a bass part in a composition which is continually moving along.
Waltz	(French = Valse) A dance in 3/4 time; very popular in nineteenth century Vienna. The *Strauss* family were famous composers of waltzes.
Western swing	This genre, which emerged in the American south-west in the 1930s and 1940s, contains elements of *jazz, ragtime,* and *blues,* as well as hillbilly and *country.*
Whole-tone scale	A scale consisting entirely of tones – e.g. C – D – E – F sharp – G sharp – A sharp – C. *Debussy* frequently used it.

Glossary 3
Musical instruments

GCSE requires a general knowledge that covers music from all ages, and many cultures. This glossary does not pretend to describe all the musical instruments that the world has seen. It covers, however, all the well-known Western European ones and introduces you to some instruments of the past, some of which are being heard again as musicians continue to explore the beauties of pre-classical music with reproduction instruments. Some mention, too, is made of the more common non-European instruments. This section should help you with the general musical knowledge required for the Musical Perception, Literacy and Set Works sections of the examination. It may even give you some ideas towards your composition!

Factual information of this sort is of little use unless you hear the sound of these instruments. There is every opportunity for this by choosing suitable pieces or programmes from radio and television; you could join a record library, and go to all sorts of concerts.

Accordion   A box-shaped reed organ that has metal reeds which vibrate with air from bellows which are pushed and pulled by the player. The right hand plays the melody keyboard while the left hand operates the harmony buttons. It is frequently associated with French café music.

Bagpipes   These have existed for over 3000 years and are played all over the world – not just Scotland. It is a reed-pipe wind instrument with air stored in a bag which serves as a reservoir, to be slowly squeezed out by the player's elbow, so that the flow of sound is unbroken when the player has to breathe. Try to hear the difference in sound between the Scottish bagpipes and the gentler Northumbrian pipes. Which do you prefer?

Balalaika   A triangular, three-stringed Russian guitar in various sizes. Played on its own, and in bands.

Banjo   A fretted, long-necked lute with a parchment-skin belly and usually four or five strings. It was popular with 'Negro Minstrels' and jazz bands in America as it is quite loud and could be heard where the guitar would be overpowered.

Baritone horn   The baritone horn in B flat is one of the various saxhorns used in brass bands. Music for it tends to use the treble clef.

Bass   A general word – it can mean an electric bass guitar in pop music, or double bass in jazz; we tend to say double bass when referring to the orchestral instrument.

Bass clarinet   A larger version of the standard B flat clarinet and pitched an octave lower.

(written)   (sounds a major 9th lower)

Bass drum   A huge orchestral drum of indefinite pitch, and played with a soft headed stick. (Try the 'Dies Irae' section from Verdi's *Requiem* for its powerful effect!) In a drum kit the stick is attached to a foot pedal.

Bass guitar   A four-stringed electric guitar used for the bass part in pop music. It was developed in the 1950s, and soon overtook the double bass in popularity because of its convenience.

Basset horn   A single-reed instrument of the clarinet family pitched in F. It has been rarely used since Mozart's day.

Bassoon   A bass woodwind instrument found in the orchestra and military band. It is sometimes found as a soloist and in chamber music. It uses a double reed. (Try Mozart's Bassoon Concerto, K.191.)

Bongos	Small Cuban drums (usually a pair joined together) played with thumb and fingers.
Brass	A term which covers wind instruments made of (any) metal and using a mouthpiece: trumpet, French horn, trombone and tuba comprise the orchestral brass family, while the brass band includes the cornet, tenor horn, baritone horn and euphonium.
Bugle	A brass instrument without valves, so it produces only a few notes (usually in B flat). Used by armies as a band instrument, and for signalling movements.
Castanets	A Spanish percussion instrument. Two small hollow pieces of wood for clicking together, or (in the orchestra) attached to the end of a stick which is shaken.
Celesta	A percussion instrument which looks like a small upright piano, and sounds like a glockenspiel. Listen to Tchaikovsky's 'Dance of the Sugar-Plum Fairy' from the *Nutcracker* ballet.
'Cello	Full name violoncello. Four-stringed bowed member of the string family, and used as the lowest instrument of the string quartet, as well as a solo and orchestral instrument.

Cimbalom	A Hungarian folk instrument having horizontal strings struck with hammers. Kodaly uses it in his opera *Hary Janos*.
Clarinet	A single-reed woodwind instrument used in the orchestra military band and in jazz. The standard instrument is pitched in B flat, but one in A is sometimes used. See basset horn and bass clarinet.

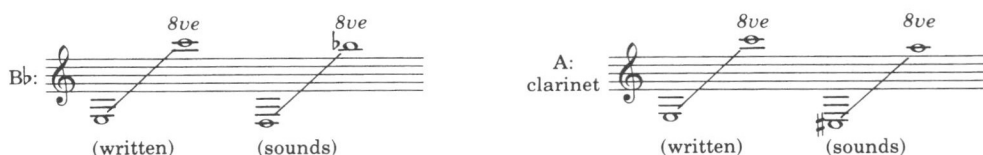

Clavichord	A small, soft-toned keyboard instrument popular from the sixteenth to eighteenth centuries. The strings are hit by metal tangents, and a vibrato effect is possible by shaking the individual keys. It was used in the home as it was too quiet for concert use.
Concertina	A type of small *accordion*, patented in 1829, and recognisable by the hexagonal shape of its ends. Buttons at either end produce single notes; chords have to be formed by the player.
Cor anglais	A woodwind instrument of the oboe type, but pitched a fifth lower. The nineteenth century Romantic composers were the first to use it regularly in the orchestra. Its name 'English horn' has never really been accounted for.

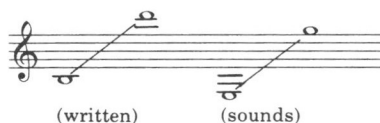

Cornet	B flat brass instrument resembling a small trumpet. Much used in brass bands, and occasionally in the orchestra.
Cornett	An obsolete wooden wind instrument having a small mouthpiece (like brass instruments) but finger-holes, not valves. Originally played in groups with sackbuts.
Crumhorn	An obsolete, curved, double-reeded, wind instrument, with the reeds covered by a windcap. It appeared in many sizes as its range was limited. It produced a quiet buzzing tone.
Curtal	Used throughout the sixteenth and seventeenth centuries as a bass instrument, this was the forerunner of the bassoon.
Cymbals	A percussion instrument. A plate of metal which can either be clashed against another, or struck with a drumstick. No definite pitch but modern composers often require several, in varying sizes. Drum kits include hi-hat cymbals.
Dobro	A modified *guitar*, dating from about 1925 in California, which was used in *bluegrass* music. It has raised strings and a metal resonator which acts as an acoustic amplifier.
Double bass	(See also *Bass*.) The largest of the modern string family; its flat back is for strength. Rarely used in chamber music. It can be bowed or plucked.

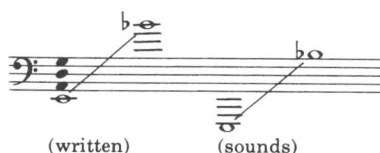

Double bassoon The lowest woodwind instrument. Similar to, but larger than the ordinary bassoon.

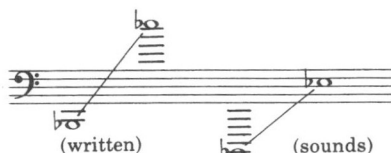

(written)   (sounds)

Euphonium A tenor tuba, mainly used in military and brass bands. It is pitched in B flat.

Flugelhorn A valved brass instrument made in various sizes and used mainly in brass bands for lyrical melodies.

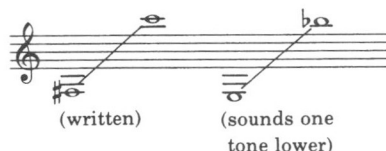

(written)   (sounds one tone lower)

Flute A horizontally-held woodwind instrument. It has no reed and the higher notes are produced by blowing rather harder (over-blowing).

French horn A coiled brass instrument. Originally played until about 1850 without valves. Horn notes are written a fifth higher than they sound.

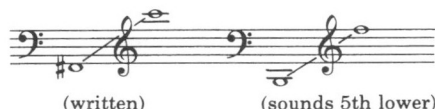

(written)   (sounds 5th lower)

Glockenspiel A pitched percussion instrument which uses beaters to strike tuned metal bars.

Gong Sometimes called tam-tam. A bronze percussion instrument in various sizes, struck with a large soft beater.

Guiro Latin-American 'scraper' percussion instrument.

Guitar Popular stringed instrument. The Spanish guitar has six strings and is played unamplified, unlike the electric guitar. The Hawaiian guitar uses a sliding metal bar (a 'steel') across all the strings to produce its characteristic sound. (See also *Bass guitar*.)

Harmonica Also called the 'mouth organ'. A small wind instrument in different sizes, using metal reeds. The better models are chromatic. The sound is continuously maintained by alternately blowing and sucking.

Harmonium A small reed organ operated by foot pedals which, when pushed alternately, pump the air.

Harp A plucked stringed instrument with a range of nearly seven octaves. Each of the seven foot pedals can lower or raise each note by a semitone.

Harpsichord A plucked-string keyboard instrument with one or two manuals. Although used frequently today, it was prominently used between about 1550 and 1750. Stops and couplers are used to change the tone-quality.

Heckelphone A rarely used type of bass oboe.

Hurdy-gurdy A portable, mechanical instrument. One hand turns a handle which activates a wheel-type bow; the other stops the strings inside by means of a tiny keyboard.

Kettledrum See *Timpani.*

Koto A Japanese zither. Thirteen strings are stretched over movable bridges that are moved with one hand; the other plucks the strings with plectra that are attached to the fingers. Six feet long.

Lute A fretted stringed instrument with a pear-shaped body; plucked by the fingers. Used as a solo instrument, or as an accompaniment to songs from about 1400–1700. The sizes and tunings of lutes varied.

Mandolin A plucked stringed instrument. Originally Italian. Eight strings tuned in pairs (G D A E) and played using a plectrum.

Maracas	Latin-American shaker percussion instrument. A pair of dried gourds with seeds inside.
Marimba	A deep-sounding xylophone with metal resonators under the keys.
Oboe	A double-reeded woodwind instrument used in the orchestra and military band, in chamber and solo music. (Listen to Britten's *Ovid Metamorphoses*.)

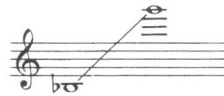

Organ	A church organ is a keyboard instrument (with one to four manuals), through which air is blown by bellows. Combinations of stops are used to vary the tone, and bass notes are produced by foot pedals; the electronic (or Hammond) organ has no bellows – sound is produced electronically.
Percussion	A general term for any instrument that is struck or shaken in some way.
Piano	Invented around 1700, the piano differs from the harpsichord because the strings are struck by hammers. Either upright (vertical strings) or grand – that is, horizontal strings.
Piccolo	A high-pitched flute used in the orchestra and military band.

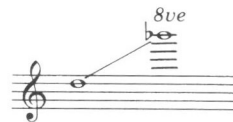

Psaltery	An ancient and now obsolete plucked stringed instrument. A simple kind of zither.
Racket	An obsolete bassoon-sounding instrument of amazingly short dimensions for its low pitch.
Rebec	An obsolete forerunner of the violin with three or four strings.
Recorder	A family of flute-type instruments in various sizes, ranging from sopranino down to the bass.
Regal	An obsolete portable organ (fifteenth to seventeenth centuries.)
Sackbut	An early trombone; virtually unchanged.
Saxophone	An instrument which gets its name from its maker, Sax, who produced several sizes of saxophones in the 1840s. It is a single-reed woodwind although made of brass; popular in jazz and the military band. Not so common in the orchestra.
Serpent	An obsolete curved woodwind instrument played with a brass-type mouthpiece.
Shawm	An old, loud-sounding woodwind instrument with a double reed. Superseded by the modern oboe.
Side drum	(Snare drum). A small drum, played to the side when used by marching bands, also used in jazz, rock, and the orchestra. There are two skins on the drum, the lower one in contact with wires (or snares) which give it its distinctive rattling sound.
Sitar	An Indian stringed instrument. Rather like a long-necked lute, but with seven strings and about twenty movable frets which arch over a wide neck. These frets enable the player to 'bend' the notes.
Sousaphone	A type of tuba which actually fits over the player's body with a big forward-facing bell. Associated originally with the American band led by J.P. Sousa.
Spinet	A small harpsichord, but wing-shaped not rectangular. A popular domestic keyboard from the sixteenth to eighteenth centuries.
Synthesiser	Popular modern electronic instrument which constructs sounds when given precise instructions by the player.
Tabla	A set of two Indian hand drums capable of producing a range of different tone colours, within the range of about an octave.
Tamboura	An Indian instrument with four to six strings. It functions as a *drone*, sounding the *tonic* constantly.
Tambourine	A small circular drum with metal jingles around the edge.
Tam-tam	Another name for a *Gong*.
Tenor horn	Really a tenor saxhorn – a brass band instrument pitched in E flat.
Theorbo	A large lute, popular in the seventeenth and eighteenth centuries.
Timpani	Italian for kettledrums. Tuned drums played with softsticks. Pedal 'timps' enable quick tuning, and make possible the use of a glissando.

Triangle   An untuned metallic percussion instrument, struck with a metal beater.

Trombone   A brass instrument which produces notes by means of a slide, rather than valves. Used in jazz, the orchestra and military bands.

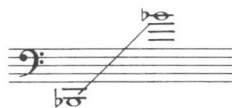

Trumpet   A three-valved brass instrument; extremely popular in jazz, and indeed all types of ensemble. Pitched in B flat (although 'Bach' trumpets in D are used for Baroque high trumpet parts).

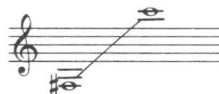

Tuba   The lowest brass instrument, dating from about 1835. It is only rarely used as a soloist, but Vaughan Williams wrote a concerto for tuba.

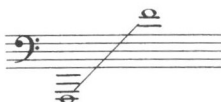

Tubular bells   A set of suspended bells (tuned metal tubes) which are struck with mallets to give a sound rather like church bells.

Ukelele   A very small four-stringed guitar-like instrument. Popular earlier this century with singers like George Formby.

Vibraphone   Or vibes for short. A tuned percussion with flat metal bars like a glockenspiel. Beneath the bars is an electrically powered motor which gives a vibrato effect to the tone.

Viol   A family (or 'consort') of bowed stringed instruments which came before the violin family. There are three principal sizes, the lowest being the *viola da gamba*. They have frets (unlike the violin) and use a different type of bow. Even the smallest size was played vertically like a cello, and had six strings.

Viola   A bowed stringed instrument, larger and therefore lower and mellower in tone than the violin. Its strings are tuned to C G D A.

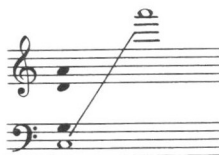

Viola da gamba   A sixteenth century bass viol, played when resting it vertically on the knees. It had six strings.

Violin   The smallest of the violin family; tuned to G D A E. See *Stradivarius* in Glossary 2.

Virginals   A simple domestic keyboard instrument without legs, similar to the harpsichord, and popular in the days of Elizabeth I. Basically a rectangular box (and often highly decorated) with a short keyboard.

Woodblock   A simple non-pitched percussion instrument. A piece of hardwood with a cavity for resonance, hit with a wooden beater.

Woodwind   Collective term for piccolo, flute, clarinets, oboe, cor anglais, saxophones and bassoons.

Xylophone   A wooden tuned percussion instrument. Different sized rosewood bars are struck with beaters.

Zither   A central European folk stringed instrument plucked when resting on the knees or a table. Some of the strings can be 'stopped' like the violin – others are fixed in pitch.

Glossary 4
Well-known performers, past and present

You should be aware of the top performers (past and present) of different instruments, as sometimes you are asked to name who might have recorded (or conducted) a particular extract. The list is kept deliberately brief; you should try to remember who was playing, singing and conducting when you listen to any music.

Δ jazz player

Baritone	John Shirley-Quirk, Brian Rayner Cook, Dietrich Fischer-Dieskau, Geraint Evans.
Bass	Stephen Varcoe.
Bassoon	Archie Camden, Roger Birnstingl.
Brass bands	William Fairey Engineering Band, Brighouse and Rastrick Band, Black Dyke Mills Band, Grimethorpe Colliery Band.
Cello	Jacqueline du Pré, Rostropovich, Paul Tortelier.
Clarinet	Jack Brymer, Benny Goodman Δ, Woody Herman Δ, Thea King.
Conductors	Simon Rattle, André Previn, Herbert Von Karajan, Leonard Bernstein, Bernard Haitink, George Solti.
Contralto	Kathleen Ferrier, Janet Baker.
Counter tenor	Alfred Deller, James Bowman.
Double bass	Rodney Slatford, Charles Mingus Δ.
Drums	Buddy Rich Δ.
Flute	James Galway, Jean-Pierre Rampal, Susan Milan.
French horn.	Dennis Brain, Barry Tuckwell, Alan Civil, Ifor James.
Guitar	Julian Bream, John Williams, Django Reinhardt Δ.
Harp	Marisa Robles.
Harpsichord	Trevor Pinnock.
Mezzo Soprano	Felicity Palmer, Sarah Walker.
Oboe	Heinz Holliger, Evelyn Rothwell, Nicholas Daniel.
Opera companies	Royal Opera House (Covent Garden), English National Opera (Coliseum), La Scala, Milan, New York Metropolitan (The Met).
Orchestras	London Symphony, Berlin Philharmonic, Chicago Symphany, Cleveland, New York Philharmonic, Vienna Philharmonic.
Organ	Peter Hurford, Simon Preston, Marie-Claire Alain.
Percussion	James Blades, Tristan Fry.
Piano	John Ogdon, Earl Wild, Alfred Brendel, Jorge Bolet, Oscar Peterson Δ, Fats Waller Δ.
Rock guitar	Jimi Hendrix, Eric Clapton.
Saxophone	alto: Charlie Parker Δ, tenor: Stan Getz Δ.
Soprano	Elizabeth Soderstrom, Emma Kirkby, Frederica Von Stade, Elly Ameling, Heather Harper.
String quartets	Allegri, Amadeus, Borodin, Endellion, Lindsey.
Sythesiser	Jean-Michel Jarre, Rick Wakeman, Keith Emerson.
Tenor	Peter Schreier, Peter Pears, Robert Tear.
Trombone	Jack Teagarden Δ, Tommy Dorsey Δ.
Trumpet	Don Smithers, Bram Wiggins, Miles Davis Δ, Dizzy Gillespie Δ.
Tuba	Paul Lawrence.
Viola	Lionel Tertis, Peter Schidlof.
Violin	Yehudi Menuhin, Itzhak Perlman, Stephane Grappelil Δ.

Index